Welcome to the *EVERYTHING*® series!

These handy, accessible books give you all you need to tackle a difficult project, gain a new hobby, comprehend a fascinating topic, prepare for an exam, or even brush up on something you learned back in school but have since forgotten.

You can read an *EVERYTHING*® book from cover-to-cover or just pick out the information you want from our four useful boxes: e-facts, e-ssentials, e-alerts, and e-questions. We literally give you everything you need to know on the subject, but throw in a lot of fun stuff along the way, too.

We now have well over 100 *EVERYTHING*® books in print, spanning such wide-ranging topics as weddings, pregnancy, wine, learning guitar, one-pot cooking, managing people, and so much more. When you're done reading them all, you can finally say you know *EVERYTHING*®!

FACTS
Important sound bytes of information

ESSENTIALS
Quick handy tips

ALERT
Urgent warnings

QUESTIONS?
Solutions to common problems

Dear Reader,

Thank you for picking up this book.

It's never too late to start playing the piano. I was nineteen when I started taking piano lessons at the Hartford Conservatory of Music. While studying, I would go from one practice room to another and experience different pianos. I played on a variety of Steinways, Baldwins, Webers, Emersons, and Hardmans. Most of the models were parlor grands with a few studio and upright verticals mixed in. They were all in very good playing condition and very different from one another. I was usually the last student to leave the building; the custodian would knock on the practice room door and tell me it was closing time.

I wrote this book with the intention of getting you acquainted with the piano. As you will discover, there is a lot to get acquainted with and a lot of piano music to listen to. I'm hoping that you will have a pleasurable relationship with this fascinating, versatile instrument. Throughout the course of reading this book, I hope that you will be inspired to sit down and play the piano again, again, and again.

Sincerely,

Brooke Halpin

THE
EVERYTHING®
PLAYING PIANO
AND KEYBOARDS
BOOK

From popular songs to classical music—
learn to play in no time

Brooke Halpin

Adams Media Corporation
Avon, Massachusetts

EDITORIAL
Publishing Director: Gary M. Krebs
Managing Editor: Kate McBride
Copy Chief: Laura MacLaughlin
Acquisitions Editor: Bethany Brown
Development Editor: Lesley Bolton

PRODUCTION
Production Director: Susan Beale
Production Manager: Michelle Roy Kelly
Series Designer: Daria Perreault
Layout and Graphics: Brooke Camfield,
Colleen Cunningham, Daria Perreault

Published by Adams Media Corporation
57 Littlefield Street, Avon, MA 02322 U.S.A.
www.adamsmedia.com

ISBN: 1-58062-651-3
Printed in the United States of America.

J I H G F E D C B

Library of Congress Cataloging-in-Publication Data

Halpin, Brooke.
    The everything playing piano and keyboards book : from popular songs
to classical music—learn to play in no time / by Brooke Halpin.
        p.   cm.   —(An everything series book)
Includes index.
ISBN 1-58062-651-3
    1. Piano. 2. Piano—Instruction and study. 3. Keyboard instruments.
I. Title. II. Everything series.
ML650 .H24 2002
786.2'193–dc21   2002003931

Illustrations by Barry Littmann.
Music typesetting by Woytek Rynczak of WR Music Service.
All other music transcription © 2002 Halpin House Music. All rights reserved.

This book is available at quantity discounts for bulk purchases.
For information, call 1-800-872-5627.

Visit the entire Everything® series at everything.com

Contents

Acknowledgments

I would like to acknowledge the following who have, in one way or another, contributed to my writing this book.

♪ Thanks to my mother, who consistently supports my creativity and individuality.

♪ Thanks to The Beatles, who are a constant source of inspiration. Without The Beatles, I would not have become a musician or have written this book.

♪ Thanks to my music teachers, who gave me encouragement and direction.

♪ Thanks to my friend Bob Auletta for his resourceful information.

♪ Thanks to my agent Wendy Keller, who offered me this writing opportunity and made it happen.

♪ And thanks to Bethany Brown at Adams for her support and for believing in me.

Introduction

Music is a universal language that anyone from anywhere in the world can understand, and the piano is a universal instrument that anyone can play and appeals to a wide variety of people. It doesn't matter what language you speak, where you come from, what your ethnic background is, what income bracket you're in, or what your religious beliefs are, you can play the piano.

The next time you attend a piano recital or performance, take a look around at the people sitting in the audience. You'll see a wide variety of people from different walks of life, all gathered together to listen to the pianist.

Musical expression has the ability to communicate a variety of human emotions, from sadness and longing to happiness and exuberance. Some people feel more comfortable expressing themselves through music versus the spoken word. Music is less confrontational than speaking and is open to personal interpretation. That's part of the magic of music—you have your own personal interpretation of the music you're hearing and what it means to you. A gifted pianist knows how to communicate with an audience through his or her piano playing.

Some people are natural performers. They have a personality that puts them at ease when in front of a group of people. Natural performers play the piano because they have a strong desire to shine in the spotlight and want to give the best performance they possibly can. They love an audience. They also want the audience to love them. The natural performer doesn't need to be asked to play the piano. If there's a piano in the room, he or she will sit down and start playing. While this behavior does have a tendency to raise a few eyebrows, once the piano playing begins, the performer almost always wins the ears and hearts of those in the room.

Other people play the piano for themselves. They dread the thought of having to play for others. They tend to be shy and do not aspire to be a performer. And that's perfectly okay. It can be a big mistake to push someone into performing when he or she has no interest or desire to do so.

Playing the piano for yourself can be very gratifying. How wonderful it is to be able to play the piano and release some of your emotions. Afterward, you might feel relieved, having released a human emotion or two or three by playing the piano. And that in itself is a gift to yourself—having the ability to get something off your chest, perhaps an abstract or deep feeling that you prefer not to talk about.

Everyone who plays the piano wants to sound good. It is far better to play a simple piece of music well than to play a complicated piece poorly. And believe me, the listener will agree. There's nothing wrong with wanting to play a challenging piece of music. Just be sure of yourself before you perform it. Practice, practice, practice, and eventually, you'll be prepared to give a good performance. And what a good feeling it is to have conquered a complicated piece of music. Knowing you have succeeded is very satisfying. But you have to know when to put a piece of music aside and acknowledge that it's not your cup of tea. Because there's such an abundance of piano music written for varying levels of technical proficiency, you can select pieces that you're attracted to, match your level, and enjoy playing. After all, playing the piano should feel good and not be an uncomfortable chore.

Everyone has his or her own natural style of playing. Find out what your style and preferences are. Some pianists play fast effortlessly, running their fingers up and down the keyboard like smooth lightning, but have difficulty keeping even time when playing slow tempos. Some pianists are naturally inclined to play slow and moderately paced music, but struggle with fast thirty-second–note passages. And that's why there are piano teachers in the world, to strengthen a player's weak spots.

The musical expression through playing the piano is a powerful, wonderful gift for the audience and yourself. I know because I play for myself, and I play for others.

CHAPTER 1

History of the Piano

If you are interested in learning to play the piano or keyboard, it helps to have a little background information. This chapter is going to give you a brief history of the piano, as well as introduce you to all the instruments within the keyboard family.

The First Piano

We have pianos today because of Bartolomeo Cristofori. In the evolution of keyboard instruments, the harpsichord preceded the piano. Bartolomeo Cristofori built harpsichords in Italy during the late 1600s. As an inventor, he was determined to create a keyboard that went beyond the dynamic range and mechanisms of the harpsichord. With that in mind, in 1698, he started to build a keyboard that would eventually be called the piano.

Cristofori wanted to create a keyboard that could be played both soft and loud, giving the player a wider range of dynamic expression. In Italian, the word for soft is *piano*, and the word for loud is *forte*. The original name in Italian for this new keyboard was *gravicembalo col piano e forte*. When translated to English, this means "harpsichord with soft and loud." Even though Cristofori had created a new instrument, he still referred to it as a harpsichord, but with modifications. In 1709, he completed the new keyboard, dropped the word *harpsichord*, and renamed it the *pianoforte*.

ESSENTIALS It's interesting to note how Cristofori's new instrument influenced composers at the time. The Italian composer Lodovico Giustini was one of the first to compose music for the new instrument. He composed twelve sonatas for the pianoforte and wrote the words *piano* and *forte* on the music to indicate where he wanted the music to be played soft and loud.

As with creating anything new, Cristofori's pianoforte had a few problems. Unlike the harpsichord, which creates its sound by plucking the strings with a plectrum, the piano strikes the strings with a device called a hammer. One of the problems Cristofori encountered was that once the hammer hit the strings, it would bounce back and hit the strings again. To prevent the bounce from happening, Cristofori created a device called an escapement. This device succeeds in preventing the hammer from bouncing on the strings a second time.

Another challenge he faced was how to make the new instrument produce a soft sound. To accomplish this, Cristofori created a device that shifts the keyboard's action to strike fewer strings, thus reducing the instrument's volume output. On today's pianos, this shift device is activated by pressing down on the soft pedal.

Even with the improvements Cristofori made with his new instrument, the pianoforte was not accepted in Italy. Keyboard players, who were accustomed to harpsichords, complained that the pianoforte was difficult to play, and they didn't like the instrument's tone. As Cristofori continued to refine his instrument, a German organ builder named Gottfried Silberman discovered Cristofori's pianoforte and used it as a model to create his own piano.

Silberman was looking for a composer to endorse his new instrument and arranged a meeting with the famous German composer Johann Sebastian Bach. Bach was not impressed with Silberman's piano and complained that the upper register sounded weak, and that the keys were too heavy, making the instrument difficult to play. Soon afterward, Silberman was able to see a more detailed account of the action (the mechanism that connects the keys to the strings) Cristofori had created. As a result of incorporating the principles of Cristofori's action, Silberman made modifications to his piano and met with Bach a second time. Bach's response to the revised piano was much more positive.

With time and improvements, the piano was gradually accepted by composers and keyboardists alike, and eventually became the keyboard of choice. The action of pianos being built today uses the same basic principles Cristofori created with his first piano.

Without Cristofori, pianos wouldn't exist, and without composers, piano music wouldn't exist. Composers contributed greatly to the popularization of the piano. After all, without composers to write music for the relatively new instrument, pianists wouldn't have any music to play.

The Square Piano

During the later part of the 1700s, the popularity of the piano spread throughout Europe. The design of pianos made during this time period were grand pianos; they were large and occupied a lot of space. Piano manufacturers experimented with making smaller pianos, thus the square piano was born.

Johannes Zumpe, who studied piano making with Silberman in Germany, moved to London and made the square piano very popular in England. Given its smaller size, the square piano fit comfortably in parlors and living rooms. Zumpe's square pianos were so popular that some of them were exported to the United States.

The Sustain Pedal

With Zumpe's influence and the growing demand for the piano, London became a haven for piano manufacturers by the late 1800s. The London-based piano manufacturing company Broadwood added the sustain pedal to their line of pianos. This new addition set a precedent that other manufacturers followed. Soon thereafter, the soft pedal was added, which is based on Cristofori's shift device and designed to make the sound of the piano soft.

QUESTIONS?

What is a sustain pedal?
A sustain pedal releases the damper pads, allowing the strings being played to sustain their sounds and resonate until the sounds naturally dissipate or until you take your foot off the pedal.

The Iron Frame

As the overall piano evolved, so did its parts. The iron frame is a very important part located inside the piano. It's a harp-shaped object that the strings are stretched over and attached to at both ends.

The very first piano frames were made of wood and supported with metal braces. Wooden frames cause problems for pianos because wood expands and contracts according to changes in climatic conditions. The expanding and contracting of wooden frames has a direct impact on the strings, making the piano go out of tune.

A Boston piano maker named Alpheus Babcock came up with the idea of replacing the wooden frame with a metal one. Subsequently, in 1825, Babcock made the first metal-frame piano. It was a big success, as the metal frame greatly improved the tuning stability of the instrument. Other piano manufacturers were quick to make use of Babcock's metal frame to the extent that it became an industry standard.

With grand pianos, the iron frame is very critical in its structural ability to support tons of tension created by over 200 stretched strings.

FACTS

Upright Pianos

Even though the square piano was a success, piano manufacturers wanted to build a smaller instrument without compromising its sound quality. Piano makers conducted numerous experiments including the repositioning of the placement of the strings and action. They moved them from a horizontal position to a vertical position, making the piano very tall.

One of the first vertical pianos to emerge was called the giraffe piano. This bizarre-looking instrument was not very popular. It was Robert Wornum, a London-based piano maker, who redesigned the giraffe piano to make it much shorter and smaller. Thus the upright piano was born.

Piano Manufacturers

The popularity of the piano created a strong supply-and-demand for the instrument, and as a result, piano manufacturing flourished. By the early 1900s, there were over 200 piano manufacturers in the United States. At that time, the piano was the single source of entertainment in the home. Unlike today, there were no radios, televisions, cassette players, CD players, or VCRs.

With the advent of radio and television, the piano began to lose its popularity. It's startling to note that only a handful of piano makers exist today. The following is an incomplete list of piano manufacturers still in existence today.

Baldwin (American)   Samick (Asian)
Bechstein (German)   Schimmel (German)
Blutner (German)   Seiler (German)
Charles Walter (American) Steinway (American)
Grotrian (German)   Weber (American)
Kawai (Asian)   Yamaha (Asian)
Knabe (Asian)   Young & Chang (Asian)
Mason & Hamlin (American)

The Family of Keyboard Instruments

There are three distinct categories of keyboard instruments.

1. Stringed keyboards: clavichords, harpsichords, virginals, spinets, and pianos.
2. Wind keyboards: organs, harmoniums, and accordions.
3. Electronic keyboards: electric pianos, electric organs, digital pianos, and synthesizers.

In a separate category of keyboards is the celesta, which has metal bars instead of strings. This relatively small instrument is commonly found in the percussion section of orchestras.

Stringed Keyboard Instruments

The clavichord is the oldest and most primitive keyboard instrument. It was a very popular instrument during the seventeenth and eighteenth centuries. Unlike the harpsichord, the strings of the clavichord are struck, producing a percussive sound. Because of its light tone, the clavichord was ideal for practicing and playing solo.

During the sixteenth, seventeenth, and eighteenth centuries, the harpsichord was a very popular keyboard instrument throughout much of central and southern Europe, especially in Italy, Germany, and France. This instrument produces a very distinctive plucked sound. When pressing down on a key, a jack containing a small plectrum is lifted and actually plucks the corresponding string. The harpsichord is more versatile than the clavichord, with some models having as many as three keyboards. It also has levers, which determine the number of strings to be played. When only one string per note is selected, the sound is soft, warm, and expressive. When playing two or three strings per note, the sound is rich, full, and relatively louder.

The spinet is a smaller version of the harpsichord, having only one string per note in most cases. Spinets were popular because of their size, light weight, and easy mobility.

The virginal is also a smaller variation of the harpsichord. During the sixteenth and early seventeenth centuries, the virginal was more popular than the harpsichord in northern Europe.

Wind Keyboard Instruments

Organs are comprised of four basic parts: pipes that produce sounds, a wind chamber, mechanically generated pressure, and a keyboard that accesses and directs wind to designated pipes.

Ktesibios, a third-century Greek engineer, is credited with creating the first organ. He named this very primitive instrument the hydraulis. Over the course of time, the basic principles of the hydraulis developed and manifested themselves in many different types of organs. All of today's organs use the same four basic characteristics that Ktesibios used with his hydraulis.

Of all the keyboard instruments, the organ is considered to be the most complex. Organs produce sounds as a result of applying pressurized air into the organ's pipes. The size of the pipes range from very small to very large and are made of either metal or wood. Devices called stops open and close individual pipes, resulting in a specific sound or combination of sounds. Aside from pipes versus strings, one of the biggest differences between the piano and the organ is the way the keys are played. To produce sound with the organ, you have to keep the keys depressed; the longer you keep the keys depressed, the longer the sound lasts.

The harmonium is a reed organ, using reeds instead of pipes. The sound of the harmonium is produced by foot pedals that pump air into the instrument. During the nineteenth century, harmonium manufacturers in France, Germany, and England developed and refined the instrument. Harmoniums became very popular because they were relatively inexpensive keyboard instruments that produced rich colorful sounds. Due to their small size, harmoniums have an abbreviated keyboard.

The accordion is comprised of three main parts: the right-hand keyboard for playing melodies; the bellows, which produce the pressurized air; and the left-hand buttons for playing chords and harmony.

At the beginning of the twentieth century, the accordion gained popularity worldwide. But it wasn't until 1953 that the accordion peaked in production due to product demand. For example, in that year alone, Italy exported 200,000 instruments, and German manufacturers exported the same amount.

The electronic keyboards category includes electric pianos, electric organs, synthesizers, and digital keyboards. Chapter 8 covers these instruments in detail.

CHAPTER 2

Classical Repertoire for the Piano

Any classical piano student will gain a superior knowledge of the piano by studying some of the piano compositions listed in this chapter. Repeated listening of recordings of these works is highly recommended. If you're taking piano lessons or writing keyboard music, these piano compositions and performances should be a great source of inspiration.

Piano Sonatas

One of the earliest forms of music written for the piano is called a piano sonata. When translating the word *sonata* from Italian to English, it means "something played." Prior to the classical period, the sonata form was comprised of a series of dances, which included gigues, sarabands, minuets, and marches. During the classical period, composers restructured the sonata form and used primarily an A-B-A form.

Structurally, a piano sonata is comprised of three sections and two principle themes of music. The A section states the first theme, followed by the B section, which states the second theme. The third section, which is also called the A section, returns to the first theme. In the third section, the return to the first theme is also called the recapitulation. These three sections constitute the A-B-A sonata form.

**SSENTIALS** The most famous pieces of music written for the piano are by composers who were also proficient pianists. For example, Beethoven, Brahms, Chopin, Clementi, Haydn, Liszt, Mozart, Prokofiev, Rachmaninov, Schumann, and Tchaikovsky represent the classical repertoire for the piano.

The two themes used in the sonata form are heard with some variation throughout the piece. The variations can be changes in key, rhythm, tempo, and/or harmony. For instance, if the sonata is in the key of C major, the first and third section will be in the key of C, while the second section is in the key of C major's relative minor, A minor. Piano sonatas written during the classical and romantic periods typically use a moderate tempo for the first section, a slow tempo for the second section, and a fast tempo for the third section. In musical terms, these corresponding tempos are called moderato, adagio or andante, and allegro or presto.

In some instances, composers, such as Beethoven, wrote sonatas that contained four sections. The third section was a minuet, scherzo, or a march, incorporating dance music from the earlier sonata form. Four-section sonatas by Beethoven are found more commonly in his earlier works.

The piano sonata serves a number of functions. It provides a platform and vehicle for aspiring composers and performers who want to gain the public's attention. The format of the piano sonata was originally, and still is, ideally suited for teaching purposes, giving the student a cohesive musical structure to follow. During the classical period, it also played an important role in church music and was the favored format of church musicians.

Piano Sonata Composers

Composers Franz Joseph Haydn, Wolfgang Amadeus Mozart, Muzio Clementi, and Ludwig van Beethoven played a significant role in the development of the piano sonata.

Franz Joseph Haydn

Haydn was born in Austria in 1732 and died in Vienna in 1809. He was one of the first composers to develop the piano sonata form. Haydn's earlier piano sonatas were written primarily for teaching purposes. In total, Haydn composed sixty-two piano sonatas, ranging from his early divertimento-like, baroque-styled sonatas to the masterpieces written in his later years. One of his most popular sonatas is his last one, Piano Sonata no. 52 in E-flat Major.

Here's a list of some of Haydn's sonatas:

Piano Sonata no. 11 in B-flat Major	Piano Sonata no. 28 in D Major
Piano Sonata no. 12 in A Major	Piano Sonata no. 29 in E-flat Major
Piano Sonata no. 13 in G Major	Piano Sonata no. 30 in B Minor
Piano Sonata no. 14 in C Major	Piano Sonata no. 31 in A-flat Major
Piano Sonata no. 15 in E Major	Piano Sonata no. 32 in D Major
Piano Sonata no. 16 in D Major	Piano Sonata no. 33 in D Major
Piano Sonata no. 17 in E-flat Major	Piano Sonata no. 34 in D Major
Piano Sonata no. 18 in E-flat Major	Piano Sonata no. 35 in A-flat Major
Piano Sonata no. 19 in E Minor	Piano Sonata no. 36 in C Major
Piano Sonata no. 20 in B-flat Major	Piano Sonata no. 37 in E Major
Piano Sonata no. 24 in A Major	Piano Sonata no. 38 in F Major

Piano Sonata no. 39 in D Major
Piano Sonata no. 40 in E-flat Major
Piano Sonata no. 41 in A Major
Piano Sonata no. 42 in G Major
Piano Sonata no. 43 in E-flat Major
Piano Sonata no. 44 in E-flat Major
Piano Sonata no. 45 in A Major
Piano Sonata no. 46 in E Major
Piano Sonata no. 47 in B Minor
Piano Sonata no. 48 in C Major
Piano Sonata no. 49 in E-flat Major
Piano Sonata no. 50 in D Major

Piano Sonata no. 51 in D Major
Piano Sonata no. 52 in E-flat Major
Piano Sonata no. 53 in E Minor
Piano Sonata no. 54 in G Major
Piano Sonata no. 55 in B-flat Major
Piano Sonata no. 56 in D Major
Piano Sonata no. 58 in C Major
Piano Sonata no. 59 in E-flat Major
Piano Sonata no. 60 in C Major
Piano Sonata no. 61 in D Major
Piano Sonata no. 62 in E-flat Major

Wolfgang Amadeus Mozart

Wolfgang Amadeus Mozart (1756–1791) is one of the greatest composers to utilize the piano sonata form. His first sonatas, written when he was a young boy, were short, somewhat mechanical-like pieces for the piano. Mozart's second group of sonatas was written while he was in London. Some music critics claim that they sound like they were influenced by the compositional style of Johann Sebastian Bach.

Here's a list representing some of Mozart's piano sonatas. The numbers following the letter *K* represent catalogue listings and the chronological order of the compositions.

Sonata no. 1 in C Major, K. 279
Sonata no. 2 in F Major, K. 280
Sonata no. 3 in B-flat Major, K. 281
Sonata no. 4 in E-flat Major, K. 282
Sonata no. 5 in G Major, K. 283
Sonata no. 6 in D Major, K. 284
Sonata no. 7 in C Major, K. 309
Sonata no. 8 in D Major, K. 311
Sonata no. 9 in A Minor, K. 310
Sonata no. 10 in C Major, K. 330

Sonata no. 11 in A Major, K. 331
Sonata no. 12 in F Major, K. 332
Sonata no. 13 in B-flat Major, K. 333
Sonata no. 14 in C Minor, K. 457
Sonata no. 15 in F Major, K. 533
Sonata no. 16 in F Major, K. 547
Sonata no. 17 in C Major, K. 545
Sonata no. 18 in B-flat Major, K. 570
Sonata no. 19 in D Major, K. 576

Muzio Clementi

The Italian composer Muzio Clementi (1752–1832) also contributed to the development of the piano sonata. Clementi was born in Rome in 1752 and moved to England when he was a young boy. Clementi was a popular composer in his day and was highly acclaimed for his numerous piano compositions. His piano sonatas became very popular as a result of his frequent public performances.

Clementi composed an extraordinary number of pieces for the piano, which included more than 100 piano sonatas. His early sonatas are very dynamic and contain sweeping melodies that run up and down the keyboard, somewhat characteristic of Beethoven's early piano works. Clementi's piano sonatas exemplify his mastery of the instrument and structure of the piano sonata form. Some of his sonatas contain highly virtuoso passages, which are quite demanding technically. His later sonatas are known for their modern qualities, experimental and extended form, and technical mastery.

FACTS

Due to his tremendous creative output, Clementi gained the reputation of being the father of the piano sonata. Clementi influenced other great composers of the piano sonata form including Ludwig van Beethoven.

Here's a list of some of Clementi's sonatas:

Piano Sonata in G Minor, op. 7, no. 3
Piano Sonata in F Minor, op. 13, no. 6
Piano Sonata in B-flat Major, op. 24, no. 2
Piano Sonata in F-sharp Minor, op. 25, no. 5
Piano Sonata in D Major, op. 25, no. 6
Piano Sonata in A Major, op. 33, no. 1
Piano Sonata in B Minor, op. 40, no. 2
Piano Sonata in D Major, op. 40, no. 3
Piano Sonata in G Minor, op. 50, no. 3

Ludwig van Beethoven

Ludwig van Beethoven (1770–1827) is one of the greatest composers of all time. His musical genius contributed to the continuing development of the piano sonata. When Beethoven was a young man, he earned the reputation of being a great pianist and composer for the piano.

As a pianist, Beethoven was intense, fiery, and emotional. His compositions embodied his emotions and gave birth to a new style of music called romanticism. Beethoven's music went beyond the formality and structure of the classical period and is filled with a variety of human emotions and innovation. As a result of his musical innovations, he is regarded as the father of romanticism.

Here's a complete list of Beethoven's piano sonatas:

Piano Sonata no. 1 in F Minor, op. 2
Piano Sonata no. 2 in A Major, op. 2, no. 2
Piano Sonata no. 3 in C Major, op. 2, no. 3
Piano Sonata no. 4 in E-flat Major, op. 7
Piano Sonata no. 5 in C Minor, op. 10, no. 1
Piano Sonata no. 6 in F Major, op. 10, no. 2
Piano Sonata no. 7 in D Major, op. 10, no. 3
Piano Sonata no. 8 in C Minor, op. 13; "Pathetique"
Piano Sonata no. 9 in E Major, op. 14, no. 1
Piano Sonata no. 10 in G Major, op. 14, no. 2
Piano Sonata no. 11 in B-flat Major, op. 22
Piano Sonata no. 12 in A Major, op. 26
Piano Sonata no. 13 in E-flat Major, op. 27
Piano Sonata no. 14 in C-sharp Minor, op. 27, no. 2; "Moonlight"
Piano Sonata no. 15 in D Major, op. 28; "Pastoral"
Piano Sonata no. 16 in G Major, op. 31, no. 1
Piano Sonata no. 17 in D Minor, op. 31, no. 2; "Tempest"
Piano Sonata no. 18 in E-flat Major, op. 31, no. 3
Piano Sonata no. 19 in G Minor, op. 49, no. 1
Piano Sonata no. 20 in G Major, op. 49, no. 2
Piano Sonata no. 21 in C Major, op. 53; "Waldstein"
Piano Sonata no. 22 in F Major, op. 54
Piano Sonata no. 23 in F Minor, op. 57; "Appassionata"

Piano Sonata no. 24 in F-sharp Major, op. 78
Piano Sonata no. 25 in G Major, op. 79
Piano Sonata no. 26 in E-flat Major, op. 81a; "Les Adieux"
Piano Sonata no. 27 in E Minor, op. 90
Piano Sonata no. 28 in A Major, op. 101
Piano Sonata no. 29 in B-flat Major, op. 106; "Hammerklavier"
Piano Sonata no. 30 in E Major, op. 109
Piano Sonata no. 31 in A-flat Major, op. 110
Piano Sonata no. 32 in C Minor, op. 111

Franz Peter Schubert

Following in Beethoven's shadow, Franz Peter Schubert was a successful composer who lived his short life in Vienna (1797–1828). Even though he was a gifted composer, Schubert didn't posses the personality of Beethoven and didn't experience that level of popularity and success. Nonetheless, his compositions contain sublime melodies and compositional mastery, as demonstrated in his piano sonatas.

Franz Schubert composed twenty-one piano sonatas. Here's an incomplete list of some of his popular sonatas. The letter *D* stands for the Deutsch catalogue listing.

Piano Sonata in E-flat Major, D. 568
Piano Sonata in C Major, D. 613 (Unfinished)
Piano Sonata in F Minor, D. 625 (Unfinished)
Piano Sonata in A Major, D. 664
Piano Sonata in A Minor, D. 784
Piano Sonata in G Major, D. 894
Piano Sonata in B-flat Major, D. 960

FACTS

As musical styles developed, and as time progressed, the piano sonata form was expanded on further. With the advent of impressionist and atonal music, the sonata form was transformed to the extent that the classical A-B-A form was no longer easily recognizable. Some composers still used the term *piano sonata* without following or being restricted to its original classical form.

Romantic Composition Styles

Romantic piano composition styles went beyond the classical confines of the piano sonata form. These styles included scherzos, rondos, etudes, tone poems, nocturnes, and preludes. Composers like Chopin wrote dance pieces for the piano including polonaises, mazurkas, and waltzes. Here is an incomplete list of Chopin's most famous pieces.

Rondo for Piano in C Minor, op. 1
Piano Sonata no. 1, op. 4
Rondo for Piano in F Major, op. 5; "La Mazur"
Scherzo no. 1 in B Minor, op. 20
Etude in F-sharp Minor, op. 25, no. 7
Scherzo no. 2 in B-flat Minor, op. 31
Scherzo no. 3 in C-sharp Minor
Waltz in F Major, op. 34, no. 3
Piano Sonata no. 2, op. 35
Impromptu in F-sharp, op. 36
Impromptu in G-flat, op. 51
Scherzo no. 4 in E Major, op. 54
Piano Sonata no. 3, op. 58
Barcarolle, op. 60
Polonaise-Fantaisie in A-flat Major, op. 61
Mazurka in C-sharp Minor, op. 63, no. 3
Mazurka in C Major, op. 67, no. 3
Mazurka in F Major, op. 68, no. 3
Waltz in D-flat Minor, op. 70, no. 3

Piano Concertos

A concerto is a musical composition form that features a solo instrument with an orchestra. Piano concertos feature the piano as that solo instrument. Unlike a piano sonata, a piano concerto contains passages in which the piano is completely silent while the orchestra plays on.

The most famous piano concertos have solo piano passages in which the orchestra is completely silent. During these solo passages, sometimes called cadenzas, the pianist demonstrates virtuoso playing and technical prowess.

Typically, piano concertos have three movements. The tempos of the movements are usually allegro for the first movement, adagio for the second movement, and allegro or presto for the third movement.

During the late seventeenth and early eighteenth centuries, composers Arcangelo Corelli and George Fredric Handel composed orchestral works that featured a particular group of instruments within the orchestra. Johann Sebastian Bach took this concept one step further with concertos in which he featured solo instruments with orchestral accompaniment.

Following Bach's model, Antonio Vivaldi and Handel composed concertos featuring solo instruments with an orchestra using a three-movement form. Mozart expanded on the concerto form with his twenty-seven piano concertos, making them more expressive, longer, and more complex than Bach's, Vivaldi's, and Handel's concertos.

Beethoven is credited with developing the piano concerto format further by introducing complex, emotional passages that set the precedent for the early romantic style of writing. His five piano concertos embody the evolution of the piano concerto form.

During the romantic period, the concerto became more virtuoso in character. German composers Robert Schumann and Johannes Brahms added virtuoso passages for the piano and expanded the orchestral sections. Fryderyk Chopin, Franz Liszt, and Felix Mendelssohn further developed the role of the soloist. The concertos of Edvard Grieg, Sergei Rachmaninov, and Peter Tchaikovsky exemplify the style of great romantic piano compositions.

ESSENTIALS
Franz Liszt, the famous Hungarian composer, is credited with introducing the tone poem, a descriptive style of writing for the piano. An example is his Piano Sonata in B Minor.

As the styles of the late romantic period evolved into more abstract styles, the concerto went far beyond its classical roots. In some instances, the writing is more percussive and less melodic or lyrical. These changes are inherent in compositions by Bela Bartok, Sergei Prokofiev, and Dimitri Shostakovich.

Famous Piano Concertos

- Bela Bartok
    - No. 1 in A Major
    - No. 2 in G Major
    - No. 3 in E Major
- Ludwig van Beethoven
    - No. 1 in C Major, op. 15
    - No. 2 in B-flat Major, op. 19
    - No. 3 in C Minor, op. 37
    - No. 4 in G Major, op. 58
    - No. 5 in E-flat Major, op. 73;
        "The Emperor"
- Johannes Brahms
    - No. 1 in D Minor, op. 15
    - No. 2 in B-flat Major, op. 83
- Fryderyk Chopin
    - No. 1 in E Minor, op. 11
    - No. 2 in F Major, op. 21
- Joseph Haydn
    - No. 3 in F Major
    - No. 4 in G Major
    - No. 11 in D Major
- Franz Liszt
    - No. 1 in E-flat Major
    - No. 2 in A Major
    - No. 3 in E-flat Major (posthumously)
- Felix Mendelssohn
    - No. 1 in G Minor, op. 25
    - No. 2 in D Minor, op. 40
- Wolfgang Amadeus Mozart
    - No. 9 in E-flat Major
    - No. 15 in B-flat Major
    - No. 17 in G Major
    - No. 20 in D Minor
    - No. 21 in C Major

- No. 22 in E-flat Major
- No. 23 in A Major
- No. 24 in C Minor
- No. 25 in C Major
- No. 26 in D Major
- No. 27 in B-flat Major
- Sergei Prokofiev
    - No. 1 in D-flat Major, op. 10
    - No. 2 in C Minor, op. 16
    - No. 3 in C Major, op. 26
    - No. 4 in B-flat Major, op. 53
    - No. 5 in G Major, op. 55
- Sergei Rachmaninov
    - No. 1 in F-sharp Minor, op. 1
    - No. 2 in C Minor, op. 18
    - No. 3 in D Minor, op. 30
    - No. 4 in G Minor, op. 40
- Maurice Ravel
    - No. 1 in G Major
    - No. 2 in C Major (for the left hand)
- Camille Saint-Saens
    - No. 1 in D Major, op. 17
    - No. 2 in G Minor, op. 22
    - No. 3 in E-flat Major, op. 29
    - No. 4 in C Minor, op. 44
    - No. 5 in F Major, op. 108
- Dimitri Shostakovich
    - No. 1 in C Minor, op. 35
    - No. 2 in F Major, op. 102
- Peter Tchaikovsky
    - No. 1 in B-flat Minor, op. 23
    - No. 2 in G Major, op. 44
    - No. 3 in E-flat Major, op. 75
        (posthumously)

CHAPTER 3

Jazz and Pop Repertoire for the Piano

There is an extensive amount of music written for the piano. The styles of the pieces reflect the artistic trends of different time periods. In the last chapter, you were introduced to classical styles. In this chapter, we are going to jump ahead to more modern times and concentrate on jazz and pop styles.

Well-Known Jazz Piano Pieces

Because the number of jazz pieces that use the piano is so extensive, the following examples represent only a very small number of pieces that crossed over to mainstream popularity. The piano is a primary instrument used in jazz.

George Gershwin wrote piano music in the jazz idiom. Gershwin's most famous piano composition is his "Rhapsody in Blue." This piece of music, written for piano and orchestra, is a landmark piece of American music. It is a wonderful mixture of styles, incorporating jazz, blues, and classical elements. In terms of song standards, Gershwin's "Summertime" from his opera *Porgy and Bess* is one of the most performed and recorded songs of all time.

Duke Ellington was one of the greatest jazz pianists of all time. One of his most famous songs is "It Don't Mean a Thing (If It Ain't Got That Swing)," with lyrics written by Bob Russell. Other Ellington songs include "Satin Doll," "Mood Indigo," and "Sophisticated Lady."

Jazz pianist Dave Brubeck is credited with reawakening the public's interest in jazz after World War II. Hailing from California, his style of music was called "West Coast Cool Jazz," depicting American jazz in the 1950s and 1960s. His hit instrumental recording "Take Five" (released in 1959) sold over one million copies.

The Ramsey Lewis Trio was very popular in the 1960s. Lead by Ramsey Lewis on piano, their biggest hit is "The In Crowd." This light jazz instrumental was recorded and released in 1965.

Rock and Roll Piano

In piano sonatas and piano concertos, the piano is the featured solo instrument. In rock and roll songs, the piano is used primarily as an accompaniment instrument to a singing voice. Some songs also contain piano introductions and piano solos, while others use the piano only as a rhythm instrument. The following material on rock and roll piano music refers to the piano in all of these roles.

In 1955, with his pounding rhythm-and-blues–style piano playing, Fats Domino put the piano in rock and roll history with his hit single "Ain't

That a Shame." Other songs include "I'm Walkin'" and his biggest hit single, "Blueberry Hill," which was released in 1956.

ESSENTIALS

Another rock and roll song that featured the piano is "Great Balls of Fire" by Jerry Lee Lewis. This single was a big hit in 1957 and inspired hundreds of future rock and roll piano players. "Whole Lotta Shakin' Goin' On" is another of Lewis's piano rockers, made up of the same powerful ingredients as "Great Balls of Fire."

When Elvis burst onto the rock and roll scene with his guitar, pianos took a backseat position while hip-swinging, guitar-playing, singer/songwriters dominated the recording industry and record charts.

The Beatles and the Piano

When The Beatles used any instrument, it became a music industry standard because of their tremendous popularity and influence. As they used more keyboards and pianos in their recordings, the piano gained popularity and equal status with the guitar.

When The Beatles came along, everything changed. During their first tour of the United States in 1964, they performed using guitars, bass, and drums—not a piano was in sight. However, when they were in the recording studio, piano tracks were added to some of their songs. As early as their *Meet The Beatles* LP recorded in 1963, a piano solo (played by their record producer George Martin, a classically trained musician) was overdubbed in the John Lennon song "Not A Second Time." As their music developed, so did their arrangements and instrumentation.

On *The Beatles' Second Album*, released in the United States in 1964, you can hear a driving piano track in "Money," and a rhythm-and-blues–styled piano in "You've Really Got a Hold on Me." Once again, George Martin played the piano tracks.

The rather obscure George Harrison song "You Like Me Too Much," released on the 1965 LP *Beatles VI*, has two piano tracks: electric piano played by Lennon and acoustic grand piano played by Paul McCartney and George Martin.

In performance scenes from their second movie, *Help*, we see Lennon playing electric piano in the song "The Night Before." Lennon's playing is background rhythmic accompaniment to McCartney's lead vocal. Later that same year, in 1965, with the release of the LP *Rubber Soul*, the piano is prominent in "You Won't See Me." On the same LP, a very classical-sounding piano solo, played by Martin, takes place in Lennon's moving ballad "In My Life."

FACTS

The Beatles's use of the piano in the studio eventually carried over into their live performances. During their last tour in 1966, Lennon put his guitar down for a few songs and played organ in the screaming "I'm Down." Lennon's keyboard technique was quite extraordinary—he played glissandos up and down the keys using his elbow.

On The Beatles's *Revolver* LP, released in 1966, the piano takes center stage in McCartney's ballad "For No One." Adding to its central piano sound, McCartney overdubbed a clavichord. The *Revolver* LP features the piano again in the honky-tonk–styled piano solo in "Good Day Sunshine" played by Martin. Another *Revolver* song that uses the piano prominently is Harrison's "I Want to Tell You."

The opening chords of "Strawberry Fields," played by McCartney on a mellotron, a precursor to the synthesizer, is another example of keyboard use with The Beatles' songs. On the same astonishing single is McCartney's "Penny Lane," with the piano as the centerpiece of the song.

Their critically and publicly acclaimed masterpiece *Sgt. Pepper's Lonely Hearts Club Band* LP uses piano in "A Day in a Life," "Lovely Rita Meter Maid," and "When I'm Sixty-Four." The use of the piano increased with the songs "The Fool on a Hill," "Your Mother Should Know," "Hello Goodbye," and the amazing "I Am The Walrus" on The Beatles' *Magical Mystery Tour* LP, released in 1967.

The combination of these brilliant songs and the use of keyboards had a strong influence on thousands of guitar players and songwriters. Other bands followed The Beatles' lead, and keyboards were used more prominently in rock and pop songs.

While The Beatles are generally classified as a rock or pop musical group, some of their songs incorporate baroque, classical, romantic, and electronic styles and elements. To a large extent, this was the result of Martin's influence combined with the creative musical genius of The Beatles. Their recordings serve as an extraordinary study of music that, due largely to its timeless quality, will more than likely last forever.

The Year of Piano Pop

Nineteen sixty-eight was a very big year for pianos and keyboards in pop music.

The Beatles returned to the top of the music charts in February 1968 with the driving, rhythmic piano sounds of "Lady Madonna." Soon afterward, McCartney's piano playing took center stage with "Hey Jude," which is almost entirely a piano song accompanied by rhythm acoustic guitar, lead electric guitar, bass, and drums.

ESSENTIALS   If there is one pop song to elevate the status and role of the piano to a primary instrument, it's The Beatles' "Hey Jude."

Prior to the release of "Hey Jude," a sophisticated, astonishing piece of music called "MacArthur Park," sung by Richard Harris and written by Jimmy Webb, dominated the airwaves and remained in the number one chart position for almost two months during the summer of 1968. This epic piece of music uses the harpsichord as its primary instrument, with added orchestration, bass, and drums. Opening with the main theme heard on the harpsichord, "MacArthur Park" takes the listener on a melodramatic ride through key changes, a driving-up-tempo instrumental section, and a soaring vocal ending complete with full orchestra. It shattered the three-minute formula pop song with its seven minutes twenty seconds of music.

During that same summer of 1968, The Moody Blues released their *Days of Future Passed* LP. This thought-provoking classic rock recording features the piano on "Tuesday Afternoon." *Days of Future Passed* was recorded with The London Festival Orchestra, which provided orchestral accompaniment and thematic passages throughout the recording. The mellotron was also used on this extraordinary recording.

The Beatles ended this piano year with the release of *The Beatles*, otherwise known as the "white album." This double-record set features the piano on McCartney's upbeat "Ob-La-Di, Ob-La-Da," "Martha My Dear," "Honey Pie," and "Back in the USSR," Lennon's "Sexy Sadie," Harrison's "While My Guitar Gently Weeps," and harpsichord on "Piggies."

Piano in the 1970s

When it comes to the 1970s and piano music, the list is long and includes several superstars. This decade is filled with examples of piano and keyboard in the pop music culture. A few of the prime players are highlighted below.

As early as 1970, Elton John brought the piano into the spotlight with his many hits including "Bennie and the Jets," "Daniel," "Don't Let the Sun Go Down on Me," "Goodbye Yellow Brick Road," "Honky Cat," "Levon," "Sorry Seems To Be the Hardest Word," "Tiny Dancer," and "Your Song."

Billy Joel didn't reach mass commercial success until the release of *The Stranger* LP. Produced by Phil Ramone, *The Stranger* contained the top-selling keyboard single "Just the Way You Are." Joel's earlier recording, the *Piano Man* LP, contains some of his greatest songs such as "Ain't No Crime," "Piano Man," "The Ballad of Billy the Kid," and "Travellin' Prayer." Every song on the *Piano Man* LP features Joel's brilliant piano playing.

Carole King released a series of hit songs with the piano songs on her *Tapestry* LP including "It's Too Late," "I Feel the Earth Move," "You've Got a Friend," and "So Far Away."

Barry Manilow is another 1970s piano man with hit songs including "Mandy," "Could It Be Magic," "I Write the Songs," "Weekend in New England," and "Tryin' to Get the Feeling Again."

The amazing Stevie Wonder released his *Songs in the Key of Life* LP in 1976, containing such keyboard gems as "Knocks Me Off My Feet" and "Summer Soft." Other Wonder keyboard hits include the syncopated clavinet sounds of "Superstition" and "Higher Ground," and Wonder's smash hit song, "You Are the Sunshine of My Life."

The 1970s also produced keyboard-oriented groups like Electric Light Orchestra; Emerson, Lake, and Palmer; and Supertramp. In addition to the songs already mentioned above, what follows are some keyboard songs from the 1970s.

"1985" by Paul McCartney (Wings)
"All By Myself" by Eric Carmen
"Angie" by The Rolling Stones
"Breakfast in America" by Supertramp
"Child of Vision" by Supertramp
"Desperado" by The Eagles
"Evergreen" by Barbara Streisand
"Evil Woman" by Electric Light Orchestra
"God" by John Lennon
"Imagine" by John Lennon
"Layla" by Derek and the Dominos
"Love Will Keep Us Together" by Captain and Tennille
"Maybe I'm Amazed" by Paul McCartney
"Morning Has Broken" by Cat Stevens
"My Little Town" by Paul Simon
"Oh My Love" by John Lennon
"Our House" by Crosby, Stills, Nash and Young
"Photograph" by Ringo Starr
"Ride Like the Wind" by Christopher Cross
"Saturday in the Park" by Chicago
"Still Crazy After All These Years" by Paul Simon
"Take the Long Way Home" by Supertramp
"The Low Spark of High-Heeled Boys" by Traffic
"Warm and Beautiful" by Paul McCartney
"Without You" by Harry Nilsson
"You Light Up My Life" by Debby Boone

Into the '80s and '90s

The 1980s brought us the keyboard wizardry and writing talents of Bruce Hornsby with his hit single "The Way It Is." Given Hornsby's keen ability to improvise, during the 1990s he toured with the legendary band The Grateful Dead.

Of course, there are several other piano and keyboard musicians during this time who made a significant impact on the music industry. A small sample of keyboard gems from the 1980s and 1990s is provided below.

"Angel in My Heart" by Mick Jagger

"Beautiful Goodbye" by Amanda Marshall

"Boxing" by Ben Folds Five

"Chariots of Fire" by Vangelis

"Climb On (A Back That's Strong)" by Shawn Colvin (with Bruce Hornsby on piano)

"End of the Innocence" by Don Henley

"Laura" by Billy Joel

"Leningrad" by Billy Joel

"Pressure" by Billy Joel

"Russians" by Sting

"Shadows in the Rain" by Sting

"Thank U" by Alanis Morissette

"The Last Polka" by Ben Folds Five

"Watching the Wheels" by John Lennon

"Your Congratulations" by Alanis Morissette

CHAPTER 4
Famous Classical Pianists

C lassical music reflects a specific period in the history of music and the fine arts. The classical period spans from approximately 1750 to 1820. Unlike music and art created during the preceding baroque period, which is ornamental and decorative, the style of the classical period is cleaner and more precise.

The Classical Composers

Some of the finest examples of classical music for the piano are piano sonatas composed by Wolfgang Amadeus Mozart. Mozart's music reaches a fine degree of harmonic perfection. The form and structure of his piano sonatas and concertos are very precise, logical, and accessible. This makes Mozart's music very appealing to pianists and a pleasure to listen to.

Another great classical composer was Franz Joseph Haydn. During his life, he wrote sixty-two piano sonatas. His earlier sonatas reflect the baroque style that was beginning to wane as the classical style was gaining popularity. As is the case with most styles and periods, there is no fine line when one style ends and another one begins.

On a smaller scale of popularity is Muzio Clementi. As you know, Clementi contributed greatly to the development of the piano sonata.

Recordings of the Classics

The works of these composers have been played (and sometimes recorded) extensively by both amateur and professional pianists. It's fascinating to listen to the same piano piece played by different pianists. Even though the music is exactly the same, each pianist makes it his or her own by marking it with individual personality and interpretation. With fine-tuned listening, one can hear the differences from pianist to pianist.

The pianist Murray Perahia has recorded several of Mozart's piano sonatas including Sonata no. 13 in B-flat Major, K. 333, and Sonata no. 15 in F Major, K. 533. Perahia has also recorded all of Mozart's piano concertos with the English Chamber Orchestra. This ten-box CD set is available on the Sony Classical label.

Because of Mozart's brilliant compositional structure and clearly defined form, most pianists have a strong desire to play his music.

Pianist Rudolph Buchbinder has recorded Haydn's Piano Sonatas numbers 17 through 62. This comprehensive recording is available on the Teldec Classics International record label.

The pianist Jeno Jando has recorded nearly all of Haydn's piano sonatas, with the exception of his very early pieces. Jando's recordings include Haydn Piano Sonatas numbers 11 through 62 and are available on the NAXOS Classical label.

The Russian pianist Nikolai Demidenko has recorded Clementi's Sonata in D Major, op. 40, no. 3; Sonata in F-sharp Minor, op. 25, no. 5; and Sonata in B Minor, op. 40, no. 2. Demidenko's recordings are available on Hyperion Records.

FACTS

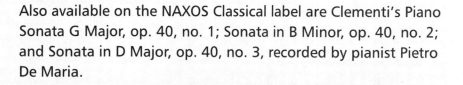

Also available on the NAXOS Classical label are Clementi's Piano Sonata G Major, op. 40, no. 1; Sonata in B Minor, op. 40, no. 2; and Sonata in D Major, op. 40, no. 3, recorded by pianist Pietro De Maria.

The pianist Peter Katin has recorded Clementi's F-sharp Minor, op. 25, no. 5; B-flat Major, op. 24; G Minor, op. 7, no. 3; D Major, op. 25, no. 6; and F Minor, op. 13, no. 6. For this recording, Katin played on a square piano, an instrument that was very popular during the time Clementi composed these piano pieces. Not only did Clementi compose volumes of piano music, he was also a piano manufacturer. The square piano that Katin played on is a Clementi piano, built in 1832. This recording is available on the Athene Record label.

Pianist Michael Leuschner recorded Clementi's Piano Sonata in D Major, op. 40, no. 3; Piano Sonata in G Minor, op. 7, no. 3; and Piano Sonata in D Minor, op. 50, no. 2. This recording is available on the Brioso Record label.

On the NAXOS Classical record label, pianist Balazs Szokolay has recorded the following Clementi piano pieces:

Piano Sonata in B-flat Major, op. 24, no. 2
Piano Sonata in G Major, op. 25, no. 2
Piano Sonata in F-sharp Minor, op. 25, no. 5
Sonatina no. 1 in C Major, op. 36
Sonatina no. 2 in G Major, op. 36
Sonatina no. 3 in C Major, op. 36
Sonatina no. 4 in F Major, op. 36
Sonatina no. 5 in G Major, op. 36
Sonatina no. 6 in D Major, op. 36
Piano Sonatina in D Major, op. 37, no. 2

Victor Borge

Victor Borge was certainly a very unique pianist. He combined his keen musical talents with original humor and became a one-of-a-kind entertainer.

Borge was born in Copenhagen, Denmark. At the very young age of three, his mother introduced him to the piano. The Royal Danish Music Conservatory recognized the young boy's talent and awarded him with a scholarship. Continuing on with his studies, Borge studied with Frederic Lamond and Egon Petri. As he grew into his twenties, Borge's unique sense of humor and pianistic finesse earned him leading film roles and stage appearances throughout Scandinavian countries.

When it came to humor, Borge's style was satirical. This did not work in his favor when the Nazi invasion spread across Europe. During his performances at that time, Borge made cutting remarks about Hitler. The Nazis found out about it and put Borge on their blacklist. Fortunately, Borge was able to escape from Finland on what turned out to be the last passenger ship to sail from Europe before the outbreak of World War II.

Borge was considered an ambassador of goodwill for both his native Denmark and his adopted new homeland, America. As a result, many people throughout the world referred to him as the "Great Dane." In recognition of his goodwill toward the United States, Borge received the Medal of Honor by the Statue of Liberty Centennial Committee at a gala ceremony at Ellis Island. Borge also received the honor of being knighted by the five Scandinavian countries—Denmark, Finland, Iceland, Norway, and Sweden.

While living in the United States, Borge performed extensively. He performed on radio and television stations, put on concerts in opera houses and sports arenas, made several film appearances, and performed at the White House. Borge was also active on Broadway, giving 849 performances of his one-man-show entitled "Comedy in Music," which still holds the record for the longest running one-man-show in the *Guinness Book of Records*.

As a pianist, Borge performed with the New York Philharmonic, London Philharmonic, Royal Danish Philharmonic, and the Cleveland, Philadelphia, San Francisco, and Chicago Symphony Orchestras.

Borge worked with PBS on a number of televised specials including one hosted by Itzhak Perlman and the Chicago Symphony Orchestra. For this special, Borge performed his popular "Borgeism" treatment of Mozart's music and teamed up with Perlman for a violin/piano duet. Other PBS specials included "Bernstein" (which took place in Tanglewood, Massachusetts, and featured Borge performing with the Boston Symphony Orchestra) and the "Victor Borge: Then and Now" fundraiser series. Borge also created and released a successful videotape designed specifically for children entitled *Victor Borge Tells Hans Christian Andersen Stories*.

ESSENTIALS

As a testament to his commitment to education, Borge established scholarship funds at a number of colleges and universities. Additionally, in 1963, he created the multimillion dollar Thanks To Scandinavia Scholarship Fund, acknowledging Scandinavians who risked their lives while saving thousands of people who were victims of the Holocaust.

Victor Borge died on December 23, 2000. On that day, the world lost an individual who had the gifted ability to bring millions of people together through his musicianship and original humor.

Alfred Brendel

On January 5, 1931, Alfred Brendel was born in Wiesenberg, Moravia. His background is multi-ethnic with a mixture of Austrian, German, Italian, and Slavic roots. Soon after Brendel was born, he and his family moved to Yugoslavia where his father owned and operated a hotel. Brendel started playing the piano when he was six years old. To round out his music studies and satisfy his interests, he began formal studies in piano, music composition, and conducting.

In 1948, Brendel made his debut and performed keyboard compositions by Bach, Brahms, and Liszt. For this debut, he also performed an original composition—a double fugue for piano.

While Brendel was in Vienna, he had the opportunity to attend concerts given by Alfred Cortot, Wilhelm Kempff, and Arthur Schnabel.

From these fine performers, he gained keyboard insights and applied them to his piano-playing technique.

Brendel's international career was launched when he won the coveted Busoni Piano Competition in 1949. For the next several years, he went on to perform solo piano recitals across Europe and in the United States. He also performed piano concertos with some of the world's best orchestras.

In recognition of his pianistic talents, Brendel received several professional and academic honors. Some of them include the Grand Prix of the Liszt Society, the Prix Mondial du Disque, the Edison Award, the Grand Prix de l'Académie Charles Cros, the Japanese Record Academy Award, and the Gramophone Award. He also holds honorary degrees from Oxford and Yale Universities.

ESSENTIALS
Brendel's creative interests were not limited to music. In his late teens, he studied literature and began painting. Some of his early watercolor paintings were exhibited at an art gallery in Graz, Austria.

Brendel is known for his performances and recordings of Beethoven's piano music. He is credited with being the first pianist to record all of the Beethoven piano sonatas. The first time he did this was for the VOX record label in the 1960s. But Brendel wasn't satisfied with his playing, so he recorded all of the sonatas a second time for Philips Records in 1970.

As a performer, Brendel sustains a remarkable output. For instance, he performed seventy-seven recitals throughout the world during the 1982–83 performance season. Brendel performed the Beethoven piano sonatas on this tour and attracted sell-out crowds everywhere he played. Seven years later, he replicated the same Beethoven program for his 1990 world tour. Illustrating his unrelenting passion for Beethoven's piano music, in 1996, he recorded the complete Beethoven piano sonatas again for Philips Records. This second recording for the Philips Records label captures Brendel's years of playing the sonatas and his evolved interpretations and insights on Beethoven's piano music.

It's a fascinating and telling experience to listen to three different recordings of the same piano music covering the span and maturity of over thirty years of Brendel's playing the Beethoven piano sonatas.

When he's not playing Beethoven's piano music, Brendel performs compositions by Bach, Brahms, Haydn, Liszt, Mozart, Mussorgsky, Schoenberg, Schubert, Schumann, and Weber.

ESSENTIALS

When he takes time out from his busy performing and recording schedules, Brendel writes books about music. He has written *Musical Thoughts and Afterthoughts* (Robson Books, 1976) and *Music Sounded Out* (Robson Books, 1990), which exemplify the same sly wit found in his piano playing.

It's interesting to note that despite his world acclaim as a fine pianist, Brendel claims that he is not a good sight reader, doesn't have a photographic memory, and doesn't consider himself to be a fast piano player.

Alfred Brendel currently resides in London with his wife, Irene.

Glenn Gould

On September 25, 1932, Glenn Gould was born in Toronto, Canada. From the very beginning of his life, Gould was exposed to music; his mother played the piano, and his father played the violin.

His parents noticed the very young Gould's extraordinary musical gifts. When he was five years old, he was composing music and playing the piano for his friends and family members. Gould started his formal piano lessons when he was ten and studied at the Royal Conservatory of Music in Toronto. Two years later, he entered the Kiwanis Music Festival Competition and won a trophy in the piano category. This was the only competition Gould performed in, as he decided not to compete in any capacity going forward. At the age of fourteen, he received a diploma with highest honors from the Royal Conservatory of Music. During his time as a teenager, Gould listened to and was very influenced by Arthur Schnabel, Rosalyn Tureck, and Leopold Stokowski.

Surprisingly enough, at his first public performance, Gould didn't play the piano. Instead he played the organ at a recital in Toronto in 1945. The following year, he made his formal Canadian debut as a soloist and performed Beethoven's Fourth Piano Concerto at the Royal Conservatory of

Music. Gould had a very long, successful relationship with the Canadian Broadcast Company (CBC). His first broadcast on the CBC took place in 1950.

When Gould was twenty-two, he gave his United States debut performance in New York City on January 11, 1955. Given his piano artistry, Gould was offered a recording contract with Columbia Masterworks the day after his debut. Five months later, he released his first recording, *Goldberg Variations by Johann Sebastian Bach*. This recording was such a big success, it made the bestseller's list. This was the beginning of an extensive recording career with Columbia Masterworks where he produced over sixty recordings.

FACTS

Gould was a rather unorthodox pianist. Breaking with tradition, Gould decided to stop giving live performances during the middle of his career. He was much more comfortable in the recording studio.

In 1957, Gould embarked on his first European tour, starting with a performance in the Soviet Union. This was the first performance to take place in the Soviet Union by a Canadian. His concert was a big success, and Gould was very well received by the Soviet audience. Part of this tour included a performance with Herbert von Karajan and the Berlin Philharmonic, in which Gould performed Beethoven's Third Piano Concerto.

Three years later, Gould collaborated with Leonard Bernstein and the New York Philharmonic and made his first American television appearance. However, by the mid-1960s, Gould was losing interest in performing. As a result, he made his last public performance in Los Angeles, California, on April 10, 1964. At that time, he realized and acknowledged his preference for the recording studio over the concert hall. Through his recordings and televised broadcasts, he was able to reach his audience worldwide.

Glenn Gould was a strong individualist who touched and inspired the lives of many people throughout the world with his extraordinary piano playing. At the age of fifty, Gould passed away on October 4, 1982, a victim of a stroke.

CHAPTER 5

Famous Romantic Pianists

The romantic period in music began in the early 1800s and lasted into the early twentieth century. Several pianists left their mark on the music of this time period. And modern pianists enjoy recapturing the essence of this genre of music. This chapter will highlight a few of the more popular romantic pianists.

Fryderyk François Chopin

On February 22, 1810, Fryderyk François Chopin was born in Zelazowa Wola, Poland. However, some musicologists argue that his exact birth date is not known.

At the age of six, Chopin began his piano studies with the Czech teacher Wojciech Zywny. In 1822, he completed his piano studies with Zywny and began private composition lessons with Josef Elsner. A year later, Chopin became a student at the Warsaw Lyceum, studying classical literature, singing, drawing, music theory, and harmony. Chopin finished his studies at the Warsaw Lyceum on July 27, 1826. Later that year, he entered the Fine Arts Department of the Warsaw University. His first piano composition, Polonaise in B-flat Major, was written when he was seventeen years old. Two years later, Chopin began to perform for the aristocracy in Warsaw.

His first visit to Vienna took place in 1829, and there he played several concerts. Chopin's performances were well received by both critics and audiences alike. On March 17, 1830, the premiere performance of his Concerto in F Minor took place at Warsaw's National Theater.

ESSENTIALS The difference between classical and romantic music is the form and content. Some composers wanted to be more expressive and infuse their emotions into their compositions and go beyond the confines of the classical form. In doing so, the tightly knit A-B-A classical form was expanded to accommodate these expressions.

While Chopin was in Vienna, he led a very active social life and was a familiar face among the local musical community. In the summer of 1830, he left Vienna and traveled to Salzburg, Munich, Stuttgart, and Paris. Chopin eventually settled down in Paris. Later that year, signs of his failing health began to appear.

On February 26, 1832, Chopin gave his first performance in Paris at the Salle Pleyel and played his Concerto in E Minor. The noted composers Franz Liszt and Felix Mendelssohn were in the audience. In Paris, Chopin's popularity grew, and he became a well-known teacher. He regularly frequented the best Parisian aristocratic, social, and political circles. During this time period, Chopin met Liszt and was very impressed with Liszt's musical interpretation of his Etudes op. 10, so much so that he dedicated the entire set to Liszt.

For the next three years, Chopin was very productive. In addition to performing on a regular basis and teaching piano to the Parisian aristocracy, Chopin composed several of his piano compositions during this time period. In 1836, due to his deteriorating health, Chopin drafted a will and testament.

For the next ten years, Chopin continued to perform and received rave reviews in Paris. His growing successes and popularity spread throughout Europe and reached his homeland, Poland.

On February 16, 1848, Chopin played his final concert in Paris at the Pleyel Salon. A year later Chopin was so ill that he had to stop teaching. In 1849, he sketched his last piano piece, Mazurka in F Minor, and burned all of his unpublished and uncompleted compositions. On October 17, 1849, Chopin died.

Van Cliburn

Van Cliburn, whose complete name is Harvey Lavan Cliburn Jr., was born on July 12, 1934, in Shreveport, Louisiana. He started playing the piano when he was three years old, and his piano teacher at that time was his mother, Rildia Bee O'Bryan Cliburn. Rildia studied piano with Arthur Friedheim, who was a pupil of the famous Franz Liszt. His first public performance took place when he was only four years old. By the time he was six years old, it was obvious to him and his parents that he was destined to be a concert pianist. At the age of twelve, Cliburn made his orchestral debut with the Houston Symphony Orchestra, as a result of winning first prize in a statewide piano competition for young Texan pianists. His mother continued to be his piano teacher until he was seventeen years old, at which time he left home to study at the Julliard School in New York City where he furthered his piano studies with Mme. Rosina Lhevinne.

In 1958, when the Cold War was all a rage, Cliburn, at the age of twenty-three, won the hearts of the Russian people when he won the first International Tchaikovsky Competition in Moscow. By winning this coveted prize, his career was launched, and Cliburn made front-page news worldwide. In New York City, he was given a ticker-tape parade, which was unheard of for a classical musician. Despite the Cold War, Premier Khrushchev invited Cliburn to return to the Soviet Union several times for an extended number of concerts. When he recorded Tchaikovsky's Piano Concerto no. 1, it was the first classical recording to reach platinum status, and since then, has sold over three million copies.

FACTS

Van Cliburn is a celebrated pianist worldwide in recognition of his outstanding accomplishments and his interpretation of piano works by romantic composers.

Because of Cliburn's outstanding achievement in winning the competition in Moscow, he was at the very center and limelight of the classical music world. His international concert tours were always met with sold-out crowds, and his recordings went to the top of record sales charts. For the next twenty years, Cliburn performed with every major orchestra and leading conductor at concert halls throughout the world. During this same time period, Cliburn was in high demand for formal performances with presidents, royalty, dignitaries, and heads of state from countries in Europe, South America, and Asia. Despite his demanding performance schedule, Cliburn made time to establish the Van Cliburn International Piano Competition in 1962 as a testament to his commitment to support and develop young talent.

Reflecting his continued commitment to the needs of aspiring young pianists, Cliburn has provided scholarships at the Julliard School, the Cincinnati Conservatory, the Franz Liszt Academy, Louisiana State University, the Moscow Conservatory, and the Leningrad Conservatory. Furthermore, he has established scholarships at the Interlochen Arts Academy, where the Van Cliburn Scholarship Lodge is located.

Vladimir Horowitz

On October 1, 1903, Vladimir Horowitz was born in the Ukraine. He began playing the piano at the age of five and was taught by his mother. He studied with her until 1912, at which time he entered the Kiev Conservatory to further his piano studies. Two years later, he met and played for the famous Russian composer Alexander Scriabin. He graduated from the conservatory in 1919 and performed Rachmaninov's Piano Concerto no. 3 at his graduation.

In 1920, Horowitz made his solo debut performance in Kiev. By 1922, he was performing throughout Russia. In 1925, he left Russia and went to Germany. A year later, Horowitz made his first solo western European performance in Berlin. With only ninety minutes' prior notice, he performed Tchaikovsky's Piano Concerto no. 1 with the Hamburg Philharmonic in 1926. Horowitz received a standing ovation for this performance, which launched his career as a concert pianist in Germany and throughout Europe.

In 1928, Horowitz traveled to New York and performed Tchaikovsky's Piano Concerto no. 1 with the New York Philharmonic. Following the success of this performance, he embarked on an extensive tour of the United States.

FACTS

Horowitz met Russian composer Sergei Rachmaninov. Soon after this meeting, Horowitz recorded Rachmaninov's Piano Concerto no. 3 with the London Symphony Orchestra and received great reviews. These two great musicians remained close friends until 1943, when Rachmaninov died.

During the early 1930s, Horowitz performed with the world's greatest orchestras and conductors. In 1932, the great conductor Toscanini, hearing of Horowitz's extraordinary talents, asked him to perform with the New York Philharmonic at Carnegie Hall. The fiery Italian conductor took a strong liking to Horowitz, which was the beginning of a long-lasting artistic relationship between these two great musicians. As fate would have it, Horowitz married Toscanini's daughter Wanda on December 21, 1933.

When World War II began in 1939, the Horowitz and Toscanini families fled Europe and came to the United States. In 1943, at the height of the war, Horowitz and Toscanini performed Tchaikovsky's Piano Concerto no. 1 at Carnegie Hall and raised over $10 million to help victims of World War II. In 1945, Vladimir Horowitz became a citizen of the United States.

Horowitz performed regularly in the United States and gave the American premiere performances of Sergei Prokofiev's Sixth, Seventh, and Eighth Piano Concertos. After years of performing, he decided to retire from the concert stage in 1953.

ESSENTIALS Horowitz was the recipient of fifteen Grammy Awards including one for his recording of Chopin's piano music for Sony Classical, which won the best solo classical album category in 1991.

During the 1950s and 1960s, Horowitz recorded for both CBS Masterworks and RCA Records. In 1965, Horowitz returned to the concert hall with his "Historic Return" performance series. He also performed a one-hour concert for television on CBS in 1968.

Honoring the Golden Jubilee of his American debut, in 1978, Horowitz performed Rachmaninov's Piano Concerto no. 3 with Eugene Ormandy and the New York Philharmonic Orchestra. Later that year, he performed at the White House for President and Mrs. Carter. In 1982, at the invitation of Prince Charles, Horowitz performed a televised broadcast in London for the royals.

After an absence of sixty years, Horowitz returned to Russia and performed for sold-out audiences in Moscow and Leningrad. While at home, on November 5, 1989, Vladimir Horowitz died of a heart attack.

Franz Liszt

Franz Liszt, regarded by many as the greatest pianist of all time, is one of the most awe-inspiring and influential pianists of the nineteenth century. He was born Ferencz Liszt on October 22, 1811, in Raiding, Hungary. At the age of six, Liszt was declared a child prodigy. He received his early piano instructions from his father, Adam, who was a professional cellist. Recognizing his son's amazing talents, Adam arranged a series of public exhibitions for his son with hopes of getting backers to help finance Liszt's musical education. Adam succeeded, and a group of Hungarian noblemen set up a fund allowing the Liszt family to move to Vienna. When Liszt was eleven years old, he and his family relocated to the thriving musical capital of Vienna, where he studied piano with Carl Czerny, who had studied with Ludwig van Beethoven. Supposedly, Czerny was so impressed with Liszt's innate talents that he offered to teach him at no cost.

By 1823, Liszt was astonishing audiences, musicians, and kings with his superb musicianship and his keen ability to improvise on the spot. Soon afterward, the Liszt family traveled to Paris with the intention of admitting Franz in the Paris Conservatory of Music. The conservatory rejected him on the grounds that he was considered a foreigner, not being a French citizen.

When he was only fifteen years old, his father died, and Liszt was left with the responsibility of having to take care of his mother. He tried to make a living by teaching piano, but the young Liszt was plagued with depression and disillusionment. He actually began to lose interest in music. Liszt's newfound interest was reading, and he immersed himself in the subjects of literature and religion.

In 1830, with the outbreak of the French Revolution, Liszt rebounded with a new commitment to music. During this time period, Liszt heard the Italian violinist Nicolò Paganini, who inspired Liszt to develop the same virtuoso technique for the piano that Paganini had done with the violin. Liszt is credited with exploring, developing, and expanding piano playing and technique to its fullest potential. Liszt accomplished this at the expense of breaking strings and even piano legs by performing with such powerful technique, passion, drama, and force.

After becoming a virtuoso pianist, Liszt embarked on whirlwind tours throughout Europe, conquering wildly enthusiastic audiences by storm. By 1844, "Lisztomania" was in full force, and Liszt reached a level of fame unprecedented by any other performing artist. Liszt's command of the instrument and dazzling showmanship resulted in sold-out audiences everywhere he performed.

Anyone who creates innovative changes and does something new and different from the norm is going to be met with resistance from the status quo. Thus, the critics did not accept Liszt's dramatic theatrics. The famous German composer Johannes Brahms went so far as to publish a manifesto against Liszt. These critics and the intellectuals of the day didn't take Liszt's crowd-pleasing pieces seriously. Some critics also didn't approve of his playing for the general mass audience instead of catering only to the kings, queens, and aristocracy.

But over time, the older classic traditions eventually faded, giving way to the new musical movement led by Liszt, called the Late Romantics. It should be noted that Liszt did win the approval of a group of composers including Berlioz and Schumann, who acknowledged his superb musicianship and ingenious compositions.

Liszt was also a humanitarian and philanthropist. For example, he raised money from his performances to aid Hungarian victims of the 1838 Danube flood and to underwrite the cost of erecting a Beethoven memorial statue in 1839.

ESSENTIALS

Liszt knew how to cater to the public and win their high approval with his brilliant showpieces. He could play from memory for hours. Women often threw themselves at the famed virtuoso.

In 1847, much to the surprise of the European music community, Liszt stopped performing and retired at the age of thirty-six. That same year, Liszt met the Russian princess Carolyne Sayn-Wittgenstein, who became his companion for the rest of his life. The following year, Liszt and Carolyne moved to Weimar where he held the esteemed position of Court Kapellmeister in Altenberg. In 1860, Liszt and Carolyne attempted to get married in Rome. However, their plans were unsuccessful because Carolyne had difficulty in obtaining the necessary divorce papers.

After thirteen years in Weimar giving numerous performances of music by Berlioz, Debussy, Wagner, and his own compositions, Liszt resigned from being Kapellmeister after repeated attacks from conservatives who were threatened by his musical innovations.

FACTS

Liszt studied theology in Rome. In 1866, Liszt was conferred the religious title of Abbé by Pope Pius IX. After 1867, Liszt divided his time between Rome, Weimar, and Budapest, conducting, teaching, composing, and promoting Richard Wagner's music. In Budapest, he established the Conservatory of Music and was elected to be the school's first president.

In addition to his accomplishments as a virtuoso pianist, Liszt taught more than 350 students, composed over 400 pieces of music, and was responsible for creating today's popular solo piano recital. He repositioned the piano sideways, giving the audience more visual and acoustic pleasure.

At every stage of his pioneering life, Liszt attracted two opposing groups of people: jealous cynics and open-minded, enlightened followers.

On July 31, 1886, Franz Liszt died of pneumonia in Bayreuth, Germany.

Ignacy Jan Paderewski

Ignacy Jan Paderewski was born in November 1860 in the small village of Kurylowka in Padolia, Poland. Paderewski's childhood was very unsettling. Soon after he was born, his mother died, a victim of the Russian Revolution, and his father, the administrator of several large estates and a member of minor nobility, was sent to prison. Under the circumstances, an aunt took care of him and raised the young Paderewski.

When he was three years old, Paderewski started to play the piano. Unlike some of his contemporaries, Paderewski had a late start with his formal piano studies. His first piano lesson took place during his early teenage years at the Warsaw Conservatoire. Much to his dismay, his first piano teacher told him he didn't have the hands required to be a pianist. Crushed, Paderewski wanted to discontinue studying the piano. Fortunately, another piano teacher told him he had a natural gift to be a pianist, and he resumed his piano lessons.

When he was sixteen, Paderewski, along with a violinist and cellist, went on a tour of Poland and performed at a variety of venues. Some venues had inadequate pianos or no piano at all. Determinedly, Paderewski approached wealthy local residents and pleaded to borrow their pianos.

In 1878, he graduated from the Warsaw Conservatoire and accepted an offer to be one of its piano teachers. Two years later, he married a student named Antonia Korsak. The following year, Antonia died while giving birth to a baby boy. Soon afterward, Paderewski left his son with his mother-in-law, resigned from the Warsaw Conservatoire, and went to Berlin.

While continuing his musical studies in Berlin, he met the pianist Anton Rubinstein, who assured Paderewski that he had a great future as a pianist. With Rubinstein's encouraging words, Paderewski moved to Vienna to study piano with Leschetizky, reputed to be one of the best piano teachers. Leschetizky told Paderewski that he could have been a great pianist if he had taken piano lessons at an earlier age. However, after a period of teaching the eager Paderewski, Leschetizky was amazed at Paderewski's remarkable progress and acknowledged the prowess he commanded at the keyboard.

A Great Career Begins

Paderewski accepted a teaching position at the Strasbourg Conservatoire in 1885. At this time, he performed frequently, attracted a strong following, and quickly rose to fame. Because of a dispute with the directors about not paying him two months' vacation pay, Paderewski resigned from the Strasbourg Conservatoire, returned to Berlin, and continued his studies with Leschetizky.

In Berlin, Leschetizky arranged to have Paderewski perform at an important concert, which turned out to be a big success. He then traveled to Paris and made his debut at the Salle Erard in 1888. In the audience were local celebrities including Tchaikovsky and the famous conductor, Lamoureux. Paderewski was so well received by the audience that he played for an additional hour after the program had officially ended. Lamoureux, so impressed with Paderewski's performance, made arrangements to have Paderewski appear at his concerts. After another successful performance in Paris, he returned to Vienna. With the success of his Paris performances under his fingers, Paderewski wowed the audiences in Vienna.

His next trip was to London, where Paderewski gave a series of recitals at the Old James Hall. He then embarked on a successful tour of Germany and Romania. On his return to Berlin, Paderewski rehearsed with the Berlin Philharmonic Orchestra, conducted by Hans Von Bulow. After the rehearsal, a successful booking agent named Wolff (who had previously refused to work with Paderewski) approached him, requesting to manage his career. Paderewski declined Wolff's offer. At the performance, when Paderewski was playing the concerto, the orchestra played out of tune and played wrong notes, souring Paderewski's performance. To add insult to the injured performance, Von Bulow walked off the stage during Paderewski's solo.

At the Top of His Game

In 1891, Paderewski traveled to the United States for an extensive tour. Paderewski's performances attracted the largest crowds in concert history. At his New York City performance, while playing Beethoven's "Appassionata" piano sonata, Paderewski tore some of the tendons in his right arm and injured one of his fingers. He was advised by a doctor to stop playing for several months, but Paderewski did not take the doctor's advice. Despite this critical handicap, he continued on with the tour. Because of the injuries, Paderewski could only use three fingers on his right hand and required medical attention before each concert. After this strenuous tour and with little rest, Paderewski went back to England for two concert performances. By this time, his injured finger had become completely dysfunctional, and medical specialists told Paderewski that there was no chance of a complete recovery. With time, he regained the full strength of his right arm, but his finger remained useless until Paderewski developed his own physical therapy and finger exercises. As a result, the damaged finger became somewhat functional, but remained much weaker than his others.

During his second United States tour, Paderewski's finger got infected. Despite the condition of his finger, he continued playing. Sometimes while playing, the finger bled and covered the keyboard with blood. After this tour, he continued playing with performances in Warsaw, Moscow, and St. Petersburg. Paderewski finally returned to his home near Lake Geneva, Switzerland, and married the Baroness Helena Gorska.

While performing in the United States, Paderewski was attracted to the climate and beauty of California, particularly the area of Paso Robles. He also liked the soothing sulfur bath waters, which relieved his rheumatism.

As World War I was about to explode, Paderewski purchased 2,800 acres of sprawling hills in Paso Robles, California. At this same time, he raised more than $60,000 to help free Poland from the hardships and destruction of the war. In response to his commitment to the people of Poland, Paderewski was made Poland's Prime Minister in 1919. He restored civility and order and helped to shape a new future for Poland by taking part in the historical signing of the Versailles Peace Treaty, which also took place in 1919. A year later, Paderewski went to Paso Robles and gave his full attention to his music. He returned to the concert stage and continued to attract large audiences wherever he played.

FACTS

Despite his overwhelming popularity with the mass population, some critics complained that he played using too much rubato— taking the liberty of slowing down and speeding up passages of music that were actually written to be played evenly or in strict time. This style of personalization is popular with pianists who take a dramatic, romantic approach.

When Germany invaded Poland and World War II began, Paderewski was living in Switzerland, and his health was failing. The people of Poland turned to Paderewski, seeking his leadership. In 1940, he became president of the new Polish Parliament-in-Exile. A year later, even though he was ill, Paderewski traveled to New York in his continuing efforts to help Poland. Shortly thereafter, he became extremely ill, and at the age of eighty, Paderewski died.

His funeral was held at St. Patrick's Cathedral and was attended by 4,500 people, including statesmen, political leaders, and famous musicians from all over the world. There were also 35,000 people standing outside the cathedral.

President Roosevelt made a declaration that Paderewski's remains were to be temporarily laid to rest at the *USS Maine* Monument in Arlington National Cemetery. In 1992, when Poland was once again a free country, Paderewski's remains were transported to his homeland and finally laid to rest in a crypt at St. John's Cathedral in Warsaw—except for his heart. Following his wishes, his heart is encased in a bronze sculpture at the Church of the Black Madonna in the predominately Polish-American community of Doylestown, Pennsylvania.

Arthur Rubinstein

On January 28, 1887, Arthur Rubinstein was born in Lodz, Poland. He began to study the piano at the age of three, and gave his first public performance when he was eight years old. Two years later, Rubinstein and his mother traveled to Berlin to audition for the famous violinist Joseph Joachim. The young Rubinstein made a strong impression on Joachim, and as a result, he agreed to take Rubinstein under his wing and be responsible for his overall musical education.

Soon afterward, Joachim introduced Rubinstein to a prominent piano teacher in Berlin named Heinrich Barth. After three years of studying with Barth, Rubinstein made his debut performance with the Berlin Philharmonic. He performed pieces by Chopin, Mozart, Schumann, and Saint-Saens. Local critics were very impressed with Rubinstein's performance. As a result, his concert pianist career was launched, and Rubinstein went on to perform throughout Europe, receiving the highest public and critical acclaim.

Rubinstein traveled to New York City in 1906, where he performed at Carnegie Hall for the first time and received a lukewarm reception. He then continued touring and performing throughout the United States.

When Rubinstein returned to Paris, he became friends with the conductor Serge Koussevitzky and composer Igor Stravinsky. In 1914, World War I began, and Rubinstein left Paris, embarking on a concert tour of Spain. The audiences of Spain responded to his playing with enthusiasm and approval. His playing had matured. He played with more passion, not like the controlled sedate playing of traditional pianists, but instead with an intense, freewheeling style. Rubinstein's new charismatic, passionate performance style attracted a large body of listeners in Spain. He then went on an extended tour of South America.

When he returned to Paris, Rubinstein felt his piano playing had become stale. This all changed when he met his future wife, Nela Mlynarski, who was nearly twenty years younger than him. They married in London in 1932. Soon after the birth of their first child, Rubinstein felt the need to return to the discipline of piano studies. He began practicing the piano twelve to sixteen hours a day.

Rubinstein made his return performance to Carnegie Hall in 1937, and this time he was hailed as a musical genius. The critics called him a master musician, performing a ground-breaking interpretation of Chopin's piano music. With the growing threat of the Nazi occupation, Rubinstein quickly relocated his family to the United States and settled in Los Angeles, California. He became a citizen of the United States in 1946, but spent most of his later years in Europe. After World War II and the loss of his entire family in Lodz, Poland, Rubinstein's performances supported the new state of Israel.

Despite his failing health, Rubinstein continued to perform during his seventies and eighties. Even when he lost his eyesight, he still traveled the world teaching and lecturing. He died in Geneva, Switzerland, in 1982; his ashes are buried in an Israeli forest that honors his name.

Rudolf Serkin

On March 28, 1903, Rudolf Serkin was born in Eger, Bohemia. His parents, Mordko and Augusta, were Russian Jews who fled Russia for Bohemia because of the pogroms.

At the young age of four, Serkin was playing the piano and reading music. The celebrated Viennese pianist Alfred Grunfield heard young Serkin play and encouraged his parents to send him to Vienna to study piano with Richard Robert. Taking Grunfield's advice, the Serkin family relocated to Vienna, where Rudolf studied piano with Robert and composition with Arnold Schoenberg.

When Serkin was only twelve years old, he made his concert debut with the Vienna Symphony Orchestra and played Mendelssohn's Piano Concerto in G Minor. Serkin performed so well that he was invited to tour Europe, but he turned down the opportunity in order to continue his studies in Vienna.

Serkin began his professional career as a pianist when he was seventeen years old, performing solo recitals and with chamber orchestras. At this time, he also played a series of violin sonatas with the violinist Adolf Busch. During the next two years, Serkin toured Europe, dazzling and impressing audiences with his intense style of playing.

In 1935, Serkin made his first American appearance at the Coolidge Festival, performing with Busch. His solo concert career was launched in 1936 when he performed Beethoven's Piano Concerto no. 4 and Mozart's Piano Concerto no. 27 with the New York Philharmonic. Serkin received praise from the New York critics who acknowledged his unusual and impressive talents, and powerful technique. That same year, Serkin married Irene Busch, the daughter of his violin partner.

Serkin performed his first New York solo recital in 1937 at Carnegie Hall. Again, the New York critics hailed him as a pianist possessing magnificent control and the keen ability to focus on each individual piano composition. The following year, Serkin and Busch played a series of concerts in New York, performing violin sonatas composed by Beethoven and Schubert.

Serkin became an American citizen in 1939 and moved to Philadelphia, where he soon became the head of the piano department at the Curtis Institute of Music. He taught piano there for thirty years before becoming the institute's director in 1968. During this time, Serkin continued making tours of the United States, performing Beethoven and Schubert piano sonatas.

Throughout the years, Serkin continued to teach at the Curtis Institute, until he had to stop due to his failing health. As a result of his declining physical condition, Serkin was forced to retire from touring in 1987. On May 9, 1991, Serkin died at his home in Guilford, Vermont, a victim of cancer.

CHAPTER 6

Famous Pop and Jazz Pianists

Because there are so many famous pianists, and because of space constraints, all of them cannot be represented here. With that in mind, what follows are some of the most well-known pianists representing the musical styles of jazz, pop, and rock and roll.

Types of Jazz

Jazz is a broad term representing many different styles of music including ragtime, Dixieland, stride, big band, blues, swing, bebop, and fusion. There is also a category of popular songs called standards. Standards include songs written by Irving Berlin, Duke Ellington, George Gershwin, Jerome Kern, and Cole Porter.

Some of the best examples of stride piano playing can be heard in the recordings of Fats Waller and Dick Hyman. Fats Waller is largely responsible for putting the stride piano style on the music map. When playing stride, the left hand does a good deal of jumping octaves in the lower resister, up and down the keyboard, playing the root and leaping up an octave to play the corresponding chord. In addition to Fats Waller, Dick Hyman is known for his expertise in stride piano playing.

FACTS

Some up-tempo Dixieland and ragtime music has a stride feel to it. In simple terms, the stride sound is sometimes referred to as "ump-ah-ump-ah" (root-chord-root-chord), which gives it a very bouncy sound.

The music of Duke Ellington and Count Basie are examples of big band and swing with pianists as leaders of the band. There are many other examples of big band music lead by clarinetists and brass players including The Tommy Dorsey Band, The Benny Goodman Band, The Harry James Band, and The Glen Miller Orchestra.

Bebop music is fast-paced with complex harmonies and intricate melodies. A good example of bebop is the music of pianist Thelonious Monk and Bud Powell.

Fusion is a term representing a combination of musical styles. One could say that George Gershwin's music is fusion. Keith Jarrett could also easily fall into this category. Jarrett plays so many different types and styles of music from standards to classical to pure improvisation that he is not limited to any one category. Chic Corea and Herbie Hancock also play multiple styles of music.

Ray Charles

Ray Charles created a new genre of music called soul, which is a mixture of rhythm and blues, gospel, and light jazz. As a result, he pioneered a new style of piano playing incorporating these different styles of music.

In 1930, Ray Charles Robinson was born in Albany, Georgia. When Charles was six years old, he started to lose his eyesight due to a glaucoma condition.

At the age of fifteen, Charles was off on his own, performing in bands in Florida. Three years later, with $600 in his pocket, Charles moved to Seattle. In Seattle, he formed the Maxim Trio, modeling the Nat King Cole sound. In 1949, the Maxim Trio had a hit single called "Confession Blues," which was released on the Downbeat record label.

In 1952, Atlantic Records bought Charles's recording contract from Swingtime for only $2,500. Charles decided to move on from the Nat King Cole style and started to mix gospel music with blues lyrics. Charles's next hit single, "I've Got A Woman," crossed over rhythm and blues into pop music charts and gave Charles a broad-based listening audience.

During the 1950s, Charles was gaining popularity with jazz fans, and he performed at the 1959 Newport Jazz Festival. His next hit single, "What I Say," was a huge hit single that clearly established Charles as a popular recording artist.

SSENTIALS In 1982, Charles was inducted into the Blues Foundation's Hall of Fame, and in 1986, he was inducted into the Rock and Roll Hall of Fame. To this day, Ray Charles inspires people throughout the world with his singing and soulful piano playing.

In 1959, Charles left Atlantic Records and began recording on the ABC-Paramount record label. In the early 1960s, he had a run of top hit singles including "Georgia on My Mind," "Hit the Road Jack," "Ruby," and "Unchain My Heart." He also had a hit instrumental single, "One Mint Julep," which was very popular with his growing number of jazz fans.

Wanting to have more control with his music, Charles formed Ray Charles Enterprises, comprised of Tangerine Records, Tangerine Music Publishing, and Racer Music Company. He opened RCE recording studios and offices in Los Angeles in 1963. At this time, Charles was using a forty-piece orchestra and full chorus with his recordings. As a result of his full commercial sound, he had huge hit records including *I Can't Stop Loving You*, *Born to Lose*, and *You Don't Know Me*.

Scott Joplin

Scott Joplin was born into a very musical family. Everyone played an instrument or sang. Joplin's father, Jiles, played the violin, and his mother, Florence, played the banjo and sang.

He was born in 1867, in the vicinity of Linden, Texas. In 1872, the Joplin family moved to Texarkana, Texas. Joplin's mother was a housekeeper. Some of these homes had pianos, and that's where Joplin practiced the piano. Ten years later, Florence bought a piano for Joplin.

Toward the end of the 1880s, Joplin left home. At that time, Joplin performed with various musical groups and traveled around the Midwestern states. Supposedly, he attended the Chicago World's Fair in 1893, playing the cornet in one of the many bands. In 1895, his travels took him to Syracuse, New York, where he sold two of his original songs, "Please Say You Will" and "A Picture of Her Face."

FACTS

Joplin finally settled in Sedalia, Missouri, where he worked as a pianist at the Maple Leaf and Black 400 Clubs, which were social clubs for black gentlemen. At this time, he reportedly attended George R. Smith College.

Original Rags was Joplin's first ragtime piece of music, which he sold to a publisher in 1898. John Stark & Sons published his second ragtime, *Maple Leaf Rag*, in 1899. He received a one-cent royalty for each copy sold, plus ten free copies. This was a better-than-average publishing deal at the time for a black composer. More often than not, white publishers took advantage of black composers, paying them a one-time flat-fee from $10 to $20 per piece with no royalties. For *Maple Leaf Rag*, Joplin earned approximately $360 a year for the duration of his lifetime.

At the beginning of the twentieth century, Joplin continued with his creative output and wrote his first opera, *A Guest of Honor*. This opera was a full-fledged production, consisting of a touring company of over twenty-four performers. After a five-state tour, *A Guest of Honor* failed because someone stole the box office receipts, seriously impairing the financial affairs of the company. Unfortunately, this opera is lost because it was never registered with the copyright office at the Library of Congress.

ESSENTIALS No one could possibly have known that nearly sixty years after Joplin's death, his ragtime song "The Entertainer" would be such a huge success as the theme song to the feature film *The Sting*. As a result, ragtime music was revitalized and appreciated by millions worldwide.

Joplin moved to New York City in 1907 and lived there for the remainder of his life. New York was inspiring for Joplin. There he wrote and published several new songs, as well as his second opera, *Treemonisha*, in 1910. This opera contained the gems "Overture," "Aunt Dinah Has Blown De Horn," and "A Real Slow Drag." Despite the wonderful music, *Treemonisha* was not a success because the lyrics were not easily understood.

The failure of *Treemonisha* hit Joplin hard and slowed his creative output. For the next six years, only three of his songs were published: "Felicity Rag," "Kismet Rag," and "Magnetic Rag."

He was also terminally sick, suffering from syphilis. In 1916, Joplin suffered from dementia, paranoia, paralization, and other syphilis-related symptoms. In January of 1917, he was admitted to Manhattan State Hospital and died there on April 1.

At the time of his death, ragtime was losing its popularity, and the United States had entered World War I. Joplin is buried in St. Michael's Cemetery located in Astoria, Queens, New York.

Oscar Peterson

On August 15, 1925, Oscar Peterson was born in Montreal. His father, Daniel, played the piano and was Peterson's first piano teacher. When Peterson was a high school student, he studied piano with an accomplished classical pianist named Paul de Marky. Mr. de Marky developed Peterson's technique and overall keyboard proficiency. He also recognized Peterson's talent and convinced him to share his musical gift with the rest of the world.

When Peterson was a teenager, his father played him recordings by Art Tatum. Supposedly, Peterson was so intimidated by Tatum's superb piano playing that he didn't play the piano for over a month. Fortunately, the intimidation soon turned into inspiration, and Peterson was once again playing the piano.

ESSENTIALS

During the early 1950s, Peterson met Tatum. They eventually became close friends; however, it took Peterson some time before he felt comfortable enough to play piano with Tatum in the same room.

Peterson attended Montreal High School, where he played piano in a band called the Serenaders. During that same time period, his older sister Daisy arranged an audition and entered him in a national amateur contest that the CBC (Canadian Broadcasting Company) was holding. Peterson won, and as a result, became a regular performer on a weekly Montreal radio program and performed on a national CBC television show. This media exposure launched his musical career.

By 1942, Peterson was playing piano with The Johnny Holmes Orchestra in the greater metropolitan area of Montreal. Maynard Ferguson was playing trumpet in the same group.

Eventually, Peterson went out on his own and formed a trio with Ozzie Roberts on bass and Clarence Jones on drums. They performed regularly at the Alberta Lounge in Montreal. Soon afterward, a local radio station began to broadcast live from the Alberta, sending Peterson's music across the airwaves. Norman Granz, the producer of Jazz at the Philharmonic, heard one of the radio broadcasts and went to hear Peterson and his trio live at the Alberta.

Impressed with what he heard, Granz arranged to have Peterson play with Jazz at the Philharmonic as a surprise guest at a Carnegie Hall performance in New York City.

The audience and critics were thrilled with Peterson's playing, and he joined the Jazz at the Philharmonic and toured North America.

For two years, Peterson played with Ray Brown on bass. In the third year, Granz suggested that Peterson play with a trio, and Charlie Smith joined him on drums. Peterson soon replaced drums with guitar, and Irving Ashby joined the trio as guitarist. Ashby and Barney Kessel played guitar with the trio for about a year, and then, at the suggestion of Ray Brown, Herb Ellis became their guitar player. This lineup of The Oscar Peterson Trio became one of the best working trios in the business.

For five consecutive years (1950–1955), Peterson was voted best pianist in the *Down Beat Magazine* reader polls. He went on to receive this same award, again, five years in a row from 1959 to 1963.

During the 1950s, The Oscar Peterson Trio toured Europe with the Jazz Philharmonic and made their debut performance in Japan in 1953. In addition to a rigorous touring schedule, the trio recorded extensively, producing dozens of albums, both live and in the studio, and became known as one of the greatest jazz trios. In 1958, Herb Ellis reluctantly retired and was replaced with Ed Thigpen on drums. With Thigpen on drums, a new trio was born.

FACTS

In the early 1990s, a joyous reunion took place with Peterson, Brown, and Ellis, which resulted in four new album releases. Oscar Peterson stands in high regard as one of the greatest jazz pianists of all time.

In 1962, The Oscar Peterson Trio recorded seven studio albums and four live albums all in one year's time. Two years later, Peterson accepted an invitation from a German millionaire/audio engineer named Hans Gerg Brunner-Schwer. This was the beginning of a long prosperous relationship, which resulted in capturing some of Peterson's finest playing. In 1965, Thigpen, tired of life on the road, left the trio, and the following year, Brown did the same.

During the remainder of the 1960s, Peterson continued to record with Hans, who had formed his own record label. Together they produced fifteen albums.

In 1972, Peterson was finally recognized by his country for his outstanding achievements and was honored as an Officer of the Order of Canada. Around the same time period, Granz launched a new record company and recorded Peterson's newly formed trio with Joe Pass on guitar and Niels Pederson on bass. This trio toured North America extensively for approximately eight years.

In the early 1980s, Peterson played more solo recitals and did less touring. His affliction with arthritis made it difficult for him to walk. Sometimes he had to cancel a performance due to excessive pain in his hands. During the 1980s, Peterson was presented with numerous awards and honors from institutions and organizations in Canada and the United States. As a recording artist, Peterson has received eight Grammy Awards, including the 1997 Lifetime Achievement Award.

Art Tatum

Art Tatum was born on October 13, 1909, in Toledo, Ohio. Despite being blind in one eye and partially blind in the other, Tatum established himself to be one of the most amazing pianists of the twentieth century.

His ears and hands made up for any inadequacy he had with his eyes. Aside from learning to read music with the aid of glasses and Braille, Tatum was for the most part self-taught. He learned from playing piano rolls and listening to records. Tatum was greatly influenced by the jazz pianist Fats Waller.

Tatum moved to New York City in 1932 and recorded his first solo recording for the Brunswick record label. During this time period, he performed regularly at the fashionable New York City jazz clubs of the day, including the Three Duces. The vast majority of the time he performed as a soloist. However, in the mid-1940s, he did form a successful trio with Tiny Grimes on guitar and Slam Stewart on bass.

Tatum's solo recordings are a true testament to his musical genius. He recorded a series of solo recordings for Verve Records that captured his technical abilities, his full command of the keyboard, and his unlimited capacity to develop and expand both melody and harmony. Tatum had an unprecedented style of piano playing that astonished and amazed his fellow jazz pianists, as well as the great classical pianist Vladimir Horowitz. The world lost this great pianist when he died in Los Angeles, California, on November 4, 1956.

Piano in Pop

With some of the rock and pop songs, you'll hear a variety of keyboards from organs to harpsichords to synthesizers instead of or in addition to the piano. The piano and/or keyboard play different roles in these songs, including background, repeated rhythmic patterns, single minimal phrases, introductions, and foreground full-blown solos. Some recording artists use the piano sparingly, bringing it in and out of the song or only for the introduction or solo, while other artists use the keyboard throughout the entire song as a rhythm instrument, with or without drums and bass. All these different uses of pianos and keyboards surely demonstrate how versatile the keyboard is.

Though there are numerous examples of pianists in pop and rock and roll, there isn't time or space to go into detail of each. The next sections highlight two of the more famous pianists in pop.

Billy Joel

Billy Joel is one of the most proficient popular pianists living today. His early turbulent background set the stage for some of the greatest pop-rock songs ever written.

Joel was born in the Bronx and raised in a very nondescript tract home development in Levittown, New York. He was a rebellious, antisocial, hell-raising teenager. Fortunately for him and the music world, Joel was deeply influenced by The Beatles and the English bands that made up the powerful "British Invasion."

His father, a classically trained pianist, had encouraged Joel to take piano lessons as a child. With the fever of Beatle-mania raging, Joel applied his early piano training to form his first rock and roll band, called The Echoes. When he was eighteen, he joined a popular local band called The Hassles. They recorded two albums that didn't go anywhere and the band broke up. Distraught and disillusioned, Joel fell to the depths of despair and depression.

Putting himself back together with a new sense of hope and determination, Joel forged ahead and formed another band called Attila. This two-man psychedelic band recorded and released an album, but ended up a failure.

His next attempt was a solo album entitled *Cold Spring Harbor*. Plagued with technical recording and mastering errors, *Cold Spring Harbor* was added to Joel's growing list of failures. Feeling angry and defeated, Joel, along with his future wife and manager, Elizabeth Weber, went to Los Angeles. Making a fresh start, Joel used the pseudonym Bill Martin and played in piano bars, which inspired his very famous song "Piano Man." His talents were finally recognized in 1973, and he signed a recording contract with Columbia records. As a result, the *Piano Man* album was released, selling over a million copies. But because of the way the deal was structured, Joel made very little money on this very successful recording.

ESSENTIALS

On a more personal note, it should be mentioned that in 1985, Joel married supermodel Christie Brinkley, who inspired his hit single "Uptown Girl" from the *Innocent Man* album. Together they had a daughter, Alexa Ray, named after Joel's friend Ray Charles. Joel's marriage to Christie ended in divorce in 1994.

His next recording with Columbia was *Streetlife Serenade*, which included his first hit single, called "The Entertainer." He went on to record *Turnstiles*, which contains a collection of brilliant songs, but surprisingly didn't produce any hit singles.

While Joel appreciated the progress he was making, he was by no means a superstar. That all changed in 1977 when record producer Phil Ramone worked with Joel on *The Stranger*. By the end of 1979, it had sold more than five million copies. Five songs from *The Stranger* generated top hit singles for Joel, including his Grammy Award–winning song, "Just The

Way You Are." He went on to write, record, and perform some of his finest work with his subsequent albums *52nd Street* (1979), *Glass Houses* (1980), *Songs in the Attic* (1981), *Nylon Curtain* (1982), *An Innocent Man* (1983), *The Bridge* (1986), *Kohuept* (1987), and *Storm Front* (1989).

Joel's most recent recording to date is the critically acclaimed *River of Dreams* (1993). Since then, he has focused his musical talents on classical music, with intentions of composing and orchestrating instrumental music.

Elton John

Elton John, whose real name is Reginald Kenneth Dwight, was born on March 25, 1947, in Pinner, Middlesex, England. His father, Stanley Dwight, a squadron leader in the Royal Air Force, wanted John to be a Royal Air Force pilot or a bank teller. Stanley insisted that John not play or listen to the new American music called rock and roll. Against his father's wishes, John and his mother listened to the music of Elvis Presley and Buddy Holly. (This was pretty easy to do since John's father was away from home most of the time traveling with the Royal Air Force.)

John started playing piano at a young age, and when he was eleven years old, won a scholarship from the Royal Academy of Music, where he studied until he was fifteen. Buddy Holly was a big influence on John. At the age of thirteen, he copied Holly's look and wore dark-rimmed glasses, even though he had perfect vision and didn't need to wear glasses.

In 1960, John formed his first band, called The Corvettes, and eventually renamed the band Bluesology. During the 1960s, John provided backup vocals for Long John Baldry, The Drifters, The Inkspots, Patti LaBelle, and Major Lance. John decided to quit Bluesology in 1967 and teamed up with a lyricist named Bernie Taupin. The two of them met at Liberty Records in London, responding to an advertisement seeking songwriters. Liberty turned down both John and Taupin. At that time, John, who was still known as Reginald or Reggie, changed his name to Elton Hercules John. He chose Elton from his friend Elton Dean's name and John from Long John Baldry.

In 1970, John and Taupin released their first album, called *Empty Sky*. Later that year, they released a second album, simply called *Elton John*, which gave them their first hit single, "Your Song." John's first American performance took place at the Troubadour in Los Angeles on August 25, 1970. Five years later, he received his star on the Hollywood Walk of Fame.

During the 1970s, John recorded several top-ten hit singles and award-winning albums, including *Tumbleweed Connection*, *11-17-70*, *Madman Across the Water*, *Greatest Hits*, *Captain Fantastic*, *Brown Dirt Cowboy*, and *Rock of the Westies*. In 1973, John launched his own record label, called Rocket Records. On Thanksgiving Day, 1974, he succeeded in getting a reclusive John Lennon onstage during a Madison Square Garden concert. This turned out to be Lennon's final public performance.

ESSENTIALS

In 1992, John formed the Elton John AIDS Foundation in honor of his friend Ryan White, who died of the disease. Profits from John's single records are donated to the foundation.

In 1994, John was inducted into the Rock and Roll Hall of Fame. As a gesture of creative appreciation, he later gave the award to Bernie Taupin.

In 1995, John was named Commander of the British Empire. Three years later at Buckingham Palace, John was given the honorary title of Knight Bachelor, making him Sir Elton John, CBE.

Nineteen ninety-nine was the year that John and Tim Rice released the soundtrack to the Disney stage musical *Aida*. Various recording artists sang the songs, including John, Tina Turner, LeAnn Rimes, Sting, Janet Jackson, and The Spice Girls.

In July of 1999, John had an operation to install a pacemaker due to an irregular heartbeat. The operation was a success, but the pacemaker activates alarms every time he walks through a security device at airports. Not very tuneful for the melodious Elton John.

CHAPTER 7
Types of Pianos

Given the wide variety of sizes, shapes, and designs, there really is a piano for everyone. Pianos fall into two basic categories: verticals and horizontals. This chapter will explain the types of pianos in each of these categories, as well as explain the external and interior parts that make a piano a piano.

Vertical Pianos

Vertical pianos are spinets, consoles, studios, and uprights. The next few sections will give you an overview of each of these types. Let's start with the smallest piano, the spinet, and work our way up to the upright.

The Spinet Piano

The size of a spinet piano ranges from 36 inches to 38 inches in height and is approximately 58 inches wide. Spinets are the smallest pianos made, and given their size, they are very popular with apartment dwellers. They are also very practical for beginners and fit nicely in a spare bedroom. Spinets are made in a wide variety of furniture styles and finishes.

 **ESSENTIALS**

Though spinets are popular because of their small size, there aren't many to choose from in the market. If you're looking for a new small piano, you'll have far more to choose from if you consider a console.

However, there are very few companies manufacturing new spinet pianos. This is due in part to spinet pianos using what is called an indirect blow action. To make the spinet piano shorter, the keys have to go through more steps before striking the string. Because of this, you get less power and accuracy. This deficiency is referred to as lost motion.

Console Piano

Console pianos are the next size up, ranging in size from 40 inches to 43 inches in height and approximately 58 inches wide. These pianos are made with a direct action, which produces a balanced feel in the keys. Consoles have long strings and a soundboard larger than the spinet, which gives the console an enhanced tone. They are made in a variety of furniture styles and finishes.

Studio Piano

Compared to consoles, studio pianos are built with longer strings and have a larger soundboard. They range in size from 45 inches to 48 inches in height and approximately 58 inches wide. Studio pianos are very popular with teachers, professionals, and music schools because of their good tone quality and durability.

Upright Piano

Upright pianos are tall, ranging in size from 50 inches to 60 inches in height and approximately 58 inches wide. A few manufacturers are still making new uprights, but most uprights can be up to eighty years old. Most uprights have experienced years of playing, resulting in a tired and beaten sound. This takes a toll on the action, which slows down the response. However, when properly restored by a skilled craftsman, uprights can produce a deep rich tone and are more than adequate.

Horizontal Pianos

Grand pianos come in varying lengths. The smallest grand is called the petite grand and ranges in size from 4 feet 5 inches to 4 feet 10 inches. The next size up is the popular baby grand, ranging in size from 4 feet 11 inches to 5 feet 6 inches. Next is the medium grand which is 5 feet 7 inches.

FACTS

Baby grands are popular because they sound good, look good in a living room, and are more affordable than the larger grands.

The parlor grand, also known as the living room grand, ranges in size from 5 feet 9 inches to 6 feet 1 inch. Getting even bigger is the ballroom or semiconcert grand, which is 7 feet long. And the biggest of all grand pianos is the concert grand, which is a striking 9 feet long.

The size, distinctive shape, and design make the grand the most prized piano of all. Grand pianos come in a wide variety of styles and finishes. Of all the pianos, grand pianos have the finest piano tone and the most responsive key action.

Exterior Parts of a Piano

The exterior structure of a piano is called the cabinet or casing. This refers to the wood that makes up the top, front, and sides of the piano. Matching moldings complete the cabinet. The models determine the shape of the cabinet.

Once the wood cabinet is assembled, a finish, which is a stain, is applied to the wood. The standard types of finishes are mahogany, walnut (light, medium, and dark), oak, cherry, and ebony. Rosewood finishes, once popular, were eventually discontinued.

Fallboard

The fallboard is the long, horizontal, movable wooden piece located directly where the keys end. When placed in the down position, the fallboard completely covers the keys, protecting them from dust and other unwanted materials. Some piano manufacturers make fallboards that have a lock-and-key mechanism. When the fallboard is locked, there is no access to the keyboard and the instrument cannot be played.

Keys

The keys are the exterior part of the piano action. The best-made pianos have ivory white keys—strips of ivory are placed on top of the wooden keys, ebony for the shorter black keys. But due to the scarcity and difficulty of getting ivory, it's more common to find plastic covering on both the white and black keys. Every acoustic piano has eighty-eight keys.

Music Desk

The music desk is the movable piece of wood that looks like the top part of a music stand. It is located directly above the fallboard. On grand pianos, the music desk is adjustable and can be moved forward or backward to meet the player's preference. It can also be folded down to a completely flat position.

Adjustable Lids

All grand piano models have adjustable lids. The lid can be opened partially, halfway, or all the way. When the lid is open, it is supported by the prop stick, which is located inside the piano and is mounted to the right side of the casing. Some grand pianos have three prop sticks, but most of them have two, which allows the player to set the lid on the short one or the long one. When the lid is closed, the sound is somewhat muted and not very loud. This lid position is ideal when the pianist is accompanying a singer; the piano isn't overbearing and doesn't drown out the singer.

FACTS

On grand pianos, a hinged movable piece called the flyleaf is part of the lid. When the flyleaf is in the down or closed position, the top of the piano is completely closed. The flyleaf must be open if the pianist wants to access the music desk and to set the lid on the prop stick.

The piano will put out more sound and volume when the lid is put on the short prop stick. This position is good when the pianist is accompanying a solo instrumentalist such as a violinist, cellist, flutist, or acoustic guitarist. This lid position also works well when playing with a small group of instrumentalists, such as a string quartet or small chamber group.

When the lid is set on the tall prop stick, the piano resounds with a full sound, and when playing forte, the piano is at its loudest. This lid position is ideal for solo piano playing. If the piano player wants to sing while playing, and doesn't want to be drowned out by the piano, it is suggested that the lid be lowered to the short prop stick position.

The vast majority of console, studio, and upright pianos have one prop stick located beneath the top lid. When the lid is opened and set on the prop stick, the piano will resonate with more sound.

Pedals

All pianos have pedals that are located at the bottom of the piano. The first pianos had two pedals: the sustain pedal and the damper pedal, also called the soft pedal. The sustain pedal is positioned on the right. When depressed, it releases the damper pads, allowing the strings being played to sustain their sounds and resonate until the sounds naturally dissipate or until you take your foot off the pedal. The damper, or soft pedal, on grand pianos is positioned on the left. When depressed, it actually shifts the entire keyboard to the right. As a result of this shifted position, the hammers strike less strings, making less sound. On smaller piano models, when depressed, the damper pedal moves the hammers closer to the strings, shortening the striking distance. As a result, when the keys are struck, the hammers produce a smaller sound.

Around the turn of the twentieth century, piano manufacturers, influenced by the impressionist movement in the arts and French impressionist composers, added the third pedal, called the sostenuto pedal. This pedal, which is the middle pedal, is designed to create a "ring-over" effect that sustains the first chord or series of notes played, and sustains common notes among different chords. For example, press down on the middle pedal and leave it depressed. Play a C-major chord, followed by an F-major chord and an A-flat–major chord. Release your fingers after playing each chord, and you'll hear the note C ring through.

ESSENTIALS

Pianos sit on casters or wheels, made of either steel or rubber. Without casters, it would be extremely difficult to move a piano.

The sostenuto pedal is similar to the sustain pedal, but differs because it sustains only the common notes within chord progressions and not the entire chord. Very few piano players use this pedal, unless indicated to use it in piano music. Despite its lack of use, it remains today as one of the three piano pedals found on grand pianos.

The middle pedal on vertical pianos is called the practice pedal. When depressed and pushed to the left, a felt device is placed between all of the hammers and the strings, making the sound softer and lighter.

On grand pianos, the pedals are located in a section called the lyre, which extends from the bottom of the grand casing down to just above the floor. Depending on the style and design of the grand piano, some lyres are very ornate and decorative.

Interior Parts of a Piano

You are familiar with the beautiful sounds that resonate from a piano. But do you know what makes those sounds possible? The next few sections are going to take you on a tour through the inside of a piano.

Strings

The strings are the voice of the piano. Piano strings are made of steel, and the bass strings have copper wrapped around them. Inside the piano, you will find 200 to 230 strings, which are graduated in length and thickness. The number of strings varies according to the manufacturer. The length of the strings varies according to the model. The longest and thickest strings are located in the bass section, which begins with the lowest note on the piano (A). The strings get shorter and thinner as you move up the keyboard. The shortest string, located in the top of the treble section, is the highest note on the piano (C).

Piano strings last a long time, but eventually they lose their brightness and tone quality and need to be replaced. Generally speaking, if a piano is twenty years old and has its original strings, the strings probably need to be replaced. This can be a rather costly proposition, so beware when buying a used piano that is twenty or more years old.

Action

The piano action is an intricate, complex mechanism comprised of up to 10,000 parts. These parts include keys, spoon, bridle, catcher, capstan, back check, rails, wires, hammers, jacks, whippens, dampers, felts, flanges, levers, and springs. In simple terms, the action is the mechanism that connects the keys to the strings. When a key is struck, a series of motions occur in the action, resulting with the hammer hitting the string, thus producing sound.

Soundboard

The soundboard is a large piece of wood that stretches across the width and length of the piano. It is located underneath the strings and metal plate. The soundboard, made of spruce, acts as a resonator and amplifies the sound of the piano. When the strings are struck, the sound travels through wooden bridges that are attached to the soundboard.

Piano manufacturers have various methods of making soundboards. Some manufacturers laminate the soundboard, using more than one layer of wood. Laminated soundboards are stronger and more durable than solid soundboards and less expensive to make.

FACTS

All soundboards are made with a curvature. This process of curving the soundboard varies from manufacturer to manufacturer. Some companies make solid soundboards with extremely thin laminations added to the upper and under surfaces, while others make soundboards that are tapered in thickness from the center out to its edges.

Bridge

The bridge is a curved piece of wood that supports the strings. It is located directly under the strings and connects the strings with the soundboard. The bridge transmits the strings' vibrations to the soundboard.

The bridge has to be very strong to support the intensity of downward pressure created by the strings, and yet be very efficient in transmitting the sound vibrations down to the soundboard. Most bridges are made with a series of laminations, making them stronger and more efficient in transmitting sound vibrations.

These laminated thin layers of wood are constructed both horizontally and vertically. Horizontal laminated bridges run parallel to the soundboard, while the vertical ones run perpendicular to the soundboard. Vertical laminated bridges are more effective in transmitting a good sound because the vibrations travel directly down to the soundboard without having to traverse layers of horizontal glue, which is the case with horizontal bridges.

Some bridges are also capped with another layer of wood placed horizontally on top of the bridge. This cap is designed to give more support to the pins that are driven into the bridge, which hold the strings in their designated positions. A vertical, laminated, capped bridge is considered to be the best for producing a maximum-quality sound.

Iron Plate

The plate is the cast iron frame that holds and supports the tension of the strings. The plate is also known as the harp—when it is extracted from the piano case, it looks like a harp. The strings are stretched from one end of the plate to its opposite end and held in position by pins at each end. Each string has about 170 pounds of tension. The combined total amount of tension from all of the strings is approximately 40,000 pounds.

Therefore, the plate has to be very durable in order to support this tremendous amount of tension. The plate is securely fastened to the inside of the piano case.

Hammers

When you press down on piano keys, piano hammers are activated; they hit the strings and make them resonate. Piano hammers are made of wooden stems, usually hard maple, and have rounded felt heads made of compressed layers of fine wool. The finest hammers are made with two layers of felt. The outer layer is white and the inner layer is green, purple, or magenta. Putting the felt onto the hammer is achieved by hammer presses that apply a tremendous amount of pressure from several different angles.

The quality of sound a hammer produces has a lot to do with the hardness of the hammer. Hard hammers produce a bright quality sound, whereas soft hammers produce a dull sound. New pianos and fully restored pianos have hard hammers, giving the piano a bright quality sound. Used pianos have older hammers, which more than likely have gotten soft from years of use and need to be voiced, or better yet, replaced with new hammers.

QUESTIONS?

What is voicing?
Voicing a hammer is the process of shaving the felt head and removing the soft edge. Once the hammer is voiced, the felt head is harder, and as a result, the tone of the piano is brighter.

Dampers

Dampers are made of wooden blocks with felt pads attached to each end. When the dampers are resting on the strings, they stop the sound of the strings from resonating. Conversely, when the dampers are lifted from the strings, the strings resonate.

When the piano player presses down on a key, a metal rod attached to the damper raises the damper off the strings, allowing the string to vibrate. Once the key is released, the damper resumes its stopped position, resting on the string. Take a look inside the piano, and you'll notice that the highest notes don't have any dampers. That's because the strings are short and don't resonate that much. When you play these high notes without any dampers, you'll hear the notes continue to resonate after you lift your fingers from the keys.

As mentioned in the pedal section of this chapter, the right pedal is called the sustain pedal. When depressed, this pedal raises all of the dampers off of the strings. When the sustain pedal is in this position, all notes played will resonate, even after you lift your fingers from the keys. The notes will continue to resonate until the sustain pedal is released, which lowers the dampers back onto the strings and stops their sounds.

On grand pianos, the sostenuto pedal, which is the middle pedal, also activates the dampers. When you play any series of notes and then press down on the sostenuto pedal, the dampers above those notes are lifted up and stay in that position until the pedal is released, which lowers the dampers back down to the stop position.

Tuning Pins

The tuning pins, which are usually nickel plated, are located at the front of the piano. This location provides easy access to the pins when the piano needs to be tuned. The tuning pins are securely housed in the iron plate and extend down through the plate and into the pin block. Each piano string is wrapped around a separate tuning pin. Keys that have three strings per key have a tuning pin for each string. As a result, pianos can have as many as 225 tuning pins, and in some cases, even more.

ESSENTIALS The pin block is located underneath the iron plate. It is made of layers of laminated wood, which are bonded or glued together. The pin block has to be strong enough to support approximately 40,000 pounds of pressure exerted on the tuning pins by the tightened piano strings.

Backposts

The ribbed soundboard is exposed on the backside of vertical pianos and the underside of grand pianos. Extra heavy backposts provide support to the soundboard and the rest of the piano. The backposts are made of solid spruce wood.

Famous Models

Now that you know the basic structure of a piano and how it works, here are some of the more famous piano models.

- Louis XVI: Louis XVI models are made in a variety of sizes, including 5 foot 9 inch, and 6 foot 2 inch grands. These models incorporate the style of the Louis XVI era (1774–1792) with simple lines and classic columns.
- Queen Anne: This model captures the distinctive style of furniture made during the reign of England's Queen Anne (1702–1714) with elegant swan-necked cabriole legs on both the piano and matching piano bench.
- French Provincial: This beautiful furniture style began during the latter part of the seventeenth century. French Provincial pianos reflect this style with decorative music desks, legs, and lyre.
- Chippendale: Originating in England during the eighteenth century, the Chippendale style is characterized by its graceful lines, elaborate ornamentation, detailed music desk, lyre, and leg design.

CHAPTER 8

Electronic Keyboards

With the advent of electricity, it was only a matter of time before it would be applied to musical instruments. This chapter will introduce you to several electronic instruments, including electric pianos, digital pianos, and synthesizers.

Electric Pianos

The basic principle of the electric piano is to imitate the sound of an acoustic piano and amplify the sound through speakers. Electric pianos are very different from acoustic pianos. They are not acoustic pianos that are electrified by attaching a microphone device. Electric pianos have no strings or soundboard.

FACTS

In 1927, the first electric piano was made and called the Superpiano, followed by the Neo-Bechstein-Flugel in 1931 and the Elektrochord in 1933. These instruments produce electronic sounds generated by striking reeds or metal bars, creating sound vibrations that are then amplified through speakers.

As the manufacturing of the electric piano developed, the sound and touch of the instrument improved dramatically. When rock and roll exploded onto the pop music scene in the mid-1950s, the acoustic piano was still the preferred keyboard instrument. For example, during that time period Fats Domino, Jerry Lee Louis, and Ray Charles always played acoustic pianos.

It wasn't until the 1960s, when rock groups turned up the volume, that electric pianos gained their popularity. This happened for a number of reasons. The textural sound of electric pianos blend very well with the popular electric guitars. Electric pianos have the ability to turn up their amplified sound to match the volume level of the electric guitars, augmented with external amplifiers and speakers. And unlike acoustic pianos, electric pianos are lightweight, small, easy to transport, and never go out of tune.

Electric Piano Versus Acoustic Piano

When choosing between these two very different keyboards, consider the following before making a purchase.

Difference in Sound

The sounds of an acoustic piano and an electric piano are two different, distinct sounds. The sound quality of an acoustic piano is very difficult to replicate with any electronic keyboard. If you really want the sound of an acoustic piano, don't even bother thinking about buying an electric piano because you won't be satisfied. On the other hand, if you're open to the sound of electric pianos, then you should familiarize yourself with electric piano products. Another factor regarding sound: most electric pianos can be played using headphones, which is a good option to have when practicing.

Difference in Touch

Electric piano keys and actions are easy to play; however, they don't have the range of dynamics that you have when playing an acoustic piano. An electric piano's volume is determined by how you set or adjust the volume level. The sound is then electrically generated through speakers. If the volume level is set low, even if you play with full force and pound the keys, the sound will be low. If you have the volume level set high and you play the keys very lightly, the sound will be loud. With acoustic pianos, there is much more of a direct relationship between how you play the keys and the corresponding sound you generate.

Difference in Size

Electric pianos are much smaller than acoustic pianos. If you have space constraints in your home and you like the sound of electric pianos, then you should probably buy an electric piano. Given their small size and relative light weight, electric pianos are very portable and can easily fit in the trunk of a car. Even though acoustic pianos are movable, they're not easy to move because of their size and weight. If you are going to move an acoustic piano, it's best to have it moved by a professional piano mover.

Digital Pianos

In terms of electronic keyboard evolution, digital pianos and synthesizers were among the next wave of products. Digital pianos, being less complicated than synthesizers, were first in bringing their products to the buying public.

Roland made the first digital piano in 1974. Using the same digital technology, many other manufacturers followed with their own line of digital pianos, including Casio, Korg, and Yamaha.

Unlike acoustic pianos, digital pianos have no strings or hammers. The sound is generated by prerecorded sampled sounds, which are amplified through speakers. A digital piano attempts to duplicate the sound and feel of an acoustic piano.

ALERT

It should be noted that if you play very aggressively and pound on electric piano keys, you could damage a key or two. When this happens, no sound is generated when you press down on the damaged key. It can be rather costly to have these keys repaired.

Digital pianos are comprised of numerous components. The keys have a weighted key action that imitates the action of acoustic pianos. Unlike electric pianos, digital pianos have electronic sensors that detect the rate of velocity when the keys are struck, resulting with the corresponding soft or loud degree of volume. A digital sound bank contains numerous sampled keyboard sounds, including grand piano, electric piano, harpsichord, and organ. Digital effects are also available, including reverb, chorus, delay, and flanges. The digital sounds are amplified through speakers or headphones.

As with most products, there are pluses and minuses. Here are some pluses regarding digital pianos.

1. They are portable, weighing less than 200 pounds, compared with an acoustic vertical piano, which can weigh as much as 500 pounds. Digital piano legs can easily be removed, making it even easier to transport the instrument.

2. They don't need to be tuned. The digital sounds, which do not go out of tune, are stored on microprocessing chips.
3. They can be played silently, by using the headphones option. When playing with the headphones on, the sound is diverted from the speakers to the headphones. This allows the player to play as loud as he or she likes without disturbing anyone else in the room.
4. They are, for the most part, maintenance free.
5. Most digital pianos have a MIDI interface, which provides the technical capability to connect with other MIDI instruments.
6. Digital pianos have multiple built-in sounds stored in sound banks, which can be very quickly accessed by simply pressing a button.

Here are some digital piano minuses.

1. Even with the latest sampling sound technologies, the sound quality does not equal the sound quality of acoustic pianos.
2. The recorded sampled sounds are set and cannot be enhanced or colored by the subtle playing techniques of the player.
3. When there is a problem, because of the complicated technology of the instrument, digital pianos are difficult and expensive to repair.
4. Because digital pianos are a product of the time and incorporate the ever-changing digital technology, they become outdated very quickly.

Digital Piano Versus Acoustic Piano

As technology continues to advance, improvements in overall quality occur in the manufacturing of digital keyboards. The sound is better, the action feels better, and the price of digital pianos is more affordable. You can buy a quality digital piano for about $2,000. For the same price, you can also buy a good used acoustic piano. In choosing between the two keyboards, it really depends on your personal aesthetics, and what sounds and feels better to you.

Because of the never-ending evolution in technology, digital pianos are a constant work-in-progress and become outdated with each technological advancement. With acoustic pianos, the evolution hasn't changed that much over the past 100 years, so you're dealing with an instrument that is relatively constant and timeless.

Polyphony

Another very important distinction between the two keyboards is something called polyphony. With acoustic pianos, you can play as many notes as your fingers are capable of playing all at the same time. Digital pianos are limited to the number of keys that can be played simultaneously. This is due to some models having a limited polyphony capability, allowing only a certain number of keys that can be played at the same time. This big difference can be the deciding factor between buying a digital or acoustic piano.

SSENTIALS

Before you shop for a digital piano, it would benefit you to first buy a set of quality headphones. This will allow you to hear what the instrument sounds like when using the headphones option.

To further compound the decision-making process, some acoustic piano manufacturers make acoustic pianos with a digital device attached to the keyboard. With this attachment, digital disks can be inserted into the device and the piano can play by itself, much like the old player pianos. It also gives the player the option to play using headphones. These pianos are more expensive than your average acoustic piano because of the digital addition.

Comparing Models

As you compare the different digital piano manufacturers and models, notice the difference in the quality of the sampled sounds, the action of the keys, the number of keys (some of the lower-end models have less than the standard number of eighty-eight keys), the quality and number of sound speakers, the power and output of the amplifier, and the quality of the sound when using headphones.

Some of the digital piano manufacturers to choose from include Baldwin, Casio, Kawai, Korg, Kurzweil, Roland, Samick, Suzuki, Technics, Wersi, and Yamaha Clavinova.

If you can't make up your mind between buying a digital or acoustic piano, take turns alternating between playing digital pianos and acoustic pianos. The differences between the two keyboards should be quite striking and should help you in the decision-making process.

Synthesizers

As advances and improvements were made in applying electronics to keyboard instruments and generating sound, the synthesizer was born. Synthesizers allow the player to produce, control, and modify sounds, going far beyond the capabilities of other keyboard instruments.

Analog Synthesizers

The first synthesizers operated using analog technology comprised of voltage-controlled oscillators (VCOs), voltage-controlled filters (VCFs), and voltage-controlled amplifiers (VCAs). Each oscillator produces a waveform, or sound, which can be free of harmonics or overtones. The oscillators can also generate white noise, a somewhat flat, grainy, non-pitched sound that can whisper or roar. The sounds are then processed through filters, which change and modify the shape of the sounds. This filtering process can apply pitch, rhythm, and effects to the sounds, and determine the degree of attack, decay, and level of volume. The VCAs generate the sound through speakers.

In 1955, RCA Laboratories introduced its first synthesizer. It looked nothing like the synthesizers we have today. The early models were large, complicated, and very expensive. The very first synthesizers were, for the most part, experimental and in the development stage, and not available to the buying public.

These synthesizers were found in the most advanced electronic music studios and educational institutions. They were not very reliable or consistent instruments. They required a long period of time to warm up, and they didn't stay in tune. In order to produce sounds, patch cords had to be connected to sound modules. Each sound module produced a specific sound. Once a sound was created, you couldn't save it by simply pressing a save button, like we can with today's synthesizers. You had to write down the patch cord configuration and parameter settings in order to reconstruct the sound at a later time. This process had to be done with every sound generated by this early breed of synthesizers. This required a lot of experimentation, time, numerous patch cord changes, writing down each sound configuration, and patience. To a large degree, the first synthesizer players were actually sound programmers.

FACTS

Hugh Le Caine is credited with building the world's first voltage-controlled music synthesizer in 1945. This early-stage electronic instrument also had a touch-sensitive keyboard and variable speed multitrack tape recorder.

During the 1960s, synthesizers became user-friendly with the creation of the Buchla and Moog synthesizers, but they were still large. In the early 1970s, Robert Moog made the MiniMoog, which became quite popular, due in part to its relatively small size and its being the first portable synthesizer. But indicative of synthesizers made at the time, the MiniMoog was a limited monophonic instrument and could only produce one sound at any one given time. If you wanted to play more than one note simultaneously, you had to have additional synthesizers. Another way to produce more than one sound at a time was to multitrack several notes by recording them individually and then playing them back all together. This recording technique is also called overdubbing.

The next generation of synthesizers were polyphonic, a huge technological breakthrough, which arrived toward the end of the 1970s. The Prophet 5, made by Sequential Circuits, was very popular because with The Prophet 5, you could play more than one note at a time. Because they were highly advanced and new to the marketplace, they were very expensive.

Digital Synthesizers

Then digital technology arrived. Synthesizer manufacturers began to incorporate the new digital technology in their latest models. As a result, analog synthesizers were eventually phased out of production and replaced with digital synthesizers, which operate on microprocessing chips called digital circuits. This new breed of synthesizer was smaller, less complicated, and more affordable.

Digital synthesizers have a very different sound compared to analog synthesizers. Digital sound is comprised of numbers, which are stored in memory sound banks. When the sounds are activated, the microprocessor retrieves the numbers from the memory and converts them to the highest quality sound. Digital synthesizers sound bright, crisp, and can even sound biting, compared to analog sounds, which sound warmer and rounder.

FACTS

The Yamaha DX-7 was one of the first fully digital, polyphonic synthesizers to quickly catch on with keyboard players around 1982. This was due in part because of its relatively affordable price, brand new sounds, and easy-to-play functionalities.

When playing a digital synthesizer in real time, the player was restricted to the preprogrammed sounds. However, there was (and still is) a pitch wheel on digital synthesizers that allows the player to raise or lower the pitch while playing in real time. With analog synthesizers, the player could make several modifications to the sounds in real time and create new sounds on the fly.

With today's synthesizers, the sounds are already programmed and preset in numerous sound banks. These sounds are accessed by scrolling through the sound banks and distributed to the keyboard. For instance, if you pick solo flute, the entire keyboard sounds like a flute. By choosing another sound, string orchestra, for example, the entire keyboard then sounds like a string orchestra. The choice of sounds is very extensive and available with the touch of a button. You also have the option to modify and change the parameters of the preset sounds. If you do, you can save the modified sounds in the memory bank.

MIDI

Digital synthesizers can interface with each other and other non-keyboard digital equipment such as a drum machine, recording deck, sampling unit, or effects unit. This digital connection is possible because of MIDI, which stands for Musical Instrument Digital Interface.

ESSENTIALS

A MIDI controller is not restricted to only keyboards; digital drum machines, samplers, sequencers, and computers can all function as controllers and can trigger all MIDI-connected instruments.

Using MIDI, several synthesizers programmed to play different sounds can be connected together. By playing one note, chord, or series of notes on the lead synthesizer, called the controller, all of the connected synthesizers can be activated simultaneously through MIDI. The combined sound possibilities are endless, considering the vast number of sounds to choose from on each individual synthesizer, sampler, or effects unit.

Synthesizer Versus Acoustic Piano

The differences between these two keyboards are vast. The two biggest differences are sound and touch.

Difference in Sound

If you have a discerning ear for pure acoustic piano sounds, then you probably shouldn't buy a synthesizer. On the other hand, if you want a wide variety of electronically produced sounds and the option of playing while wearing headphones, then you should seriously consider buying a synthesizer. The sounds vary from manufacturer to manufacturer. The number of synthesizer sounds can be overwhelming. Try to identify what your keyboard needs are and what type or types of sounds you want before trying out the different makes and models.

Even though the digital sampled sounds of an acoustic piano are improving with the latest synthesizers, they will never be able to sound the same as acoustic pianos because of the difference in sound fundamentals. Synthesizer sounds are electronically generated and amplified, while acoustic piano sounds are naturally produced with old-fashioned strings, hammers, soundboards, and wooden cases.

Difference in Touch

If you prefer the feel of a hammer-and-string action and weighted keys, you should probably buy an acoustic piano. Or, if you like the feel and light-touch ease of playing synthesizer keys, then you should consider buying a synthesizer. Most synthesizer keys are touch-velocity sensitive—the harder you press the key, the louder the sound; the lighter you press the key, the softer the sound. Aftertouch is another characteristic of synthesizer keys. When you hold down on a synthesizer key, the sound will continue until you release your finger. This aftertouch function can also give the note a variety of expressions, including vibrato, overtones, and various sound effects.

Difference in Number of Keys

Another difference between these two keyboards is the number of keys. All acoustic pianos have eighty-eight keys. Some synthesizers have eighty-eight keys, while others have seventy-six, sixty-one, forty-eight, or even as few as thirty-six keys. If you're used to playing eighty-eight keys, it will more than likely feel very strange to play a keyboard that has fewer keys. Because of your prior playing experience on eighty-eight keys, your fingers will probably have the physical expectation of being able to play notes in the upper and lower registers of the keyboard. When playing on seventy-six keys or less, adjustments have to be made in terms of registration, octave placement, and the voicing of chords, bass lines, and melodies. Typically, synthesizers with eighty-eight keys cost more than the seventy-six or less key models.

CHAPTER 9

Finding the Right Piano

A pianist isn't a pianist without a piano. But don't rush into a purchase. Several factors need to be considered when choosing a piano. You should take your time with this decision and shop around until you find the piano that is just right for you.

Decide on a Location

Before you go shopping for a piano, determine which room in your home or apartment is best suited to accommodate a piano. Typically, people put their piano in the living room, family room, or den since these are typical gathering places for family and friends. Be sure to place the piano far away from the television. There will be many times when you want to play the piano while others are glued to a sports program or favorite sitcom and do not want to be disturbed.

For the professional musician who spends a lot of time playing the piano, it might be best to put the piano in a spare room or guest bedroom. This is ideal for everyone—the pianist can concentrate without extraneous sounds and interruptions, while others in the household are undisturbed.

Determine a Price Range

Once you know where you're going to put the piano, figure out how much money you are willing to spend. If you have a big apartment or home and really want a grand piano but have a small budget, you can make a down payment and finance the remaining balance.

What you're willing to pay for a piano will also determine whether you buy a new or used piano. New pianos are generally more expensive than used or restored pianos. The exception would be if you were looking for a rare restored piano. Then the price could be considerably higher than that of a new piano.

If you're going to buy a used or restored piano, be prepared to ask the salesperson a lot of questions. A list of questions should include the following:

When was the piano built?
What is the condition of the soundboard?
Has it been replaced?
Have the strings, felts, hammers, and action been replaced?
Under normal playing conditions, how long will the piano last?
Other than the difference in price, why should I buy a used piano
    instead of a new piano?

Settle on a Size

What you can afford to spend will usually determine the size of the piano. The most affordable pianos are spinets and consoles, which happen to be the smallest acoustic pianos made. Spinets are good for beginners and for people who have space constraints. However, very few piano manufacturers make new spinets. Consoles are the next size up and cost a little more than spinets. Due to their popularity, today's piano manufacturers make new consoles.

Studio pianos are even bigger in size and price. Upright pianos are taller and more expensive than studios. Grand pianos, which are the most expensive, range in size from petite grands to concert grands.

Make sure that the size of the piano you choose is appropriate with the size of the room you're going to put it in. For instance, putting a grand piano in a small studio apartment would look very strange!

Choose an Appropriate Style

Pianos come in a variety of finishes, including high-gloss black, satin black, cherry, mahogany, walnut, or oak. The style of the casing also has several varieties, including modern, French Provincial, Italian Provincial, Queen Anne, and Louis XVI. You want to choose a piano that blends in with the overall style and design of the room you're going to put it in.

If you have wood paneling, wood-beamed ceilings, or hardwood floors, a wood finish piano would look good. On the other hand, if the style of your home is modern with white and black tones, a black satin or high-gloss ebony piano would blend right in.

In terms of the casing, again, choose a piano that matches your overall decor. For example, if your home is filled with antiques, you may want to choose a Louis XVI or Queen Anne. For the modern-style home, a contemporary-styled black piano would be appropriate.

Take Your Time

Every piano is different. The sound, feel, and action of a piano are based on your own subjectivity. Granted, most ears can hear the qualities that are inherent in high-quality pianos, which sound better than pianos of a lesser quality. However, what sounds or feels good to one person might not be the same for another. Therefore, you have to spend some time with each piano you are considering to buy.

Narrow your choices down to two or three pianos. Play the same piece of music on each one and make comparisons. Which one sounds better? Which one is easier to play? Which one feels better? Ask the salesperson to tell you the differences and the pros and cons of each piano.

If you're still undecided and you have a friend or family member who plays the piano, ask him or her to go to the piano store with you and play the pianos you are considering. Ask for his or her opinion.

It's always a good idea to shop around and not limit your potential purchase to one piano store or retail outlet. Visit a big retail outlet that carries a lot of different pianos from a variety of manufacturers. Go to a smaller, local piano store. And visit an exclusive dealership and individual manufacturer's showroom. By doing so, you'll get an excellent education, which will help you in your decision-making process.

ESSENTIALS

Be sure to ask the salesperson if the price includes the bench (seat), shipping, and tuning. When a piano is moved or shipped from the warehouse or store to your home, it invariably goes out of tune and needs to be tuned once it arrives.

Don't feel as though you have to pay the asking price. Every piano store wants your business, so you can say it's a buyer's market when it comes to pianos. In that respect, negotiate with the salesperson and make a counteroffer.

Another thing to consider is choosing an American-made piano versus a German-made or Asian-made piano. In the United States today, the primary manufacturers are Baldwin and Steinway (which includes their Boston line), and to a smaller extent, Mason & Hamlin and Charles Walter.

In addition to their American-made pianos, Steinway also makes pianos in Germany, which tend to be more expensive than their American models. Other German manufacturers include Blutner, Bechstein, Grotrian, Schimmel, and Seiler. Asian manufacturers include Kawai, Knabe (which originally made their products in the United States), Samick, Yamaha, and Young & Chang.

FACTS

The tones of pianos vary from manufacturer to manufacturer. For example, Baldwin pianos tend to be brighter in tone while Steinway pianos sound mellow. Here again, tone is another subjective call and varies from listener to listener.

New Pianos

With a very wide range of prices that will suit the buyer's budget, there really is a piano for everyone. Keep in mind that the following prices are approximate and reflect the different types of sizes, cabinets, and finishes. Regarding new pianos, prices start as low as $2,700 for a small vertical and as high as $128,000 for a 9-foot concert grand.

Let's begin with the manufacturer Baldwin. Their pianos are made in the United States. Prices for verticals—which include spinets, consoles, studios, and uprights—start at $3,990 and go as high as $16,520. Baldwin grand pianos start at $23,320 and go as high as $71,800 for a 9-foot concert grand.

Boston pianos, which are part of the Steinway product line, are made in Japan by Kawai. Vertical piano prices range from $7,320 up to $10,600. Boston grand pianos start at $14,400 and go as high as $39,990 for a 7-foot concert grand.

Bechstein pianos are made in Germany. Vertical piano prices start at $20,660 and go up to $38,400. Bechstein grand pianos start at $54,320 and go as high as $128,000 for a 9-foot concert grand.

Blutner pianos are also made in Germany. Vertical piano prices start at $16,750 and go up to $26,910. Blutner grand piano prices range from $42,050 to $89,120.

Charles Walter pianos are made in the United States. Vertical piano prices start at $6,480 and go up to $7,490. Grand piano prices range from $29,000 to $32,400.

Grotrian pianos are made in Germany. This manufacturer doesn't make vertical pianos. Grand piano prices start at $44,600 and go as high as $75,400 for a 9-foot concert grand.

Kawai pianos are made in Japan. Vertical piano prices start at $4,190 and go up to $5,050. Kawai grand piano prices start at $11,090 and go as high as $68,790 for a 9-foot concert grand.

Knabe pianos were originally made in the United States but are now being manufactured in Korea and China. Vertical piano prices start at $3,190 and go up to $3,990. Kawai grand pianos range in price from $13,580 to $23,120.

Mason & Hamlin pianos are made in the United States. Vertical piano prices start at $14,190 and go up to $14,400—comparatively speaking, a higher price range and narrower range of models. Grand piano prices range from $39,200 to $55,100.

Samick pianos are made in Korea. Vertical piano prices start at $2,790 and go up to $6,390. Grand piano prices start at $7,390 and go as high as $47,990.

Schimmel pianos are made in Germany. Vertical piano prices start at $11,380 and go up to $17,980. Grand piano prices start at $33,780 and go as high as $169,800 for a custom concert grand.

Steinway & Sons pianos are made in the United States, with a limited amount made in Germany. Vertical piano prices start at $16,700 and go up to $24,100. Steinway grand piano prices start at $34,200 and go as high as $92,700 for a 9-foot concert grand.

Yamaha pianos are made in Japan and China. Vertical piano prices start at $5,390 and go up to $9,690. Yamaha grand piano prices start at $10,390 and go as high as $97,990 for a 9-foot concert grand.

Young & Chang pianos are made in China. Vertical piano prices start at $2,700 and go up to $4,390. Grand piano prices range from $10,340 to $21,190.

Used Pianos

Used pianos come in all sizes and models, with the exception of limited custom editions and rare pianos, which are hard to find and are generally quite expensive. There are two basic categories of used pianos: "as is" and rebuilt or restored. "As is" pianos, more often than not, need to be rebuilt, at least to some extent. Some "as is" pianos need to be completely restored, which can be quite costly, and in some cases are even more expensive than buying a new piano.

Piano prices for used verticals at retail outlets can start as low as $1,000 and go as high as $5,000, depending on the manufacturer, model, and condition of the piano. Used grand piano prices can start as low as $2,500 and go as high as $35,000. Here again, the difference in price depends on the manufacturer, model, and condition of the piano.

ESSENTIALS

If you're looking for a used piano, be sure to check your local classified ads. More than likely, you can get the same piano for less when buying from a private individual versus buying from a used piano store. The person selling the piano doesn't have the overhead and expense of running a business that the piano store has.

Another thing you should do when looking for a used piano is to get in touch with your local music schools or the music department of a community college or university. Periodically, these places replace their old pianos with new ones, or are sometimes making cutbacks. This presents an excellent opportunity to get a used piano at a very good price. Or, they may know of some other institution or organization in the area that wants to sell a piano.

When I was a student at The Hartford Conservatory of Music, I let my teachers know that I was looking for a used piano. A local convalescent home had contacted the conservatory and said they had an old upright piano that no one was playing; it was stashed away in a corner collecting dust. The convalescent home just wanted to get rid of it. My piano teacher heard about this and gave me the phone number to call.

When I called, I inquired about the asking price of the piano. Now being a student, I didn't have much of a budget for a piano. When the person replied that it was for sale for $15, I nearly fell over. The only thing I had to do was to arrange for it to be moved to my father's house, where I was living at the time. It just so happened that my father had a sizable truck that had more than enough room to accommodate the old upright. It didn't cost me a cent to have it moved, thanks to my father and a few husky friends. The piano was in such good condition that the only thing it needed was a tuning once it landed in the living room. I sold the piano two years later for $145.

ALERT

There's no need to rush your decision. Take your time and feel good about your purchase. Whichever piano you choose, you'll be spending a lot of time with it, so be sure it's the one you really want.

CHAPTER 10

Taking Care of Your Piano

E ven though the piano is large and produces a strong sound, it is a delicate instrument and must be treated as such. Regardless of the size and price of your piano, it is necessary to protect and take care of it. In doing so, you will maximize the value of your piano and protect your investment.

The Importance of Humidity Control

A piano functions best under consistent climatic conditions—not too moist or too dry. The ideal temperature is 68 degrees with 42 percent relative humidity.

Pianos are primarily made of wood. Wood is greatly affected by varying degrees of humidity. Changes in humidity cause the wooden parts of a piano to swell and shrink. These changes have a direct impact on the tuning and action of pianos. When extreme swings occur in humidity levels, wood can crack and glue joints can be damaged.

Hundreds of felt and leather parts in the piano's action are also affected by changes in humidity, which can increase friction and make the piano's action feel stiff and resistant to the touch. Under very high humid conditions, condensation can build up on the metal parts of the piano and eventually rust the strings, tuning pins, and iron plate.

ALERT

You might consider it aesthetically pleasing to have a piano in a beach home, but all that moisture from the ocean air, surf, and low clouds can eventually damage any piano.

The opposite extreme is having a piano in a very dry climate. Aside from potential damage from the sun, a climate that is very arid can dry out the wooden parts of the piano and cause them to crack.

The suggested humidity level for your piano should be a consistent 42 percent, as recommended by major piano manufacturers and technicians. When your piano is kept at a constant moisture level, shrinking and swelling are minimized, and your piano will stay in tune for a longer period of time.

The best way to maintain a consistent humidity level for your piano (and ultimately prevent damage from occurring) is to install a humidity control system. This device, which can be attached directly to a piano, has three parts: a humidifier that adds moisture, a dehumidifier that eliminates excessive moisture, and a humidistat that detects the relative humidity of the air within the piano and adds or removes moisture as needed.

Effects of the Sun

Beware of direct sunlight. Do not place your piano in front of windows or below skylights. The ultraviolet rays of the sun can damage the finish on your piano. With repeated exposure to the sun, the piano casing will get bleached out, blisters may appear on the finish, and the piano may go out of tune.

Aesthetically, it's tempting to place the piano near a window. It's inspiring to look out the window instead of looking at the wall when playing the piano. This holds true when the pianist is playing from memory and not reading music or looking at his or her fingers. But even so, it isn't a good idea to put your piano in harm's way.

SSENTIALS

If you are tempted to move your piano to a window for inspiration, consider this: Would you rather be inspired and play beautifully for a short period of time or find other sources of inspiration and play beautifully for several years?

When I was living in Laguna Beach, California, my patron had an ebony Steinway grand piano placed by the window in her living room. I must admit it was very pleasing to play the piano while looking out the window and seeing the sun glistening on the Pacific Ocean. Unfortunately, this Steinway fell victim to the exposed sunlight. The color of the side of the casing had turned to a chalky white, and the piano suffered from drying out. This drying out negatively affected the action, the hammers, and the keys. The exposure to the sun also made the piano go out of tune.

Having seen the damage to this Steinway grand, I made sure not to place my Knabe grand near a window in my living room. However, I overlooked the fact that a skylight in the living room's vaulted ceiling was beaming sunlight down on the lid of the Knabe. It gets pretty hot during the summer months, and after this happened repeatedly for three years in a row, I noticed blisters popping up on the surface of the lid. I looked up, saw the skylight, and realized this was the result of the lid being exposed to the powerful sunrays. I had to have the lid refinished. Now during the summer months, I simply place a satin cover over the lid, protecting the lid from the sun. As a result, no blisters have resurfaced.

Keeping Your Piano in Tune

If you protect your piano from direct sunlight, excessive moisture, and extreme dryness, your piano is more likely to stay in tune. These extreme conditions and extreme changes in temperature can cause a piano to go out of tune.

But even under the best climatic conditions, pianos still need to be tuned at least once a year. Depending on how critical your ears are, and the age and condition of your piano, you may need to tune your piano every six months.

If your piano can be moved without much effort, and you want to reposition it in your home, it probably won't need to be tuned after moving it. However, when a piano is moved requiring the help of piano movers and putting it in a truck to transport it to another location, it will more than likely need to be tuned once it reaches its new location.

For the courageous individual who has very good ears, you might want to get a tuning hammer and tune a string or two. But beware, you could do more harm than good. Keep in mind that the overall tuning of the piano involves all of the strings.

ESSENTIALS

Aside from having your piano tuned on a regular basis, your piano may need to be voiced. This is a process in which the felt heads of the hammers are shaved in order to produce a brighter sound when the hammer strikes the string.

Also, when attempting to tune a note that sounds either sharp or flat, you could be dealing with a note that has two or three strings. You have to be able to isolate the string that sounds out of tune and match it with the other string or strings. This requires the use of a rubber insert to stop the other string or strings from resonating. You also have to compare the string with its upper and lower octaves. I must stress that it is far better to have an experienced piano technician tune your piano.

Restoration and Piano Repairs

Restoration is the skilled process of transforming older, worn-out pianos to their original condition. This process involves restoring or replacing the soundboard; restringing and repinning the frame; restoring, rebuilding, and regulating the action, damper assembly, and keyboard; stretching the strings and raising the pitch to A-440 tuning; overhauling the pedals; and stripping down and refinishing the casing to reveal the original wood grain.

FACTS

To polish your piano, most manufacturers suggest simply wiping it with a soft damp cloth. If you want to apply furniture polish or lemon oil, it's recommended that you check with your piano technician or piano salesperson before doing so to make sure you don't cause any damage to the finish.

Some used pianos may need to be completely restored, having to replace all of the parts. This can take as long as four to six months to complete. A complete restoration can be quite costly and, in some instances, can cost as much as the price of a new piano. If you're going to buy a used piano, it's best to buy one that is already repaired and restored.

A new piano shouldn't require any repairs, but a used piano is an entirely different story. Due to its age and having endured years of playing, a piano's parts may need to be replaced.

Occasionally, piano strings break. When I used to bang away on my Hardman upright grand, once in a while, I would break a string. It was a very old piano (built around 1909), and I played very aggressively. However, even when playing non-aggressively, strings can break on used pianos because of old age and changes in climatic conditions. Rarely does a string break on a new piano. When a string breaks, it needs to be replaced by a piano technician.

How to Sell Your Piano

The time may come when you have a reason or two to sell your piano. You might want to upgrade and get a bigger and better one. Perhaps you or your child has lost interest in the piano and it hasn't been played for an extended period of time. Or maybe you're moving and you'd rather sell it than have it moved to your new home. (Moving is an opportune time to upgrade and get a new piano for your new home.)

In any case, do research before selling your piano. Call your local piano stores and ask them how much they're asking for a piano model that is comparable to yours. Contact the manufacturer of your piano and find out what they think your piano is worth. And for comparison's sake, ask the manufacturer what the selling price is for a new piano that is the same as yours. You can also get your piano appraised by a piano technician or by contacting the Piano Technicians Guild of America, and they can tell you what your piano is worth. The goal is to come up with a fair market price of what your piano is actually worth. Naturally, the age and overall condition of your piano factor into what your selling price should be.

You could trade in your piano to a piano store and apply it toward the purchase price of another piano. However, by selling your piano on your own, you will get more money than what the piano store offers.

Because some buyers will offer you less than your asking price, it's always a good selling practice to ask a little more than what you're willing to settle for. Most things are negotiable, and a used piano falls into that category.

If someone is paying by check, be careful. If you don't know who they are (or, in some cases, even if you do), it's a good idea to ask the buyer for a bank check to protect yourself.

It's best to run a classified ad in your local newspaper to attract prospective buyers. Based on the response rate of the ad and the number of calls you get, you may not have to take the first offer. Some buyers aren't really serious; they're simply curious and aren't sure that they want to buy a piano. These are the type of people who make appointments then don't show up. The serious buyer will be more obvious and straightforward. He or she will set a time to meet and show up with a checkbook, or better yet, cash in hand.

CHAPTER 11
Practicing

If you want to become an accomplished pianist, you must practice, practice, practice. It also helps to have a piano teacher who complements you. Taking piano lessons with the right piano teacher builds the technique required to learn how to play the piano proficiently. This chapter will help you find that perfect teacher and improve your practicing techniques.

When to Start Taking Piano Lessons

There isn't a magic age you need to be to start taking piano lessons. The time to start is when you really want to, and when you can commit to going to lessons and practicing on a regular basis. Personal desire and wanting to play the instrument are essential in starting a good working relationship with the piano. Sustained self-motivation and discipline is what keeps an individual interested in the piano.

Children

Expose your children to the piano at a very young age by playing recordings of piano music in your home. Even though they might be too young to speak, they are very receptive to their immediate surroundings. They are also very impressionable, vulnerable, and easily influenced. With that in mind, play a variety of musical styles such as children's songs, Broadway musicals, pop songs, and classical music. While driving in your car, play piano music CDs or cassette tapes. Observe how your child responds and what style of music he or she seems to prefer. In essence, your child will let you know his or her level of interest in the piano.

ESSENTIALS
If possible, take your children to piano recitals. This experience can be very inspiring not only from the audio perspective, but also from the visual experience of the performance.

When your child is three or four years old and is showing signs of having an interest in the piano, rent a piano for six to twelve months. If the child has a natural tendency toward the piano, he or she will start playing it on his or her own. This is the best possible situation. Encourage your child to play the piano, and when he or she finishes playing, clap with approval. This will give your child the confidence he or she is seeking and the encouragement to stay at it and keep playing. When the level of desire becomes more consistent, it's time to find a good piano teacher who has an expertise in teaching children.

Adults

Adults should start taking piano lessons once they have committed to going to every lesson and making the necessary time to practice each week prior to each lesson. Here again, the level of desire to play the piano will substantially help in keeping to your commitment. As with any discipline, a routine is good because it sets a condition and habit. That being said, try to schedule your practicing for the same time each day. You'll find it will become part of your daily and weekly schedules.

There's no point in taking piano lessons if you don't have a piano to practice on. Ideally, you already have a piano sitting in your living room or family room. If not, check with your local piano store and inquire about piano rentals. For the beginner, at any age, it's wise to rent a piano before making a purchase. The vast majority of piano stores will apply the cost of the rental toward the purchase price. In this case, you're making a small investment while taking time to see how serious you really are about playing the piano.

Piano Teachers for Children

Piano lessons for children should be a positive experience. Your child should want to go to piano lessons. It's very important that your child like the piano teacher. In finding the right piano teacher for your child, start by asking your friends if their children are taking piano lessons with someone in your local community. Your friends, who already have some experience in this area, can be very beneficial to you and your child.

Once you've established that the teacher is qualified and has a good reputation in teaching children, ask to meet with the teacher and, of course, bring your child. Based on your child's initial reaction to the teacher, you'll probably know whether or not this is the right teacher for your child. Because the teacher/child relationship is so important, be sure to take the time to find a teacher that your child will have a positive response to.

At what age should a child begin piano lessons?
A child could start taking piano lessons as early as age four. But please, don't ever force your child to take piano lessons if he or she doesn't want to. By forcing the issue, the parent can actually kill any desire or curiosity the child may have toward the piano.

Piano Teachers for Adults

There are a lot of piano teachers to choose from—some are better than others. Some teachers are faculty members at accredited music conservatories, colleges, or universities. Others teach at local music stores. Some teach in their homes where they have set up a home piano studio. Depending on your comfort level, you might prefer the formality and academic setting of studying at a conservatory, college, or university. Or you might prefer the more casual environment of the local music store. Some of you may prefer the more personal teaching-from-home piano teacher.

FACTS

Teaching requires giving and nurturing, and the ability to effectively communicate with the student at each lesson. The best piano teachers are the ones who take pride in developing the talents of their students. They know how to motivate and encourage their students and give them the necessary constructive criticism.

In all cases, find out what the teachers' qualifications are and whether or not they are in good standing with professional music teachers' associations. Find out where they studied and what diplomas or degrees were earned. If you haven't already heard them play, ask them to play the piano for you. You should be impressed with the way your piano teacher plays the piano; it will be a source of inspiration and something for you to aspire to.

But even the most qualified piano teacher might not be right for you. It depends on how much discipline you want from your teacher. Some teachers are more rigid than others. Some teachers are nicer than others. Once their teaching skills are established, it really boils down to personality. You want to like and admire your teacher. While contemplating which teacher to choose, ask your prospective teachers a lot of questions. This will help you choose the teacher who is best suited for you.

1. How long have you been teaching?
2. Why do you teach the piano?
3. How many students do you currently have?
4. What is your method of teaching?
5. How often should I practice?
6. What can I expect to accomplish after six months of lessons?
7. Why should I take piano lessons from you?

How Often Should I Practice?

A tourist was visiting New York City and asked a bystander on the street, "How do I get to Carnegie Hall?" The bystander answered, "Practice, practice, practice."

It's pretty basic: The more you practice, the better you sound. If you're really serious about learning how to play the piano, then you will make time each week to practice. At a minimum, you should practice ninety minutes a week in three thirty-minute practice sessions. And don't be restricted by your practice schedule. If you get the urge to play the piano, don't hold back; go ahead and play it. For the best use of your practice time, practice at the time of day or night that is free of any interruptions. This uninterrupted time will allow you to concentrate on your lessons.

ESSENTIALS

When assisting children, be sure to make it a fun and positive experience. When they experience frustration and are feeling discouraged, give them some encouraging words. If they're having difficulty with an exercise, play it for them and explain it to them as you're playing it.

If your child is taking piano lessons, he or she is going to need your assistance. Naturally, the younger ones need the most assistance. Children should practice at least three times a week and, depending on their ability to keep their attention on practicing, each session should be twenty to thirty minutes long. Children who have a high level of interest in the piano should practice five to seven days a week. For children ten years old and up, it's best for them to practice on their own.

Keeping Your Concentration

The best way to keep your concentration is to minimize interruptions and distractions. Turn off the television, radio, all telephones (including your cell phone), and pager. If you have a family and your piano is located in a separate room, lock the door. Mental distractions can also be very counterproductive when practicing. As part of your discipline, clear your mind of any extraneous thoughts before you start practicing. This will allow you to keep your concentration, and as a result, make more progress.

ALERT

You shouldn't try to fix something in a way different from what your teacher has told you. Once you've learned something the wrong way, it's very difficult to unlearn the wrong way and make it right.

After you've taken piano lessons for two to three months and you feel fairly confident about your playing, record yourself playing your favorite piece of music. Listening to your playing is a very telling experience. When you're actually playing the piano, you're focused on playing the music to the best of your ability. When you listen to the playback of a recording, you'll hear things you didn't hear when you were playing. You can learn a lot about your playing by listening to a tape. This allows you to critique yourself, hear any imperfections, and make adjustments in your playing.

When you are having difficulty with a certain passage, do your best to work it out using the instructions given to you by your teacher. Make several attempts to get it right. If you're still having difficulty with it, move on to another section or to an entirely different piece of music. At your next piano lesson, your teacher will show you how to work out the section you're having difficulty with.

Once you start your practice session, don't stop. It's very difficult to start and stop and try to start again. This counterproductive bad habit should be avoided.

There are no shortcuts in getting to Carnegie Hall and learning how to play the piano. Learning how to play comes with time, desire, discipline, dedication, instruction, and a lot of practicing.

Physical Positioning

To avoid back pain, you have to sit at the piano with a straight spine. Do not lean forward or slouch while playing the piano. In the interest of comfort, sit on a cushion. If you purchase a used piano, be sure to get a matching piano bench and, if possible, a padded one. New pianos come with a matching piano bench, and some are padded. The best padded piano benches are adjustable. These benches are preferred because you can adjust the height according to your size and finger placement on the keyboard. In terms of height, you want to be sitting high enough so your fingers and forearms are slightly higher than the keyboard, making it easy to press down on the keys. If you don't have an adjustable bench, then use cushions or pillows to get the height you need.

Don't put your fingers too far forward toward the back of the keys. Instead, place them closer to the edge, or the front, of the keys. This will give you a quicker and better response in pressing and releasing the piano keys.

ESSENTIALS When the piano bench is not padded, and you're going to be playing for an extended period of time, be sure to put a cushion or pillow on the bench. It will make a big difference in terms of comfort.

Good Habits

1. Always sit in an upright position.
2. Make sure you're sitting at the proper height.
3. Sit on a cushion or padded bench.
4. Minimize all interruptions.
5. Find a quiet place to practice.
6. Clear your mind before you start practicing.
7. Create a routine.
8. When you get stuck with a passage, move on and come back to it later.
9. Learn to play it the right way, as instructed by your teacher.

Bad Habits

1. Stopping and starting while practicing; not having a steady momentum.
2. Repeating difficult passages, making no progress.
3. Learning something the wrong way.
4. Trying to make shortcuts. (There aren't any shortcuts.)
5. Allowing yourself to be interrupted while practicing.
6. Letting anyone discourage you from wanting to play the piano.

CHAPTER 12

Recording the Piano or Keyboard

If you're fortunate, someone other than you will function as an engineer or producer and record your keyboard playing. If you don't have an engineer or producer, then you're going to have to learn how to record your music. After a lot of trial and error, experience, and experimentation, you will acquire the basic skills required to engineer and produce yourself.

Recording Studios

If you want to get the best possible quality recording of your keyboard playing, then look into professional digital recording studios. These studios come complete with producers, sound engineers, acoustic pianos, synthesizers, samplers, and effects units. Most of them also have analog recording equipment for those who prefer an analog sound.

Because of their superior quality, equipment, and services, they are expensive. If you're lucky and really talented, some studios might be willing to work out some type of barter arrangement. For example, they provide you with an engineer/producer during off hours, usually between midnight and 6:00 A.M. You don't have to pay their hourly rate; you only pay for tape costs and tape dubs. And in exchange, the studio owners own the copyright to the material you're recording if it's original, or they take a percentage of any future sales of your recording.

FACTS

This type of barter arrangement is more likely to happen if it's a new studio with new equipment—they want to test out the studio on you. For instance, they may need to experiment with microphone placement when recording the grand piano, or they may have a new recording console board and effects units that they need to become familiar with.

Hourly recording studio rates range from as little as $50 an hour for a "home studio" to $300 and up an hour for the fully staffed professional studio. In most cases, studios are willing to work out a package rate versus hourly rates, which definitely saves you money.

Home Recording Studios

If a professional recording studio doesn't suit you, you always have the option of creating a home recording studio. The first thing you have to do is find the best room or space to set up your home studio. Ideally, it will be in a separate room, basement, or garage.

In any room, and especially the garage, you're probably going to need to install insulation. Insulation minimizes room noise, absorbs the sound, and also helps in preventing the neighbors from complaining about the "noise."

If you're going to be recording using an electric piano, digital piano, or synthesizer, the noise factor will be greatly diminished by using headphones while playing and recording, and even during playback.

It's best not to record an acoustic piano in the basement or garage because it could suffer from extreme changes in temperature and humidity. Your acoustic piano should be in your living room, family room, or spare bedroom.

You should set up your home studio in an uncluttered space. There's going to be quite a few cables, cords, extension cords, microphone cables, and so forth that can very quickly and easily get tangled up. Some people tape down the cords and cables, which prevents a tangled mess. Of course, once they're taped down, you don't have the flexibility to move them. The length of your cords and cables is important because it limits the distance between the recording deck, amplifier, and keyboard. It's always better to have more than enough cable length than to be stuck with cables that are too short.

Recording Equipment

If you choose to set up your own home recording studio, you want to make sure that you have all the equipment you will need. Of course, if you choose to go with a professional recording studio, this equipment will most likely be provided for you. Even so, it is a good idea to become familiar with the equipment used. Here's a quick checklist to get you started.

Recording Equipment Checklist
❏ Keyboard (acoustic, electric piano, digital piano, or synthesizer)
❏ Recording deck
❏ Tapes
❏ Amplifier
❏ Speakers
❏ Microphones
❏ Effects unit (optional)
❏ Sampler (optional)
❏ Mix-down unit
❏ Power strips, extension cords, connecting cables, etc.

Magnetic Tape Recorders: Audiocassette Decks

Audiocassette decks, which are analog instruments, use audiocassette tapes to record and store the data. It's always best to use the highest quality tape for recording purposes, such as metal bias, type IV or high bias, type II tapes. The number of recording tracks on audiocassette decks generally ranges from four to eight tracks. To minimize tape hiss, these decks are usually made with a noise-reduction system. Most of them come equipped with variable tape speeds, zero return, and pitch control functions.

Variable tape speed allows you to record in slow, normal, or fast mode. Recording using the fast speed setting will give you the best quality sound. Use this speed when you are well rehearsed and ready to record a finished piece of music. The normal and slow speeds are good for recording your practice sessions or for experimenting with microphone placements and recording techniques. The normal speed (and even more so, the slow speed) has more tape hiss than the fast speed setting. However, when using the normal or slow speeds, you can get more material on one tape because the tape turns slower than it does with the fast speed setting.

The zero return function is very helpful when you want to rerecord, overdub, or simply find the beginning of a piece of music. Before you start recording, set the counter numbers to zero and put the zero return setting in play. Press the record key and start recording. If you want to go back to the beginning of the piece, press the rewind key. The tape will stop at zero, right at the beginning of the piece.

The pitch control device can raise or lower the collective pitch of music recorded on tape. When you raise the pitch, you are also increasing the speed and tempo of the music; when you lower the pitch, you are also slowing the speed and tempo of the music. You can get creative with this device. For instance, if you're recording a musical passage that is difficult to play at normal speed, set the pitch to as low as possible and record it playing at a slower tempo. Once you have recorded it, increase the pitch to normal and it will sound faster (and higher) than what you recorded. If you want the recorded passage to sound even faster (and higher), increase the pitch to a higher setting.

If you're going to be recording your voice and want to sound higher or younger, record your voice with the pitch set normal and increase the pitch when listening to the playback.

Each track has EQ (equalization) settings and pan settings. Panning is used to place the sound within the stereo spectrum. With panning, you can place a track to the far right, center (down the middle), or far left. All the variables in between right, left, and center are also available.

Magnetic Tape Recorders: Reel-to-Reel Tape Recorders

Every now and then, you might come across a reel-to-reel tape recorder. These machines were very popular in the 1950s, 1960s, and 1970s. Reel-to-reel recorders use magnetic tape to record the sound. The size of the tape is usually a quarter of an inch in width. Professional recording studios have reel-to-reel recorders that use half-inch, one-inch, and two-inch tapes that are still in use today. Some people are convinced that these analog machines sound warmer than the digital decks.

As with audiocassette decks, when using any size magnetic tape, you're going to encounter tape noise. That's why noise-reduction systems, such as Dolby, were built. In addition to tape noise, magnetic tapes over an extended period of time can dry up and crack, losing some data and quality.

Because digital technology is so popular and offers so many functions not available with tape decks, quarter-inch reel-to-reel tape recorders have become fairly extinct. As a result, it's very difficult to purchase blank reel-to-reel magnetic tapes.

Digital Recording Decks

If you're going to record using a digital recording deck, you don't have to be concerned with audiotapes; digital decks record and store the data using internal computer chips, also called a hard drive. As is true with digital sound instruments, the sound that digital decks record and playback is bright, crisp, and has an edge.

One of the big differences between audiotape decks and digital decks is tape noise. Since digital decks don't use tapes, there is no tape noise whatsoever. The number of recording tracks on digital recording decks designed for home studios range from eight to twenty-four tracks. Professional studios have digital decks with as many as sixty-four tracks, and even more in some cases.

Because of the digital technology, when recording using digital decks, you have options that are not available with audiotape decks. For instance, you have the ability to copy and paste sections of music instead of having to play everything in real time, as you have to do with audiotape decks. When using the editing mode on digital decks, you can add harmony, counterpoint, bass, or rhythm parts to a previously recorded piece of music.

Digital decks come preloaded with as many 130 different rhythm patterns, incorporating a wide variety of musical styles, drum-kit combinations, and percussion instruments.

Digital decks have built-in sound effects, which can be assigned to each track. The effects can be edited and stored in the user-effect memory banks. Each track also has its own individual EQ settings; you can add treble to brighten up one track, while adding bass to deepen another. If you want to keep strict time while recording a piece of music, you can activate a built-in metronome and adjust the tempo accordingly.

Digital decks also have a punch-in/punch-out function that makes it easy to rerecord or add music to specific sections. You can set the exact record in-point and out-point with a trigger record function, which keeps the music up to the in-point, and after the out-point, completely intact and protected.

The internal hard disk of digital recorders can hold up to a specific amount of data; the bigger the size of the disk, the more data it can store. When the disk has reached its maximum storing capacity, the data can be downloaded to a DAT (digital audio tape) recorder or an external hard disk drive.

Amplifiers

Because recording decks don't have any speakers, all recording decks need to be connected to an external amplifier with speakers. Most decks do come with a built-in amplifier, which works well while listening with headphones. An external amplifier has much more wattage and sends the sound through external speakers. The amplifiers in receivers are more than adequate. Simply connect your recording deck to the receiver using the tape, or auxiliary inputs, and set your receiver to the appropriate setting. Your recording deck will send its sounds to the receiver and to the attached stereo speakers.

Another option is to use an amplifier made for guitars, keyboards, or sound systems. However, the sound probably won't be as clean as the sound you get when using the amplifier in a receiver. And if the speakers are contained in one single cabinet, you won't hear the sounds in stereo.

Microphones

When recording an acoustic piano, you need microphones. It's best to get two quality microphones and two adjustable microphone stands. There are basically two different types of microphones: directional and omnidirectional. Directional microphones are sharper in recording tighter, focused sounds. Omnidirectional microphones record more room noise, sound fuller, and have more ambience. Both types of microphones work well. It just depends on the specific type of sound you're striving for that will determine which type you ultimately use.

QUESTIONS?

What are directional and omnidirectional microphones?
Directional microphones receive sound signals from a narrow, semi-closed radius. Omnidirectional microphones receive sounds from a wider, more open radius.

Microphone prices start at the bottom end from around $49 and go up to $500 or more. The more money you spend on a microphone, the better the quality. Generally speaking, you can get a good quality microphone for about $150, which should be more than adequate in recording your piano.

One microphone should be placed in the treble section and the other placed in the bass section of the piano. This will allow you to record the full range of sound the piano has to offer. Be sure to have long enough cables to reach the distance from the microphones to the inputs on your recording deck.

Effects Units

If you're going to be recording using an audiocassette deck, it probably won't have built-in effects. More than likely, you're going to want to connect it to an effects unit. An effects unit contains numerous types of effects, including various types of reverb, echo, delay, chorus, gated effects, and so forth. Effects units are digital and MIDI compatible.

The recorded tracks on the cassette deck are sent to the effects unit, processed with a specific effect, and sent back to the deck. Each track on the cassette deck can be processed with an effect. The amount or level of the effect can be adjusted on the cassette deck.

Digital recording decks are made with built-in effects. The type and quality of effects are similar to external effects units. The built-in effects on digital decks are more than adequate, so you probably won't need an external effects unit.

Samplers

Samplers are separate sound units, similar to effects units with one big difference: They record sampled sounds. A sampler allows you to take any external sound, such as a musical instrument, a slamming door, or running water, and record and store it in memory.

The recorded sample sound is looped, making it continuous. Using the sampler as a controller, the sampled sound is sent through MIDI to a digital keyboard. When the keyboard is programmed to play the sampled sound, the entire keyboard will produce the sampled sound, like running water for instance. You can play high-pitched, fast-running water sounds or low-pitched, slow-running water sounds.

Sampling is really an extraordinary technical accomplishment. The possibilities of this technical capability are endless and are only limited by your imagination. And for analog fans, any analog sound can be sampled and then played on digital synthesizers. The sampling of sounds is possible because of digital technology and the use of MIDI.

ESSENTIALS A good example of sampled keyboard sounds are the soundtracks to Ericka Beckman's films *Out of Hand*, *You the Better*, *Cinderella*, and *Hiatus*. These soundtracks, which were composed by yours truly, use sampled sounds from striking metal pipes, chirping birds, water sprinklers, and running water. The sampled sounds were manipulated through sound and effect processors.

At the low end of the price spectrum, you can purchase a portable battery-operated sampler for around $299. This type of sampler is very practical for sampling (recording) outside noises such as the sound of traffic, trains, or low-flying jet engines. Jumping up in price to around $999, Yamaha and Roland make samplers that can record the sampled sound for a longer period of time, and come with many built-in special effects. For those of you who want to have a digital keyboard with a built-in sampler, you can get an Ensoniq, Kurzweil, Korg, or Yamaha starting at around $1,999. These keyboard samplers have the best editing features and come equipped with sequencing, cutting, and copying features.

Mix-Down Deck

This important piece of equipment is used during the final stage of the recording process. A mix-down deck can be an audiocassette deck/player, DAT recorder, or CD burner, and must have a record function. Connect your recording deck to the mix-down deck using the appropriate outputs, inputs, and cables. When you connect the mix-down deck to your amplifier, you can hear the incoming signal through the speakers. Or if the deck has a headphone option, you can listen with headphones.

Preparing to Record

One of the most important things to do when you purchase your recording equipment is to read the instruction manuals carefully and thoroughly. Take your time and set the equipment up properly. Explore all the different options and functions the equipment has to offer. Don't rush into the recording process without reading the manuals. If you do, you'll end up wasting time and not utilizing the full capacity of the equipment.

If you're recording an acoustic piano, make sure it's in tune. It should be tuned to A-440, which is the universal tuning for all musical instruments. This is especially important if you're going to be recording both an acoustic piano and electric keyboards. The acoustic piano has to be tuned to A-440 so it will match and be in tune with the electric keyboard instruments.

Check the pedals on your acoustic piano and make sure they're not squeaking. If they are, apply a small amount of oil and work it into the pedal mechanism. This will prevent the microphones from picking up any unwanted squeaking sounds from the pedals.

Also check your piano for any buzzes or vibrations before recording. Sometimes, unknowingly, something drops into the casing and rests on the soundboard or strings, such as a pencil or paperclip. These little objects can cause buzzing and vibrating noises.

Make sure that the nuts and bolts inside or underneath the piano bench are tight. This will prevent the bench from making squeaking sounds.

Be sure to have a few pieces of music well rehearsed before you start the recording process. If possible, have them memorized so you won't have to read the sheet music. Instead, your eyes can watch the record levels on the deck and make sure that the levels don't get too high and distort the incoming sound.

Recording an Acoustic Piano

Set up two microphones: one in the treble section and the other in the bass section of the piano. If you place the microphones close to the strings, you'll capture a direct, relatively dry sound from the strings and soundboard. When the microphones are in this position, you'll get a strong signal. You might also pick up some hammer and action sounds. The way to counter this is to tip the microphones away from the hammers and action. If you place the microphones four to six inches away from the strings, the sound will be softer, less dry, and contain some room noise or ambience. The only disadvantage to having the microphones in this position is that you'll have to increase the record level to get a strong signal, and in doing so, you'll be picking up more room noise. There will also be noticeable differences in sound depending on your choice of microphones: directional or omnidirectional.

Another variable affecting the sound of recording the piano is the position of the lid. If the lid is only slightly open, just enough to get the microphones in position, the sound will be somewhat compact and tight. If the lid is raised to its high position, the sound will be more open and fuller.

The only way to find the sound of your liking is to experiment with different microphones, and microphone and lid positions. After you find the sound you like, set the record levels to as high as possible without getting too hot of a signal and distorting the incoming sound. Assign track one to one microphone and track two to the other. If you want to get a full-spread stereo sound, set the pan dial on track one to the left and the pan dial on track two to the right. Experiment with the varying degrees of the pan settings, from extreme left and right to moving the pan toward the center. For example, place the pan setting halfway between far left and center.

In the process of finding the best possible sound, you only need to play a few chords at your normal dynamic level of playing. Once you are satisfied with the sound and settings, play the softest and loudest passages from the piece you're going to record. Make sure that you're getting enough record level during the soft section and not too much level during the loud section. It's best to set the record level to an overall level; getting enough signal for the soft sections and not too much signal for the loud sections. Here again, you have to experiment with the record levels before you record the entire piece of music.

Recording a Non-acoustic Piano

The big difference between recording with electric pianos, digital pianos, or synthesizers, and with recording an acoustic piano is that you don't have to use any microphones. Simply connect a patch cord from the output of your keyboard directly into the input on your record deck and assign it to a designated track. Going direct and not using microphones gives you a cleaner sound with less noise. The majority of these keyboards have two output jacks, which can be assigned to two different tracks on the recording deck, giving you a stereo recording.

Electric pianos don't offer much as far as built-in effects; however, digital pianos do have some built-in effects. Synthesizers come equipped with electric piano and digital piano sounds, some of which have a variety of effects already built-in.

Recording Techniques

If you're recording an acoustic piano and using a four-track audiocassette deck, use the two-microphone setup that was covered in the microphone section of this chapter. Set the pan dials to left and right to get a good stereo sound. Turning the pan dials slightly in either direction will give you varying degrees of stereo, from extreme left and extreme right to the sound of the tracks bleeding or overlapping each other. If you only have one microphone, you can still create a stereo sound by sending the incoming record signal to two different tracks. With track one, set the pan to the left. With track two, set the pan to the right. When using only one microphone, you'll be recording an overall sound of the piano versus a treble-section and bass-section recording when using two microphones.

ESSENTIALS

If you want to simulate the sound of a bass track and treble track when using only one microphone, try increasing the bass equalization on track one, and increasing the treble on track two. This technique can give your piano a simulated stereo sound.

When recording using an electric piano, digital keyboard, or synthesizer, plug directly into the recording deck. Send the incoming signal to two different tracks and experiment with different pan settings and EQ settings. As you will notice with your keyboard, some of the sounds are already processed with effects and may not need any changes. However, you might want to experiment with modifying the equalization.

You have the option to add additional sounds to your keyboard tracks by utilizing any unrecorded tracks on your recording deck. For instance, you can add a string line, string section, bass, or percussion track to accompany your keyboard tracks. This process is called multitracking or overdubbing. If you plan on multitracking and want the additional track or tracks to start at the very beginning of the piece of music, you're going to have to record, using a microphone, a count-off so you know when to start playing the overdubs. For instance, if the piece of music is in 4/4 time, count off saying, *one, two, three*. Don't say *four* because it's too close to the beginning of the recorded music and nobody wants to hear it! By doing the count-off, you set the tempo and know where the downbeat to the first measure is. A count-off can also be accomplished by using a built-in metronome or beats from a drum machine.

For those of you who are ambitious, creative-type musical arrangers, and who want to multitrack using more than the four available tracks, you can mix two tracks down to one open track. For example, you can take the two piano tracks on tracks one and two and mix them down to track three. This will give you three open tracks for overdubbing.

ALERT

Mixing two tracks down to one requires a lot of recording experience and experimentation with your equipment.

There are some disadvantages if you choose to use this mixing option when using an audiotape deck. You will lose the stereo sound of the two separate piano tracks, lose some sound quality, and increase tape noise. Mixing two tracks down to one can also be done using a digital deck. Actually, it sounds much better because there is no increased tape noise. It's a process of finding the best balance and mix of both tracks before you mix them down to one track.

The Mix

Now comes the final stage in the recording process. Once you are completely satisfied with the sound and settings of your recorded piano or keyboard tracks, you can mix down the two tracks to an audiocassette, DAT tape, or CD. If mixing down to a tape, to ensure the best quality of sound, clean the tape heads on the mix-down deck by applying some rubbing alcohol to a cotton swab and rubbing it on the tape heads. This will remove any dirt built up from repeated use. Be sure to use the highest quality tape as your mix-down tape. This tape, or CD if using a CD burner, will be your master from which you can make copies.

When you're satisfied with the pan and EQ settings, assign different effects from the effects unit to the recorded tracks. Listen to how the sound of the piano varies with each effect. Also experiment with the level of the effect. Too much effect can wash out the definition and clarity of the recorded piano sound.

Play back the source tape on your recording deck. Adjust the incoming record levels on the mix-down deck. To get a strong sound level without distorting the sound, set the level to as high as possible without going into the red for any extended period of time. (Occasional peaks into the red zone are okay.) Rewind the tape to the beginning of the recorded piece of music. Start the mix-down tape first to allow for preroll and to not miss or clip the very beginning of the music on your source tape. About four seconds later, start the source tape on your recording deck. At the end of the music, stop both decks. Rewind the mix-down tape and listen to its playback. If the sound level and quality sounds good, you have a master mix tape.

Pros and Cons of Digital Decks

The biggest advantage in recording with digital decks is that it's easier and quicker to record, edit, and mix down music tracks. This is possible because the technology has advanced functions that are not available when using analog decks.

Another big advantage with digital decks is the superior sound quality. Because digital decks record and store data by using a microchip, the use of magnetic audiotapes is completely eliminated. As a result, there is no tape hiss or tape noise to contend with.

ESSENTIALS

If you find the digital sound too bright or not warm enough, try adjusting the EQ by lowering the treble and increasing the bass or midrange.

Digital decks integrate with analog decks. You can very easily transfer pre-existing recordings from reel-to-reel tapes, audiocassettes, or any other sound source to a digital recording deck. Simply record them onto assigned tracks on your digital recorder. Once you have done that, the music is safely stored on the hard drive and can be treated with all of the options and functions available on the digital deck.

There are a few disadvantages with digital decks. There is a limit to how much data that can be stored on the microchip's hard drive. Be sure to find out how much memory is available on the digital deck before you make your purchase. Generally speaking, the larger the memory capacity, the higher the price. When the hard drive has reached its full capacity, you will not be able to make any additional recordings. In order to do so, you will have to delete some of the data on the hard drive or download some or all of the data onto an external digital disk or hard drive. This will free up the memory and allow you to make new recordings.

In terms of sound quality and recording functions, the advantages of digital recording decks far outweigh any disadvantages.

CHAPTER 13

Learning to Play the Piano

It's time for you to take a seat at the piano and learn how to play. In this chapter, you're going to learn about basic music theory as it applies to the keyboard. In doing so, you will be able to play several easy exercises.

Music Terms and Definitions

Music is a universal language. Anyone can listen to music. However, the making and playing of music requires more than listening. It requires the know-how. If you want to play the piano, you're going to have to study, take lessons, and practice.

But before you dive into the exercises, you should know some of the basic terms used in music and their definitions.

Bar lines—Bar lines are placed between measures. In 4/4 time, a bar line is placed after the fourth beat of each measure.

Bass line—The bass line, played by the left hand, accompanies the melody. Bass lines usually play the root of the chord and can also include the fifth and third of the chord and passing tones.

Beat—A beat is a measurement of time. For example, in a 4/4 time signature, there are four beats in a measure of music. The beats in music help you keep even time.

Chords—Basic chords are comprised of three notes: the root, the third, and the fifth. Three-note chords are called triads.

Clefs—There are three clefs in music: treble, tenor, and bass clefs. In piano music, the treble and bass clefs are used. The treble clef is also called the G clef; the bass clef is also called the F clef. Clefs sit at the far left end of a staff and determine the letter names of the notes.

Harmony—Usually comprised of chords, harmony supports the melody. In piano music, the harmony is generally played with the left hand.

Key signature—The key signature tells you what key a piece of music is written in. There are two kinds of key signatures: sharp (♯) and flat (♭). The key signature is written on the staff to the immediate right of the clef.

Ledger lines—These are short horizontal lines found above and below the five lines of the staff. Ledger lines accommodate notes that are above G at the top of the staff and below D at the bottom of the staff. For instance, middle C on your keyboard is written on one ledger line below the staff.

Measure/Bar—A measure of music is the same as a bar of music. A measure, or bar, contains a number of beats, as designated by the time signature. For instance, when the time signature is 4/4, there are four beats per measure.

Melody—Melody is the dominant musical line that is usually played by the right hand on the piano and is usually written in the treble clef.

Notes—Musical notes are used to determine the duration and value of the note being played. Notes and their values are: whole notes, half notes, quarter notes, eighth notes, sixteenth notes, and thirty-second notes.

Pitch—Pitch is determined by where the note is played on the piano and its corresponding written note on manuscript paper.

Rests—Rests represent silence in music. When you see a rest, stop playing for the duration and value of what the rest is equal to. There are whole rests, half rests, quarter rests, eighth rests, sixteenth rests, and thirty-second rests. Rests are of equal value to notes. For instance, a quarter rest is equal in value to a quarter note, which represents one beat.

Rhythm—Rhythm occurs when playing a series of notes.

Staff—Staffs are made up of horizontal lines and spaces. When using a treble clef, the lines on a staff from bottom to top are: E, G, B, D, and F. To help remember these letter names to the corresponding lines, think of this saying, "Every Good Boy Does Fine." The letter names of the spaces on the staff between the lines are: F, A, C, and E. When you put the letter names of the lines and spaces together, you get E, F, G, A, B, C, D, E, and F, which correspond directly with letter names of the piano keys.

Stems—Stems are attached to notes. There are quarter-note stems, eighth-note stems, sixteenth-note stems, and thirty-second–note stems.

Tempo—The tempo is the rate of speed at which you're playing music.

Time signature—The time signature tells you how many beats there are per measure.

Once you have the terminology down pat, you are ready to begin your first lesson. The following series of exercises are written for the beginner level—the aspiring pianist. As the lessons and exercises progress, they reach a more intermediate level.

Learning the Names of the Notes

FIGURE 13-1:
Abbreviated
keyboard

1. 2. 3. 4. 5. - the fingers of your
right hand

Please note that this illustration does not show the eighty-eight keys found on acoustic pianos. A full keyboard has an additional twenty-four keys above the far right C key and another fifteen keys below the far left C key. The additional keys follow the same white key/black key configuration. The highest note on an acoustic piano is C; the lowest note is A. As you can see in **FIGURE 13-1**, the notes of the piano's white keys are C, D, E, F, G, A, and B. The notes of the black keys are C-sharp, D-sharp, F-sharp, G-sharp, and A-sharp.

The black keys are located between the white keys. They are grouped in sets of two and three. For instance, C-sharp and D-sharp make up a group of two black keys while F-sharp, G-sharp, and A-sharp make up a group of three. This two- and three-group black note sequence is consistent up and down the keyboard. The black keys are called sharp keys because they're slightly higher (sharper) than the white key that precedes it. For instance, the black key C-sharp is slightly higher in sound and pitch than the white key C. When playing in flat key signatures, the black keys are also called flat keys. This is further explained in Chapter 16.

The note called middle C is located approximately in the middle of the keyboard. Actually, it's a little left of the middle—slightly left of the manufacturer's brand name on the fallboard. If you count up from the lowest note on a keyboard instrument that has eighty-eight keys, middle C will be the fortieth note up from the bottom.

Applying Your Fingers to the Keys

Looking at your right hand, let's assign numbers to each of your fingers. Your thumb is 1, index finger is 2, middle finger is 3, forefinger (ring finger) is 4, and your smallest finger is 5. Now let's assign corresponding numbers to the keys starting with middle C. C is 1 (your thumb), D is 2 (your index finger), E is 3 (your middle finger), F is 4 (your forefinger), and G is 5 (your smallest finger). See **FIGURE 13-1**.

Two-Finger Exercise

This first series of exercises will use only your first two fingers: your thumb (1) and your index finger (2).

Place your thumb on middle C, press down on the key, and release it. Repeat this action a number of times. Place your index finger on the D key and do the same. Play D a number of times. Using your thumb to play middle C and your index finger to play D, alternate playing both notes in the following sequence: C, D, C, D, C. Try to play the two notes evenly with the same measured time for each note. Keep playing this simple two-finger exercise until it feels comfortable and sounds good.

Three-Finger Exercise

Now let's add your third (middle) finger to the exercise. Place your third finger over the E key (key 3) and press and release it a few times. With your thumb positioned above middle C, your second finger above D, and your third finger above E, play the following sequence of notes: C, E, D, E; C, E, D, E; C, E, D, E, C. Another way of thinking and playing this exercise is to use the corresponding number of your fingering sequence: 1, 3, 2, 3; 1, 3, 2, 3; 1, 3, 2, 3, 1 (1 represents your thumb, 3 represents your middle finger, 2 represents your index finger, 3 represents your middle finger).

The written music for this three-finger exercise looks like this:

EXERCISE 13-1

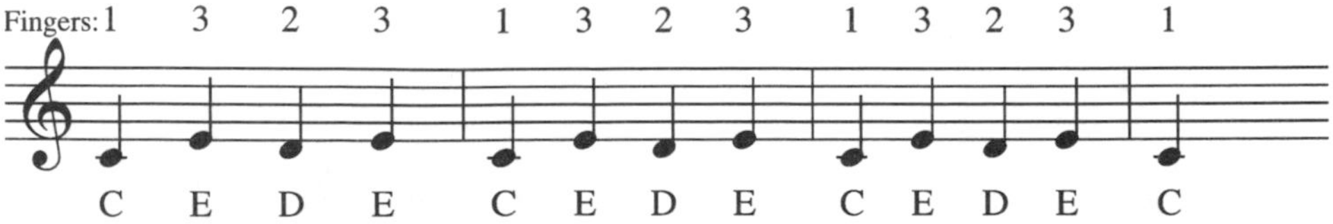

Fingers: 1 3 2 3   1 3 2 3   1 3 2 3   1

C   E   D   E   C   E   D   E   C   E   D   E   C

It's important to note that the middle C on your keyboard corresponds to the written quarter note C, located on one ledger line below the staff. This note is the first written note in **EXERCISE 13-1**.

Now play **EXERCISE 13-1** reading the music. Your fingers and hand stay in the same position, so you don't have to look down at them. Instead, keep your eyes on the music. Keep repeating this exercise until it feels good and sounds good.

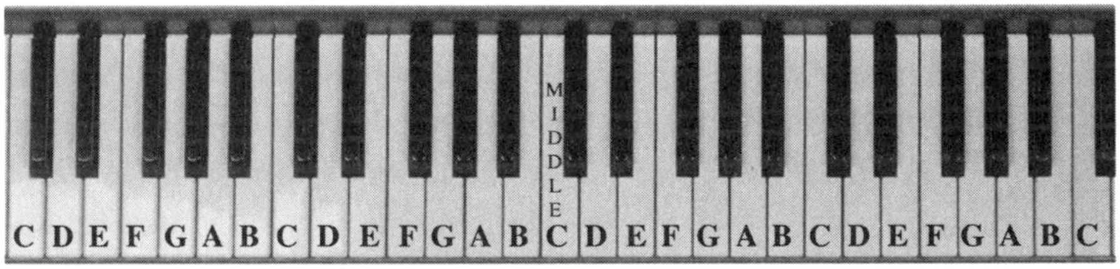

FIGURE 13-2:
Abbreviated
keyboard

C D E F G A B C D E F G A B C D E F G A B C D E F G A B C

Exercise #2 - Starting on D:	1. 2. 3. (first 3 fingers - right hand)
Exercise #3 - Starting on E:	1. 2. 3.
Exercise #4 - Starting on F:	1. 2. 3.
Exercise #5 - Starting on G:	1. 2. 3.
Exercise #6 - Starting on A:	1. 2. 3.
Exercise #7 - Starting on B:	1. 2. 3.
Exercise #8 - Starting on C:	1. 2. 3.

Using the same three fingers (the thumb, index finger, and middle finger), place your thumb above the D key, index finger above the E key, and your middle finger above the F key (see **FIGURE 13-2**). Play the following sequence of notes: D, F, E, F; D, F, E, F; D, F, E, F, D. The corresponding numbers of your fingering sequence is exactly the same as **EXERCISE 13-1**: 1, 3, 2, 3; 1, 3, 2, 3; 1, 3, 2, 3, 1 (1 represents your thumb,

3 represents your middle finger, 2 represents your index finger, 3 represents your middle finger).

The written music looks like this:

EXERCISE 13-2

Congratulations! You have just played the first in a series of sequential exercises. The fingering configuration—1, 3, 2, 3; 1, 3, 2, 3; 1, 3, 2, 3, 1— can be played on any group of three piano keys. For example, in **EXERCISE 13-1**, you played this configuration starting with your thumb on the C key. In **EXERCISE 13-2**, you played the same configuration starting with your thumb on the D key.

Noting the Symbols

Before we continue with the exercises, let's take a close look at all the symbols used in **EXERCISE 13-2**.

First, we see a treble clef sitting on the far left of the staff. The treble clef is also called the G clef because the curl wraps around and stops at the G line on the staff. This clef tells you that the letter names of the lines and spaces on the staff are: E, F, G, A, B, C, D, E, and F.

Next, we see the first note D, which is a quarter note and whose value is one quarter beat in the measure. As you can see, the quarter note is shaped like a filled-in circle with a stem attached to it. The following F, E, and F are also quarter notes. So, we have four quarter notes (D, F, E, F) in the first measure.

Immediately following the fourth quarter note in the first measure is a bar line. The bar line separates the measures on the staff and keeps the four quarter notes together in one measure. The next measure (measure 2) is an exact repetition of measure 1: same notes, same keys, same fingering, and same number of beats in the measure. The same is true in measure 3—a direct repetition of measures 1 and 2. Again, please notice the bar lines separating each measure.

In measure 4 we see only one quarter note followed by a quarter rest (the curved zigzag line) and a half rest (the small rectangular block that sits on the middle line of the staff). A quarter rest equals a quarter beat, and a half rest equals two beats. The combined value of one quarter note, one quarter rest, and one half rest gives us four beats in measure 4. The first beat has sound, which is the quarter note D. The second beat is silent, represented by the quarter rest. And the third and fourth beats are silent, represented by the half rest.

The symbol we see at the very end of the staff is called a double bar line. The double bar line means this is the end of the piece.

In reviewing the above material, answer the following questions.

1. How many bars are there in **EXERCISE 13-2**?

   ♪ ....

2. How many notes are there in bar 3 in **EXERCISE 13-2**?

   ♪ ....

3. How many notes are there in bar 4 in **EXERCISE 13-2**?

   ♪ ....

4. What kinds of notes are in **EXERCISE 13-2**?

   ♪ ....

5. How many beats are there per measure in **EXERCISE 13-2**?

   ♪ ....

6. What separates the measures?

   ♪ ....

7. What is the name of the clef?

   ♪ ....

8. What do the numbers above the notes represent?

   ♪ ....

9. What is the name of the zigzag line in measure 4, and how many beats is it equal to?

   ♪ ....

10. What is the name of the small rectangular block in measure 4, and how many beats is it equal to?

    ♪ ....

11. What is the final symbol at the very end of the staff called, and what does it mean?

    ♪ ....

(Answers can be found in Appendix A.)

Moving Up the Keyboard

Let's continue with the exercises using the same sequence starting on different notes.

As you can see in **EXERCISE 13-3**, the fingering is the exactly the same as **EXERCISES 13-1 AND 13-2**. The only differences are the pitches and letter names of the notes. You're simply moving your first three fingers up the keyboard and playing the same sequence. Play **EXERCISE 13-3** starting with your thumb playing the E key, followed by your middle finger playing the G key, and your index finger playing the F key.

EXERCISE 13-3

Remember: As you play the exercises, try to play the quarter notes evenly, since they all have the same equal value.

If you get lost during the course of playing these exercises, refer to **FIGURE 13-2**. This illustration shows you where the letter names of the notes on the staff are relative to the piano keys. For instance, the first note in **EXERCISE 13-4** is F, which is four notes above middle C on your piano.

Play **EXERCISE 13-4** starting with your thumb playing the F key, followed by your middle finger playing the A key, etc.

EXERCISE 13-4

Now try **EXERCISE 13-5**.

EXERCISE 13-5

Looks like there's something new in **EXERCISE 13-5**. Immediately following the treble clef are two fours, one on top of the other. This is a time signature. The top number four tells you there are four beats per measure, and the bottom number four represents the quarter note, telling you the quarter note gets the beat. Exercises 13-1, 13-2, 13-3, and 13-4 are also in 4/4 time.

This time start the sequence on the A key.

EXERCISE 13-6

Something new has been added in **EXERCISE 13-6**. The word *moderato* in the upper left-hand corner indicates the rate of speed at which the exercise should be played. *Moderato* is an Italian word that means "moderately"—not too fast and not too slow. This is the tempo (rate of speed) at which the music is to be played.

The first note in **EXERCISE 13-7** is B.

EXERCISE 13-7

There is a change in the placement and direction of the quarter note stems in **EXERCISES 13-5, 13-6, 13-7**. In the previous exercises, all of the quarter note stems are placed on the right side of the notes and go upward. When notes are on the middle line of the staff (B) and higher, note stems are placed on the left side of the note and go downward.

Directly below the 4/4 time signature is the symbol *mf*. This symbol stands for the Italian term *mezzo forte*, which in English means "medium loud." **EXERCISE 13-7** should be played at a moderate tempo and played medium loud.

EXERCISE 13-8 introduces another musical symbol called the repeat sign. It is located immediately to the right of the 4/4 time signature and again at the end of measure 4. As you can see, a repeat sign is a double bar line with two small circles in the A and C spaces of the staff. There is also written text telling you to repeat three times at the end of measure 4. This tells you that after you have played the exercise once, you are to repeat the entire exercise twice. In doing so, you will have played the exercise a total of three times.

Be sure to give the quarter rest and the half rest in measure 4 their full values totaling three beats of silence—one beat for the quarter rest, two beats for the half rest. It might help to count *one, two, three, four* for each beat per measure. For instance in measures 1, 2, and 3, as you're playing the quarter notes C, E, D, E, say *one, two, three, four*. When you get to measure 4, count *one* for the C note, *two* for the quarter rest, and *three, four* for the half rest.

Play **EXERCISE 13-8** starting with the C key.

EXERCISE 13-8

Introducing Octaves

There is a direct correlation between **EXERCISE 13-1** and **EXERCISE 13-8**: Both exercises have the same letter names for the notes—C, E, D, E; C, E, D, E; C, E, D, E; C. The difference is the placement of the notes on the staff and corresponding piano keys. The notes in **EXERCISE 13-8** are an octave higher than those in **EXERCISE 13-1**. *Octave* is a musical term referring to a pitch that is eight notes above a note that has the same letter name.

Place your thumb on middle C (the first note in **EXERCISE 13-1**, written on one ledger line below the staff) and count the keys moving up the keyboard until you reach the C (the first note in **EXERCISE 13-8**, written in the third space of the staff). The high C is exactly eight white keys higher than middle C, thus an octave higher.

Using these two Cs as a model, do the same with the second note E in **EXERCISE 13-1** and the second note E in **EXERCISE 13-8**. You will discover that there is the same number of white keys from the E on the first line of the staff in **EXERCISE 13-1** to the higher E in the fourth space on the staff in **EXERCISE 13-8**. Now do the same comparison with the third note D in both Exercises 13-1 and 13-8, and you will discover the same thing: There are eight white keys from the low D to the high D.

Playing a Simple Melody

Now that you have played Exercises 13-1 through 13-8, it's time to play your first piece of music. This little tune is comprised of sections from Exercises 13-1, 13-2, and 13-3. As you can see, the fingering of the right hand is not indicated beyond measure 4. This is because the fingering pattern is already established and keeps repeating throughout the piece (1, 3, 2, 3, 1).

As the time signature indicates, there are four beats per measure. Be sure to give all the measures their full four beats, including the measures that have rests.

Let's take a closer look at **EXERCISE 13-9**. This piece is written using a two-bar pattern. The two-bar pattern is a series of four quarter notes in the first measure followed by one quarter note, one quarter rest, and a half rest in the second measure. This is a rhythmic pattern—it creates a specific rhythm that is repeated throughout the piece. The rhythm of the pattern is the same; however, the pitches change. In measures 1 and 2, the pitches are C, E, D, E, C. In measures 3 and 4, the pitches rise to D, F, E, F, D. In measures 5 and 6, the pitches rise to E, G, F, G, E. Measures 7 and 8 are exactly the same as measures 3 and 4. And measures 9 and 10 are exactly the same as measures 1 and 2.

This structural analysis identifies the patterns in the piece, which should make it easier to play the music.

NICE and EASY

In reviewing this material, answer the following questions.

12. What do you call the first thing you see to the immediate right of the treble clef in Exercise 13-5?

    ♪ ....

13. What does this symbol mean?

    ♪ ....

14. In Exercise 13-6, what does the word *moderato* command?

    ♪ ....

15. What is the English translation of the Italian word *moderato*?

    ♪ ....

16. In **EXERCISE 13-7**, what does the symbol *mf* mean?

    ♪ ....

17. Why are the stems on the quarter notes in **EXERCISES 13-7 AND 13-8** going down?

    ♪ ....

18. In **EXERCISE 13-8**, what is to the immediate right of the time signature and also at the very end of measure 4?

    ♪ ....

19. What does this symbol mean?

    ♪ ....

20. When you see this symbol, how many times should you play the music?

    ♪ ....

21. What is the correlation between **EXERCISE 13-1** and **EXERCISE 13-8**?

    ♪ ....

22. What type of pattern is used in **EXERCISE 13-9**?

    ♪ ....

23. What other pattern is consistent throughout the piece?

    ♪ ....

24. How many measures are there in **EXERCISE 13-9**?

    ♪ ....

25. How many bars are there in **EXERCISE 13-9**?

    ♪ ....

26. How many beats are there in measures 2, 4, 6, 8, and 10?

    ♪ ....

27. In those measures, how many beats are silent?

    ♪ ....

(Answers can be found in Appendix A.)

Half and Whole Notes

Before we continue on with the exercises, let's take a look at notes and their relative values. You are already familiar with quarter notes, having played them in the previous exercises. As you know, a quarter note equals one beat. You also know that four quarter notes equal four beats. For example, in **EXERCISE 13-9** the time signature is 4/4, telling you that there are four quarter beats per measure. Measures 1, 3, 5, 7, and 9 have four quarter notes in each of those measures.

You are also familiar with the quarter rest, which equals a quarter beat of silence, and the half rest, which equals two beats of silence. A half note looks like a white quarter note and equals two beats of sound. The sound of a half note is sustained, or held, for two beats. For example, in **EXERCISE 13-10**, the first note is a half note and represents the first and second beats in the measure. This is followed by a quarter note for the third beat and another quarter note for the fourth beat. When playing a half note, you hold the sound through the second beat.

Whole notes look like half notes without stems. They are held for a full four beats. Whole rests look like upside-down half rests and receive four counts of silence. You can find a whole note in the next chapter, **EXERCISE 14-1**; whole rests first appear in **EXERCISE 15-9**.

Adding the Fourth and Fifth Fingers

Now let's add fingers 4 and 5 to the exercises. Place your fifth finger above the G key (five keys above middle C), your fourth finger above the F key, your third finger above the E key, and your second finger above the D key.

Play **EXERCISE 13-10** starting with your fourth finger on the F key.

EXERCISE 13-10

A new symbol has been added in **EXERCISE 13-10**: the dynamic marking *mp*. This symbol means *mezzo piano*, which translated from Italian to English means "medium soft."

At this point, you might be wondering why musical terms and symbols are in Italian. It started with the Italian Operatic composers Puccini, Rossini, and Verdi, who wrote dynamic and tempo markings in Italian for the singers and musicians who performed their operas. Other countries in Europe adopted the Italian symbols, which eventually became the universal standard.

Be sure to acknowledge the repeat sign in **EXERCISE 13-10**; at the end of measure 8, go directly back to the beginning of the piece (measure 1) and play the exercise again. Don't stop the even flow of beats when going from the end of measure 8 back to measure 1.

For the next exercise, place your fifth finger above the G key, your fourth finger above the F key, your third finger above the E key, your second finger above the D key, and your thumb above the C key (middle C). This exercise is designed to strengthen your fourth and fifth fingers, which are normally the weakest fingers in the right hand. (Reminder: Be sure to acknowledge the repeat sign.)

Play **EXERCISE 13-11** starting with your thumb on middle C.

EXERCISE 13-11

Play **EXERCISE 13-11** frequently. In doing so, you will strengthen your fourth and fifth fingers.

The following are a few things to keep in mind when playing the exercises in this chapter.

1. Start playing the exercises slowly. Once you have played the exercise correctly, then increase your tempo (speed) to moderato.
2. If you get confused with your fingering, refer to **FIGURES 13-1** and **13-2** as needed.
3. Your hand and fingers should never be flat when playing the keyboard. Be sure to keep your right hand arched and your fingers curved when playing these exercises.
4. Play the quarter notes evenly, giving them the same equal value (one beat).
5. Be sure to give the quarter and half rests their full values.
6. Enjoy playing the exercises and feel good about learning how to play the piano.

CHAPTER 14
Adding Your Left Hand

Think of the left hand as providing the musical foundation that supports what the right hand is playing. This chapter is going to introduce you to the bass line in a piece of music and how to use your left hand to play it. Then you are going to put both hands together to play a short piece of music.

Playing a Bass Line

For the most part, the left hand plays the bass line in a piece of music, which provides harmony to the melody played with the right hand. In more advanced piano compositions, the left hand plays both bass lines and chords. This is the case with most of the piano sonatas mentioned in Chapter 4. However, we're going to set the more advanced stuff aside for now and concentrate on using the left hand to play just the bass line.

FIGURE 14-1:
Abbreviated
keyboard

5. 4. 3. 2. 1. - the fingers of your left hand

Let's assign numbers to the fingers in your left hand. Your thumb is 1, your index finer is 2, your middle finger is 3, your forefinger is 4, and your fifth finger is 5. Referring to **FIGURE 14-1**, place the five fingers of your left hand above the following keys: thumb above middle C, index finger above the B key, middle finger above the A key, forefinger above the G key, and fifth finger above the F key.

When playing with your left hand, the corresponding notes are written on a staff using the bass clef. As you can see in **FIGURE 14-2**, the bass clef has two dots immediately to the right of the curved, half heart-shaped half circle.

FIGURE 14-2:
Bass clef

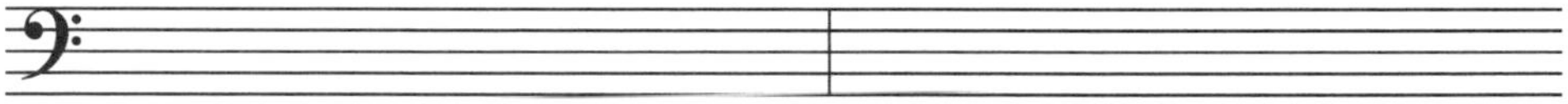

Starting with the top line and going down to the bottom line, the letter names of the lines of the bass staff are: A, F, D, B, and G. The letter names of the spaces from the top space to the bottom space are: G, E, C, and A. The F line is between the two dots of the bass clef.

Middle C plays a very important role in tying together the bass clef and the treble clef. As you can see in **FIGURE 14-3**, one ledger line above the bass clef is middle C, which is the same middle C located one ledger line below the treble clef.

FIGURE 14-3

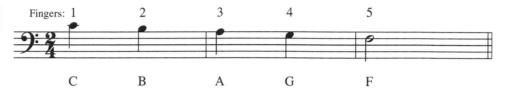

In **FIGURE 14-3**, the time signature is 2/4. This time signature tells you two things: The top number tells you how many beats there are per measure (two) and the bottom number tells you the quarter note gets the beat.

As indicated in **FIGURE 14-3**, play the notes C, B, A, G, and F with the corresponding fingers of your left hand.

In the next exercise, the fingering of the left hand starts on middle C in measure 1. In measure 3, the sequence begins with the thumb on B. In measure 5, the sequence begins with the thumb on A. And in measure 7, the sequence begins with the thumb on G.

The very last note in this exercise is C, which is one octave below middle C.

EXERCISE 14-1

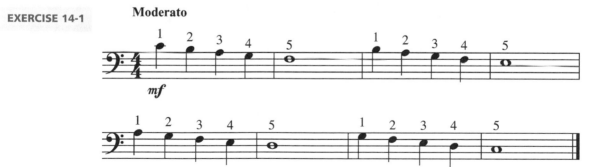

The first note in **EXERCISE 14-2** is C, located one octave below middle C. Place your fifth finger above the C key, fourth above the D key, third above the E key, second above the F key, and your thumb above the G key. Keeping your fingers in this position, play **EXERCISE 14-2**.

EXERCISE 14-2

A few new symbols have been added to **EXERCISE 14-2**. The word *allegro* indicates the tempo, which means "fast." The *f* dynamic marking, which represents *forte*, means "loud."

Start the exercise slowly. Once you have worked out the notes and rhythm, increase your speed and play the exercise loudly.

FIGURE 14-4:
Abbreviated
keyboard

* = the first note in exercise #3
** = one octave below middle C

The first note in **EXERCISE 14-3** is A, located two keys below the last note C in **EXERCISE 14-2** (please see **FIGURE 14-4**). Starting with your fifth finger on the A key, play **EXERCISE 14-3**.

EXERCISE 14-3

There's a new tempo marking in **EXERCISE 14-3**, *adagio*, which means to play the exercise slowly. Did you acknowledge the repeat sign and play the exercise twice?

Before we continue on with more exercises—and eventually a piano piece using both your right and left hands—please answer the following questions.

1. What are the letter names of the lines on a staff from top to bottom when using a bass clef?

2. What are the letter names of the spaces from top to bottom?

3. Where is middle C located when using the bass clef?

4. What does *allegro* mean?

5. What does *f* mean?

6. What does *adagio* mean?

(Answers can be found in Appendix A.)

Playing Octaves with the Left Hand

By now, you are familiar with the term *octave*, which is a derivative of the Latin word *octava*, which means "eight." For example, the low note C in **EXERCISE 14-2** is an octave below middle C.

In order to play an octave, you have to open up and stretch your left hand. The low note is played with your fifth finger, and the high note (located an octave above) is played with your thumb.

Place your fifth finger on the low C key and your thumb on middle C and play **EXERCISE 14-4**.

EXERCISE 14-4

Play **EXERCISE 14-4** often so you can get accustomed to stretching the fingers on your left hand and getting the feel of playing octaves.

Learning Eighth Notes

In the next exercise, you're going to play eighth notes. Eighth notes are a subdivision of quarter notes. In other words, two eighth notes equal one quarter note. As you can see in measures 2, 4, 7, and 9 in **EXERCISE 14-5**, there are two eighth notes for the third and fourth beats of each measure. In measure 2, the third beat is comprised of the two eighth notes E and D, and the eighth notes C and B make up the fourth beat. Your goal is to play the eighth notes evenly within the third and fourth beats of the measure.

As you can see from the fingering in **EXERCISE 14-5**, your thumb will be playing more than one key; it will play the A, G, F, and E keys. You will discover that the thumb on your left hand will be very active when playing bass lines.

EXERCISE 14-5

In **EXERCISE 14-6** you're going to play a series of eighth notes in every measure except the last measure, which has a whole note. With the steady flow of eighth notes, this exercise is designed to help you play the eighth notes evenly.

Start playing this exercise slowly. When you have worked out the placement of notes on the keyboard and the corresponding fingering, increase your speed to the designated allegro tempo.

EXERCISE 14-6

Practicing Techniques When Playing with Both Hands

By now, you should have a good feel for playing bass lines using the left hand. Are you ready to put both the left and right hands together?

Before you start playing a piano piece written for both hands, keep the following practice techniques in mind:

1. Start with only playing the right-hand part. Keep playing the right-hand part until you have perfected it and, if possible, have memorized it.
2. Once you have accomplished that, move on to the left hand. Now play only the left-hand part and keep playing it until you have perfected it.
3. Try your best to play either the right- or left-hand part automatically, without having to think about what you're playing; try to play the part instinctively. This will make it a lot easier when putting both hands together and playing both parts simultaneously.
4. Don't try to play the whole piece at once. Instead, take it one measure at a time. Once you have perfected measure 1, add the second measure. Before going on to the third measure, repeat measures 1 and 2 until they flow together without any hesitation or pauses. Keep adding measures, one at a time, until you have played them all.
5. Take your time; don't rush into the exercise.
6. Start playing it slowly. Once you are comfortable with the parts, increase the tempo.
7. If you choose to use pedals, keep in mind that when using the sustain pedal, a common practice is to press it down at the beginning of each measure and release it at the end of each measure. This pedaling technique will prevent the blurring of chords, harmonies, and melodies from measure to measure. For practicing purposes, you might want to use the soft pedal. If you have one on your piano, experiment with the sostenuto pedal. The use of pedals is determined by your subjective ear and aesthetic taste.

With all of the above tips in mind, play **EXERCISE 14-7**.

EXERCISE 14-7

Let's take a closer look at **EXERCISE 14-7**. As you can see, this is the first exercise that uses two staffs—one for the right hand (treble clef) and one for the left hand (bass clef). A bracket ties the two staffs together.

In measures 1 and 2, the right hand plays whole notes while the left hand plays quarter notes. As you can plainly see, the whole note equals four quarter notes. Likewise, the four quarter notes equal the whole note. In the third measure, the half note E, played by the right hand, equals the two quarter notes C and B, played by the left hand. The same note values occur with the second half note F, played by the right hand, and the two quarter notes A and B, played by the left hand.

As indicated by the time signature, **EXERCISE 14-7** is in 4/4 time. The first beat in measure 1 has two notes: the whole note in the right hand

and the quarter note in the left hand. Both of these notes are to be played at exactly the same time. In the first beat of the second measure, the F note in the right hand and the F note in the left hand are to be played at exactly the same time. Incidentally, the distance between the F note in the left hand and the F note in the right hand is an octave. In the first beat of the third measure, the E note in the right hand and middle C in the left hand are to be played at the same time. In the third beat of this same measure, the F note in the right hand and the A note in the left hand are to be played at the same time. Finally, in the first beat of the last measure, the exercise is concluded with the right hand playing the whole note E and the left hand playing the whole note middle C.

When playing the piano using both hands and reading the corresponding music, a vertical and horizontal sound experience occurs simultaneously. The vertical sound occurs when two notes are played at the same time. For instance in **EXERCISE 14-7**, measure 1, the right hand plays the E while the left hand plays the middle C below it. Looking at the written music, you see the vertical relationship of the E above the middle C. Once this vertical sound occurs, the horizontal sound takes place with the descending bass notes of the left hand. Your eyes are reading the music both vertically and horizontally at the same time.

The Thumb Goes Under the Fingers

There are eight white keys from middle C down to the C key an octave lower. When playing descending bass lines with your left hand that span an octave, you can run out of fingers. For instance, after playing the A with your third finger in **FIGURE 14-8**, how do you play five more notes? By putting your thumb under your third finger. If F is your lowest note and middle C is your highest note, then you don't have to alter the fingering. However, if you have to play all eight notes from middle C down to the C located an octave lower, then your thumb is going to go under your middle finger.

EXERCISE 14-8

As the fingering indicates, after playing the third quarter note in the first measure with your third finger, the next note is to be played with the first finger of your left hand. The way to do this is to move your thumb under your third finger immediately after playing the A note. In doing so, you will be repositioning the fingers of your left hand to be able to play all of the notes down to the low C without running out of fingers.

Play **EXERCISE 14-8** slowly and keep repeating it until you are comfortable with this new fingering technique. In playing the repeat, you will be leaping an octave from the last note C (played with your fifth finger) up to the first note middle C (played with your thumb).

Leaping over the Thumb

When playing ascending bass notes with the left hand, you have to leap your finger over the thumb to avoid running out of fingers. As indicated in **EXERCISE 14-9**, in the third measure after playing the G note with your thumb, move your middle finger over your thumb to play the A note. The last two ascending notes are played with your second finger playing the B note and your thumb playing middle C.

EXERCISE 14-9 will help you to learn to play both descending and ascending bass notes, moving the thumb under your fingers on the way down and moving your middle finger over the thumb on the way up.

Play **EXERCISE 14-9** slowly and keep repeating it until you get comfortable with the descending and ascending fingering.

EXERCISE 14-9

Putting It All Together

EXERCISE 14-10 is a piece of music I wrote that incorporates a lot of the material covered in this chapter. Before you play this piece, take a close look at all of the elements that make up the piece. Notice the rhythm of the right hand, which is comprised of a two-bar sequence made up of two eighth notes followed by two quarter notes, two more eighth notes, and a whole note in the second bar. The left hand plays a series of half notes, with fingering that includes the thumb going under the middle finger in measure 5. The tempo is moderate and the dynamic level is medium soft.

It's very important to look at all of the elements in a piece of music before you play it. This allows you to get mentally prepared and to anticipate what you have to do in order to perform it properly and play what's written.

Refresh your memory and look over the tips listed earlier in this chapter about practicing techniques to use when playing a piano piece with both hands.

When you are mentally prepared, play **EXERCISE 14-10** and enjoy this simple little tune.

EXERCISE 14-10

LAZY DAY

In reviewing the material covered in this chapter, please answer the following questions.

7. What is an octave?

    ♪ ....

8. What fingers on the left hand play an octave?

    ♪ ....

9. How many eighth notes equal one quarter note?

    ♪ ....

10. In Exercise 14-5, what measures have eighth notes?

    ♪ ....

11. What beats in those measures have eighth notes?

    ♪ ....

12. What should you do before practicing a two-hand piano exercise or piece?

    ♪ ....

13. What does a bracket do?

    ♪ ....

14. What do your eyes do when reading both right- and left-hand parts?

    ♪ ....

15. When does the thumb on the left hand go under the fingers?

    ♪ ....

16. Why does the thumb go under the fingers?

    ♪ ....

17. When does the middle finger on the left hand leap over the thumb?

    ♪ ....

18. What is the two-bar sequence comprised of in **EXERCISE 14-10**?

    ♪ ....

(Answers can be found in Appendix A.)

CHAPTER 15

Learning Sharp Key Signatures

You've done a great job so far! Now, it's time to take things a little further. In this chapter you are going to be introduced to the circle of fifths, learn scale degrees, and, of course, learn sharp key signatures.

C Major

All of the exercises and piano pieces you have played thus far have one thing in common: They are all in the key of C major or A minor. Why is that? Because the key of C major and its relative minor, A minor, have no sharps or flats—you only play the white keys. The vast majority of sharps and flats are located on the black keys on the keyboard.

The key of A minor is C major's relative minor because it uses the same key signature, which has no sharps or flats. Notes that have no sharps or flats are also called naturals; they're natural—not sharp or flat. So all the notes in the C-major scale and the A-minor scale are natural.

Key signatures tell you what the notes are in a specific scale and what the corresponding keys are on the keyboard. Having played the exercises in Chapter 14, you are already familiar with the key of C major. The consecutive sequence of eight notes from middle C up an octave to the C on the third space of the treble staff is called a scale. Let's take a look at the C-major scale.

EXERCISE 15-1   **Moderato**

As you can see, the notes in the C-major scale are C, D, E, F, G, A, B, and C. Scales go up, scales go down, and scales in a specific key are the same in all octaves.

The notes in scales are numbered from one to eight.

1. C is the root; also called the tonic.
2. D is the supertonic.
3. E is the mediant.
4. F is the subdominant.

5. G is the dominant.
6. A is the submediant.
7. B is the leading tone.
8. C is the octave.

All of these scale degrees have an intervallic relationship with the root C. An interval is the distance between any two pitches or notes. For instance, the intervallic distance between C and D is a second, between C and E is a third, between C and F is a fourth, and so forth.

Practice the C-major scale in **EXERCISE 15-1** with your right hand. Notice that the thumb goes under the middle finger on the third beat in measure 1, and the middle finger goes over the thumb on the fourth beat in measure 3. Repeat this exercise several times.

In the next exercise you're going to play the C-major scale with your left hand. Notice that the middle finger goes over the thumb on the first beat in measure 2 and that the thumb goes under the middle finger on the second beat in measure 3. Repeat **EXERCISE 15-2** several times.

In **EXERCISE 15-3** you're going to play the C-major scale covering two octaves, from middle C to the C two ledger lines above the treble staff. As indicated in the fingering, when you see 1 after 3 and 4, the thumb goes under the middle finger going up the scale. And going down the scale, when you see 3 and 4 after 1, the middle finger goes over the thumb.

EXERCISE 15-3

Moving on to the left hand, play the C scale covering two octaves in the bass. Before you do, notice that in the fingering on the way up the scale, the middle finger goes over the thumb in measure 2, the fourth finger goes over the thumb in measure 3, and the middle finger goes over the thumb in measure 4. On the way down the scale, the thumb goes under the middle finger in measure 5 and under the fourth finger and third finger in measure 6. The first note is two octaves below middle C.

EXERCISE 15-4

Next you are going to play the C-major scale at the distance of two octaves. Notice that **EXERCISE 15-5** is a combination of Exercises 15-3 and 15-4.

EXERCISE 15-5

As you can see in the next exercise, the fingering for the left hand and the right hand is exactly the same as the fingering in **EXERCISE 15-5**. In **EXERCISE 15-6** play the A-minor scale at a distance of two octaves between both hands.

EXERCISE 15-6

The Circle of Fifths

Music theory is very logical. All of the notes in music are in alphabetical order from A to G. The treble and bass staffs are joined by the common note middle C. Notes from high ledger lines above the treble staff to ledger lines below the bass staff follow the musical alphabetical order.

In terms of the sequence of key signatures with sharps, they follow a circle of fifths. For example, the first sharp key signature, using one sharp, is the key of G, which happens to be five notes (a fifth) above C.

Below is a visual representation of the Circle of Fifths. It is easy to see, for example, that the major key of E has a relative minor of C-sharp. Both keys contain four sharps.

Major Key	Relative Minor Key	Number of Sharps & Flats	Sharps or Flats
C	A	none	all naturals
G	E	1 sharp	F
D	B	2 sharps	F, C
A	F-sharp	3 sharps	F, C, G
E	C-sharp	4 sharps	F, C, G, D
B	G-sharp	5 sharps	F, C, G, D, A
F-sharp	D-sharp	6 sharps	F, C, G, D, A, E
C-sharp	A-sharp	7 sharps	F, C, G, D, A, E, B
F	D	1 flat	B
B-flat	G	2 flats	B, E
E-flat	C	3 flats	B, E, A
A-flat	F	4 flats	B, E, A, D
D-flat	B-flat	5 flats	B, E, A, D, G
G-flat	E-flat	6 flats	B, E, A, D, G, C
C-flat	A-flat	7 flats	B, E, A, D, G, C, F

You may ask yourself the question, "Why does the key of G have an F-sharp?" It's because it follows the same scale degrees and intervallic relationships of all major keys. Using the C-major scale as an example, the distance between C and the seventh scale degree B is a half-step. Looking at your keyboard, you can see that the B key is right next to the C key. In the key of C, there are two half-steps: between B and C, and between E and F. The relationships among the other notes in the key of C are whole steps. For example, going from

C to D is a whole step; there is a black key between the two notes. It's also a whole step from D to E, F to G, G to A, and A to B. As you can see on your keyboard, there are black keys between each of these whole steps.

All major key signatures have the very same whole-step/half-step pattern, which is:

- A whole step from the root to the second scale degree.
- A whole step from the second to third scale degree.
- A half-step from the third to fourth scale degree.
- A whole step from the fourth to fifth scale degree.
- A whole step from the fifth to sixth scale degree.
- A whole step from the sixth to seventh scale degree.
- A half-step from the seventh scale degree to the octave.

In summary, there are two half-steps and five whole steps in all major key signatures. The half-steps are from the third to fourth scale degrees and from the seventh scale degree to the octave.

G Major

Using this parallel whole-step/half-step relationship, the seventh scale degree in the key of G has to be a half-step away from the octave G. That's why the F is sharp. So when playing the G-major scale, you're going to play the black key between the F and G keys, which is called F-sharp. In **EXERCISE 15-7**, a sharp sign (♯) is on the F line in the treble clef, telling you to play the black key F-sharp. Be sure to play all of the F notes F-sharp, even though there isn't a sharp sign on the F space in the staff. With that in mind, play **EXERCISE 15-7** with your right hand.

EXERCISE 15-7

In keeping with the parallel relative logic of music theory, since C major's relative minor is A minor, G major's relative minor is E minor. The relative parallel connection is that the relative minors are built on the sixth scale degree of the major key. In the key of C major, the sixth scale degree is A, and in the key of G major, the sixth scale degree is E.

G is the root, the tonic.

A is the second, the supertonic.

B is the third, the mediant.

C is the fourth, the subdominant.

D is the fifth, the dominant.

E is the sixth, the submediant.

F is the seventh, the leading tone.

G is the eighth, the octave.

Both G major and E minor use the same key signature, which has one sharp—F-sharp. In the key of E minor, the scale degrees are:

E is the root, the tonic.

F-sharp is the second, the supertonic.

G is the third, the mediant.

A is the fourth, the subdominant.

B is the fifth, the dominant.

C is the sixth, the submediant.

D is the seventh, the subtonic.

E is the eighth, the octave.

It's important to note that all natural minor scales have a different whole-step/half-step pattern than major scales. In minor scales, the pattern is:

- A whole step from the root to the second scale degree.
- A half-step from the second to the third scale degree.
- A whole step from the third to the fourth scale degree.
- A whole step from the fourth to the fifth scale degree.
- A half-step from the fifth to the sixth scale degree.
- A whole step from the sixth to the seventh scale degree.
- A whole step from the seventh to the eighth scale degree.

In natural minor key signatures, the half-steps are from the second to third scale degree and from the fifth to sixth scale degree.

When playing **EXERCISE 15-8**, please note that the F-sharp is the second note in the E-minor scale and is played with the second finger on your right hand and the fourth finger on your left hand.

EXERCISE 15-8

Music in major keys tends to be bright and cheerful. On the other hand, music in minor keys can sound introspective, moody, and even sad. **EXERCISE 15-9**, written in E minor, should create an introspective mood. Before you start playing it, there's a lot of new information you need to grasp.

First of all, notice the 3/4 time signature. That tells you there are three beats per measure and the quarter note gets the beat. This time signature creates a different feel from the customary 4/4 time signature. Time signatures that are in 2/4 and 4/4 create an even feel—the numbers are even—whereas a 3/4 is uneven because of the number three.

In **EXERCISE 15-9** you can see a series of three quarter notes per measure in the left hand, except for measures 16 and 24, which have dotted half notes. The series of three quarter notes will help you keep a steady 3/4 time. In order to get comfortable with the 3/4 time signature, look at the quarter notes and count *one, two, three*. The first beat of each measure is a little more pronounced than the second and third beats. The first beat is called the downbeat; the second and third beats are called upbeats. Downbeats are generally stronger than upbeats.

Look at the notes in the right hand in measures 1, 3, 4, 5, 7, 8, 9, 11, 12, 13, 14, 17, 19, 20, 21, and 24, and you'll see dotted half notes.

The dot represents half the value of a half note, which is equal to one quarter note. Therefore, a dotted half note equals three quarter notes—the half note equals two quarter beats, and the dot equals one quarter beat. These three beats satisfy the 3/4 time signature, which tells you that there are three beats per measure.

In measures 3, 4, 7, 8, 11, 12, 13, 14, 19, and 20, the dotted half notes are tied to each other. This means you hold the dotted E in measure 3 through the end of measure 4. The collective value of the two dotted half notes tied together equals six beats, tying together the three beats in measure 3 with the three beats in measure 4. When you play the E in measure 3, keep that key depressed through the end of measure 4. In doing so, the sound will continue through both measures. The same is true in measures 7 and 8, 11 and 12, 13 and 14, and 19 and 20. Please observe the whole rests in the right hand in measures 15 and 16.

Also look at the fingering of both hands before playing the piece (the left-hand fingering is the same throughout). Notice the tempo marking *andante*, the metronome marking quarter note equals 108, and the dynamic marking *mp*. *Andante* means "moderately slow." If you have a metronome, set it to quarter note equals 108, and you will hear the rate of the pulse of the quarter note. The metronome marking makes the tempo marking much more specific.

In the left hand, the third note in measures 1, 5, 17, 21, and 23 is on two ledger lines above the bass staff, which is one octave above the first note in these measures. This ledger line is two whole steps above middle C. It is also the exact same pitch as the tied dotted half notes in measures 3 and 4, 7 and 8, and 19 and 20.

And because **EXERCISE 15-9** is in E minor, the key signature has an F-sharp in both the treble and bass clefs. In honoring the key signature, be sure to play the F-sharps. Even though there is only one sharp symbol on the top line of the treble clef and one sharp symbol on the second from the top line of the bass clef, *all* Fs have to be played sharp. The first and third notes played by the right hand in the second measure are F-sharps.

Once you have studied and are mentally prepared, play **EXERCISE 15-9** starting with only the left-hand part. Then add the right hand, one measure at a time.

LATE AT NIGHT

Andante ♩ = 108

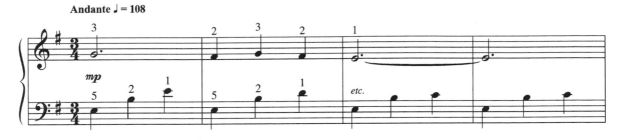

D Major

As we go through the circle of fifths, we'll be adding one sharp at a time for each new key signature.

The next key signature in the circle of fifths is D major, a fifth above G. The key of D major has two sharps: F-sharp (carried over from G major) and C-sharp. As with all major key signatures, there has to be a half-step from the seventh scale degree to the octave and a half-step from the third to the fourth scale degree. Therefore, the C is raised to a C-sharp, and the F is raised to an F-sharp.

If the relative minor of C major is A minor, and the relative minor of G major is E minor, what is the relative minor of D major? Knowing the relative minor is built on the sixth scale degree of every major scale, B minor is D major's relative minor. B minor and D major use the same key signature, which has two sharps: F-sharp and C-sharp.

In the next exercise, you're going to see a different fingering pattern for the left hand when playing the B-minor scale. As indicated, you start with your fourth finger instead of the customary fifth finger when playing C- and G-major scales and A- and E-minor scales. Be sure to catch the over-the-thumb action going up the scale and the under-the-thumb action on the way down.

With that in mind, play **EXERCISE 15-10** with the left hand, starting with the low B, located below the second ledger line below the bass clef.

EXERCISE 15-10

Move on to **EXERCISE 15-11** and put your hands together to play the B-minor scale up and down two octaves. Be sure to catch the under-the-thumb action in the right hand going up the scale and the over-the-thumb action going down the scale.

EXERCISE 15-11

In **EXERCISE 15-12**, play the D-major scale with both hands.

EXERCISE 15-12

Now that you are familiar with the D-major and B-minor scales, let's take a close look at the next exercise. This piece is designed to strengthen all of the fingers in your right hand. It is composed utilizing a sequence of a quarter note followed by six eighth notes. As the metronome marking indicates (quarter note equals 92), **EXERCISE 15-13** is slower than **EXERCISE 15-9**. Given its title, the piece is to be played lightly and, as the dynamic marking indicates, medium soft.

Make your preparations and enjoy this light little piece.

EXERCISE 15-13

QUITE LIGHTLY

We have covered quite a bit of ground so far in this chapter. Before we move on, please answer the following questions.

1. How many sharps does C major have?

2. What is C major's relative minor?

3. On what scale degree is a major key's relative minor built on?

4. What is a note called that has no sharps or flats?

5. The first scale degree in the key of C is called the tonic. What else is it called?

6. What key signatures have one sharp?

7. What is the distance between the seventh and eighth scale degrees in a major key?

8. What is the distance between the second and third scale degrees in a major key?

9. What is the distance between the second and third scale degrees in a minor key?

10. In Exercise 15-9, what is the first beat called?

11. What does a dotted half note equal?

12. What happens when notes are tied together?

13. What does *andante* mean?

14. What is "quarter note equals 108"?

15. What does it tell you?

16. In the key of E minor, are all the Fs played sharp?

17. What should you do before starting a two-hand piano piece?

18. What key signatures have two sharps?

19. When playing the B-minor scale with the left hand, which finger plays the first note B?

(Answers can be found in Appendix A.)

A Major

So far we have covered C major (A minor), G major (E minor), and D major (B minor). A fifth above D is A. Therefore, the next key in the circle of fifths is A major and its relative minor, F-sharp minor.

There are three sharps in the key of A major and F-sharp minor: F-sharp, C-sharp, and G-sharp. In the next exercise, you will be playing the A-major scale with both hands. Start playing with only the right hand, then move on to only the left hand, and eventually put both hands together.

EXERCISE 15-14

In the next exercise, please notice the different fingering for both hands when playing the F-sharp minor scale.

EXERCISE 15-15

E Major

The next sharp key is E major and its relative minor, C-sharp minor. E major and C-sharp minor have four sharps in the key signature: F-sharp, C-sharp, G-sharp, and D-sharp. Play **EXERCISE 15-16** starting with the right hand and eventually add the left hand.

EXERCISE 15-16

In the next exercise, please notice the different fingering in both hands when playing the C-sharp–minor scale. Similar to F-sharp minor, the fingering is different because the scale starts on a black key.

EXERCISE 15-17

B Major

Continuing on with the circle of fifths, the next sharp key is B major and its relative minor, G-sharp minor. The new sharp added to this key signature is A-sharp, the seventh scale degree in B major. The five sharps in B major and G-sharp minor are: F-sharp, C-sharp, G-sharp, D-sharp, and A-sharp.

By now you have probably noticed the pattern in the addition of sharps: The new

sharp is always a fifth above the previous sharp. For example, in the key of E major, the fourth sharp is D. B major uses the same four sharps in E major plus the new sharp A. A-sharp is a fifth above D-sharp.

Before playing the B-major scale, notice that the fingering in the left hand starts with the fourth finger. And watch out for those A-sharps!

EXERCISE 15-18

The fingering for playing the G-sharp–minor scale is the same as the fingering for the C-sharp–minor scale—the right hand starts with the second finger, and the left hand starts with the third finger. Here's the G-sharp–minor scale in action.

EXERCISE 15-19

F-Sharp Major

In the next key signature, you're going to discover a sharp that isn't on a black key. In the F-sharp–major scale, the seventh scale degree (which you know has to be raised a half-step) is E-sharp. As you also know, E-natural is the white key on the piano, two whole steps above C. When raising E a half-step and making it E-sharp, it happens to be the same pitch as F, which is one white key above E.

With that in mind, play the F-sharp–major scale in **EXERCISE 15-20**.

EXERCISE 15-20

Here's the D-sharp–minor scale, which uses the same key signature as F-sharp major. Notice the different fingering in both hands and watch out for those E-sharps!

EXERCISE 15-21

Let's review the key signatures. The sequence of key signatures in the circle of fifths starting with C major (and their relative minors) is:

Major Key Signature	Relative Minor
C major	A minor
G major	E minor
D major	B minor
A major	F-sharp minor
E major	C-sharp minor
B major	G-sharp minor
F-sharp major	D-sharp minor

As you can see, the relative minors also follow the circle of fifths: E minor is a fifth above A minor; B minor is a fifth above E minor, and so forth.

The major sharp key signatures and their relative minors have:

No sharps—C major, A minor
One sharp (F-sharp)—G major, E minor
Two sharps (F-sharp, C-sharp)—D major, B minor
Three sharps (F-sharp, C-sharp, G-sharp)—A major, F-sharp minor
Four sharps (F-sharp, C-sharp, G-sharp, D-sharp)—E major, C-sharp
    minor
Five sharps (F-sharp, C-sharp, G-sharp, D-sharp, A-sharp)—B major,
    G-sharp minor
Six sharps (F-sharp, C-sharp, G-sharp, D-sharp, A-sharp, E-sharp)—
    F-sharp major, D-sharp minor

Continuing the Circle of Fifths

In this chapter, we have covered the most common sharp key signatures used in piano music, and music in general. However, sharp key signatures do continue beyond F-sharp major. Continuing on with the circle of fifths, the remaining major sharp key signatures and their relative minors are:

C-sharp major, A-sharp minor
G-sharp major, E-sharp minor
D-sharp major, B-sharp minor

Even though you probably won't play piano pieces written in these key signatures, you should be aware of them.

CHAPTER 16

Learning Flat Key Signatures

Now that you have the sharp key signatures down pat, it only makes sense to move on to the flat key signatures. Take a deep breath, relax, and get ready to tackle the circle of fourths.

The Circle of Fourths

Sharp key signatures follow a circle of fifths. Sharps raise any given pitch up a half-step. Flats, on the other hand, lower a pitch down a half-step. Flat key signatures follow a circle of fourths. Refer to the chart on page 160 to visualize this system.

The first flat key is F major. Going up four notes is B; however, in keeping with the whole-step/half-step scale degree pattern of major scales, the B is flat in F major. There has to be a half-step between the third and fourth scale degrees. F to G and G to A are whole steps; A to B-flat is a half-step. The B-flat is the black key located between A and B on your keyboard. In keeping with the whole-step/half-step pattern of minor key scales, there has to be a half-step from the fifth scale degree to the sixth scale degree. So in the key of D minor (which is F major's relative minor), the fifth scale degree is A, and a half-step above that is the sixth scale degree, B-flat.

As you recall, sharps are located on the seventh scale degree in major key signatures and on the second scale degree in their relative minor key signatures. For example, in the key of G major, the seventh scale degree is F-sharp; in E minor, F-sharp is the second scale degree. Unlike sharps, flats are located on the fourth scale degree in major key signatures and on the sixth scale degree in minor key signatures.

The major flat key signatures and their relative minors are:

Major Flat Key Signature	Relative Minor
F major	D minor
B-flat major	G minor
E-flat major	C minor
A-flat major	F minor
D-flat major	B-flat minor
G-flat major	E-flat minor

F Major

Play **EXERCISE 16-1** and take special note of the B-flat.

EXERCISE 16-1

By now, you're quite familiar with the way major scales sound. You're accustom to scale degrees and the pattern of whole steps and half-steps. With that in mind, try a little experiment and play the F-major scale with B-natural (the white key), not B-flat (the black key). Your ears should tell you that the B-natural doesn't sound right because it's not in the key signature.

In the next exercise, play the D-minor scale, which uses the same key signature as F major.

EXERCISE 16-2

B-Flat Major

Moving up a fourth is the key signature of B-flat major and its relative minor, G minor. Notice that the fingering in the right hand starts with the second finger. The fingering in the left hand starts with the third finger.

As always, start playing with only the right hand. Then play with only the left hand. When you have both parts worked out, play the B-flat–major scale with both hands.

EXERCISE 16-3

EXERCISE 16-4 is a piano piece I wrote called "Octavia." (When you look at the left-hand part, you'll know why I call it "Octavia.") Let's take a close look at this exercise before you start playing it.

First of all, the key signature, which has the two flats B-flat and E-flat, tells you the piece is in the key of B-flat major. The time signature tells you the piece is in 4/4 time. The tempo is moderato, with a metronome marking of quarter note equals 108. The dynamic marking *mp* tells you to play the music medium soft. But then there's a new sign, which looks like a stretched-out part of a triangle. This is a crescendo sign, which means to play the music gradually louder by increasing the volume of sound. This pertains to the first four eighth notes: D, E-flat, F, and G. In the next measure, the *mf* dynamic marking tells you to play medium loud. So there is a gradual increase from medium soft to medium loud from the first eighth note D in measure 1 to the quarter note A in measure 2.

EXERCISE 16-4 starts out differently from the other pieces you have played so far. It starts off with rests—a whole rest in the left hand and a half rest in the right hand. What you have to do is count off and feel the first two beats, which are silent, and then play the eighth notes representing the third and fourth beats for the right hand. The four eighth notes in the first measure are called pick-up notes, which lead the way up to the downbeat (quarter note A) in measure 2.

Compositionally, **EXERCISE 16-4** uses a two-bar sequence, or motif, which is comprised of a half rest followed by four eighth notes followed by a quarter note, two eighth notes, and a half note. This two-bar sequence is repeated throughout the piece until measure 13, when the sequence is broken with two quarter notes (instead of four eighth notes) followed by a tied whole note.

Another dynamic sign appears in measure 15 that is just the opposite of the crescendo sign in measure 1. This is a decrescendo sign, which tells you to play the music softer. Because the right hand is holding the sound of the tied whole note, the decrescendo sign applies to the notes played in the left hand. In terms of volume, **EXERCISE 16-4** starts off medium soft, gets medium loud, and ends medium soft.

Notice the fingering in the right hand in measures 9, 11, and 12. The thumb goes under the second finger to play the middle C in measures 9 and 11; and, in measure 12, the second finger goes over the thumb to play the half note B-flat.

Starting slowly with the right hand only, play **EXERCISE 16-4**.

OCTAVIA

In the next exercise, which is in the key of G minor, take a close look at the fingering in the right hand before playing it. As you will discover in the first measure, it feels natural to simply move the fifth finger of the right hand down a half-step from B-flat to A. In the third measure, the first note is played by the second finger by going over the thumb on the last note played in the preceding measure. In the third measure, the fifth finger moves down a half-step from E-flat to D. When playing this exercise, please observe the repeat sign.

EXERCISE 16-5

E-Flat Major

The next flat key signature in the circle of fourths is E-flat major and its relative minor, C minor. As you can see, E-flat major and C minor have three flats: B-flat, E-flat, and A-flat. In comparison with the evolution of sharp key signatures and their corresponding sharps, the addition of flats in flat key signatures follows the evolving circle of fourths. In other words, the first flat key signature, F major, has one flat: B-flat. The second flat key signature, B-flat major, has two flats: B-flat and E-flat. And the third flat key signature, E-flat major, has three flats.

In the next exercise, notice that the fingering in the right hand starts with the second finger, and the fingering in the left hand starts with the third finger. When going up the E-flat major scale, the thumb in the right hand will go under the fingers twice per each octave, and the third and fourth fingers go over the thumb on the way down. The fingering in the left hand starts with the third finger. On the way up the scale, the fourth and third fingers go over the thumb twice per each octave. On the way down the scale, the thumb goes under the fingers twice per octave.

With that in mind, play the E-flat–major scale in **EXERCISE 16-6** starting with the right hand.

EXERCISE 16-6

In **EXERCISE 16-7**, try your hand at E-flat's relative minor, C minor. And be sure to play the B-, E-, and A-flats!

EXERCISE 16-7

As you discover each key signature, compare how they sound. The biggest difference in sound is between major and minor keys. But in addition to that, each major key has its own distinct sound. For instance, play the C-major scale. Then play the B-flat–major scale. Even though they're both major scales, they sound very different. The difference in sound is attributed largely to the two flats in the B-flat scale: the B-flat and the E-flat. You may discover that C major sounds brighter than B-flat major.

With minor scales, the difference in sound can be even more striking. For example, play the A-minor scale. Then play the C-minor scale. You'll probably hear quite a difference in sound between these two different minor scales. Here again, the difference is because of the three flats in the key of C minor. In the key of A minor, the B, E, and A are natural, and in C minor, the B, E, and A are flat. That's what creates the striking difference in sound between these two minor keys.

Let's take a look at **EXERCISE 16-8**. The key signature tells you the song is in C minor. The time signature is in 4/4 time. The tempo is andante with a metronome marking of quarter note equals 96, and *mf* tells you to play the song medium loud.

In the first measure, the first three beats are silent (as indicated by the half rest and quarter rest), and the fourth beat has two eighth notes (E-flat and F), which are pick-ups leading up to the first quarter note in the second measure. In the sixth measure, notice that the last eighth note (E-flat) is played with the first finger as it goes over the thumb.

For those of you who are vocally inclined, you might want to sing along with the melody played by the right hand.

DON'T YOU EVER LET ME DOWN

Before we continue with the remaining flat key signatures, see if you can answer the following questions.

1. Flat key signatures follow what kind of circle?

2. What do flats do?

3. In major flat key signatures, what scale degree gets the flat?

4. In minor flat key signatures, what scale degree gets the flat?

5. What is the first major flat key and its relative minor?

6. Where is the B-flat key located on the keyboard?

7. How did "Octavia" get its name?

8. What should you do when you see a crescendo sign?

9. What does decrescendo mean?

10. What are the first four eighth notes called in the first measure of Exercise 16-4?

11. In Exercise 16-4, what type of sequence is used in the melody played by the right hand?

12. How many flats does the key of C minor have?

(Answers can be found in Appendix A.)

A-Flat Major

The next flat key is A-flat major and its relative minor, F minor. The new flat in this key is D-flat, which is the fourth scale degree in A-flat major and the sixth scale degree in F minor. As you can see in the fingering of both the right and left hands, a lot of under- and over-the-thumb action takes place while playing the A-flat–major scale in two octaves.

With that in mind, please play the A-flat–major scale starting with your second finger in the right hand and your third finger in the left hand.

EXERCISE 16-9

You'll notice the fingering in **EXERCISE 16-10** is quite different from the fingering of the A-flat–major scale in **EXERCISE 16-9**. With that in mind, play the F-minor scale in **EXERCISE 16-10**.

EXERCISE 16-10

Here's a challenging piece I wrote so you can get your right hand accustomed to moving from E-flat down a fifth to A-flat. In order to accomplish this, your third finger goes over the thumb, and your thumb goes under your third finger and leaps down to A-flat. As indicated in the fingering of the right hand in measures 8 and 16, the last eighth note is played with your third finger, while your thumb quickly goes under your fingers and plays the A-flat.

The tempo of **EXERCISE 16-11** is allegro with a metronome marking of quarter note equals 126. Start playing **EXERCISE 16-11** slowly and gradually speed up to the allegro tempo. But before you do, be sure to note that **EXERCISE 16-11** is written in the key of A-flat, which has four flats. So be sure to play Bs, Es, As, and Ds flat.

As you can see, this piece starts off with the right hand, while the left hand rests for the first eight measures. Even though the left hand isn't playing at the beginning, have it ready in position, resting lightly above A-flat and E-flat for the left hand in measure 9.

Do yourself a big favor and play only the right hand for the entire piece several times before adding the left hand. Be careful with the last four eighth notes in measure 20; they're one note higher than the sequence of eighth notes in measures 4 and 12. The fingering for the left hand is the same throughout the piece, alternating between the fifth finger and the thumb.

As you play the descending eighth notes in measures 8 and 16 and the following quarter note in measures 9 and 17, you might be able to hear the title "Leaping Down a Fifth."

EXERCISE 16-11

LEAPING DOWN A FIFTH

D-Flat Major

A fourth above A-flat gives us the next key signature, D-flat major, and its relative minor, B-flat minor. D-flat major has five flats: B-flat, E-flat, A-flat, D-flat, and the new flat, G-flat. With five flats in the key signature, you'll be playing five black keys and only two white keys on the keyboard. As a result, the fingering in the right hand starts with the second finger, and the fingering in the left hand starts with the third finger. At the top of the two-octave scale, the thumb on the right hand goes under the fingers to play the C, and the second finger goes over the thumb to play the high D-flat. Similarly, the thumb on the left hand plays the high C, and the second finger goes over the thumb to play the high D.

EXERCISE 16-12

The next exercise is the B-flat–minor scale, which starts with the second finger on both hands.

EXERCISE 16-13

Enharmonic Equivalents

Before we move on to G-flat major, we need to discuss enharmonic equivalents. What's an enharmonic equivalent? Let me explain. For example, the pitch G-flat, which is located on the black key (one half-step lower than the white key G), is the same pitch as F-sharp (a half-step higher than F). G-flat and F-sharp are enharmonic equivalents; they are the same pitch—the same black key—but have different letter names.

In addition to individual notes having enharmonic equivalents, there are enharmonic equivalent scales. For example, when you play the D-flat–major scale, you're also playing the C-sharp–major scale. The pitches, the keys, and even the fingering are the same, but all of the letter names are different.

Looking at the letter names in both keys we have:

D-flat major	equals	C-sharp major
D-flat	=	C-sharp
E-flat	=	D-sharp
F	=	E-sharp
G-flat	=	F-sharp
A-flat	=	G-sharp
B-flat	=	A-sharp
C	=	B-sharp

So every note in the C-sharp–major scale is an enharmonic equivalent of the notes in the D-flat–major scale. Furthermore, the entire C-sharp–major scale is the enharmonic equivalent of the D-flat–major scale. Instead of having to play seven sharps in C sharp-major, simply play five flats in D-flat major. Looking back to Chapter 15, you can see that C-sharp major was not included in the sharp key signatures list.

The same is true with the relative minors. When you're playing the B-flat–minor scale, you're also playing the A-sharp–minor scale because B-flat and A-sharp are enharmonic equivalents.

G-Flat Major

Just as D-flat major is the enharmonic equivalent to C-sharp major, G-flat major is the enharmonic equivalent to F-sharp major. More than likely, if someone is going to write a piece of music in G-flat major, it will be written in the enharmonic equivalent key, F-sharp major.

Here are the note-for-note enharmonic equivalents in both keys:

G-flat major	equals	F-sharp major
G-flat	=	F-sharp
A-flat	=	G-sharp
B-flat	=	A-sharp
C-flat	=	B
D-flat	=	C-sharp
E-flat	=	D-sharp
F	=	E-sharp

So go back to Chapter 15 and play the F-sharp–major scale in **EXERCISE 15-20**. When playing the F-sharp–major scale, say the enharmonic equivalent letter names in G-flat major (G-flat, A-flat, B-flat, C-flat, D-flat, E-flat, and F). For all intents and purposes, you will have played the G-flat–major scale.

Do the same with the enharmonic equivalent relative minors, E-flat minor and D-sharp minor. Play D-sharp minor in Chapter 15, **EXERCISE 15-21**, and say the letter names for the corresponding scale degrees (E-flat, F, G-flat, A-flat, B-flat, C-flat, and D-flat). In doing so, you will have played the E-flat–minor scale.

Here are the note-for-note enharmonic equivalents in both relative minor keys:

E-flat minor	equals	D-sharp minor
E-flat	=	D-sharp
F	=	E-sharp
G-flat	=	F-sharp
A-flat	=	G-sharp
B-flat	=	A-sharp
C-flat	=	B
D-flat	=	C-sharp

Here are some more questions to wrap up this chapter.

13. What is the fourth flat in the key of A-flat major?

   ♪ ....

14. How many flats does F minor have?

   ♪ ....

15. What does *allegro* mean?

   ♪ ....

16. In **EXERCISE 16-11**, where does the leaping fifth occur?

   ♪ ....

17. What does the left hand do in the first eight measures of **EXERCISE 16-11**?

   ♪ ....

18. What should you do before adding the left-hand part to **EXERCISE 16-11**?

   ♪ ....

19. How many flats does B-flat minor have?

   ♪ ....

20. What is the harmonic relationship between the notes G-flat and F-sharp?

   ♪ ....

21. Are the notes E-sharp and F-natural enharmonic equivalents?

   ♪ ....

22. What is B-flat minor's enharmonic equivalent scale?

   ♪ ....

23. What is F-sharp major's enharmonic equivalent scale?

   ♪ ....

24. What is D-sharp minor's enharmonic equivalent scale?

   ♪ ....

25. What is the note A-flat's enharmonic equivalent?

   ♪ ....

26. What is the note B's enharmonic equivalent?

   ♪ ....

(Answers can be found in Appendix A.)

CHAPTER 17

Learning Chords

You've learned so much already, but do you feel like you are ready to perform in front of an audience? Probably not. Something is missing. You sound good, but you could sound better. This chapter will help you take that sound a step further by introducing chords.

What Is Harmony?

Let's start this chapter off with the definition of harmony (in the general sense): an agreement in feeling or opinion; accord; a pleasing combination of elements in a whole.

And now the definition of harmony in terms of music: the study of the structure, progression, and relation of chords; simultaneous combination of notes in a chord; the structure of a work or passage as considered from the point of view of its chordal characteristics and relationships; a combination of sounds considered pleasing to the ear. Got all that?

As you discovered in the previous chapters, melody is commonly played with the right hand on the piano or keyboard. Melodies are comprised of a specific series of singular notes, from simple tunes to more challenging melodic lines.

What's fascinating about music is the many different ways of arranging harmony juxtaposed to melody. For instance, with piano music, the right hand can play a simple melody, while the left hand can play consonant, harmonically pleasing chords or dissonant, unresolved chords.

For our purposes, let's focus primarily on harmony that constitutes "a combination of sounds considered pleasing to the ear."

Major Chords

As you already know, an interval is the measured distance between any two pitches. (For instance, in the key of D major, from the root D up to B is an interval of a sixth.) Chords are comprised of intervals. A D-major chord is the combination of two intervals: a major third from the root (D) up to the third scale degree (F-sharp), and a minor third from F-sharp up to the fifth scale degree (A). A major third contains two whole steps: D to E and E to F-sharp. A minor third contains one half-step, F-sharp to G, and one whole step, G to A. So a D-major chord contains the three notes D, F-sharp, and A. Three-note chords are also called triads.

All major chords follow the same two-interval formula: a major third followed by a minor third. Choose any pitch and make it the root of a major chord, count up two whole steps and you have the third of the chord, count up a half-step and whole step above the third and you have the fifth. For example, with A-flat as the root, the third is C, and the fifth is E-flat.

Here's a table showing the construction of major triads (chords) starting with various roots:

Table 17-1

Root	Third	Fifth
C	E	G
C-sharp	E-sharp	G-sharp
D	F-sharp	A
E-flat	G	B-flat
E	G-sharp	B
F-sharp*	A-sharp*	C-sharp*
G-flat*	B-flat*	D-flat*
A	C-sharp	E
B	D-sharp	F-sharp

* enharmonic equivalents

Now let's apply these major chords to the keyboard. Starting with C major and using your right hand, place your thumb on middle C, your second finger on E, and your fifth finger on G. Strike the keys all at the same time. This right-hand finger configuration is the same for all major chords, and the same in any octave. For example, when you play the C-major chord an octave higher, use the same fingering. Please see **FIGURE 17-1**.

FIGURE 17-1:
Root position
major chords

Do the same with the rest of the major chords listed in the table (C-sharp, D, E-flat, E, F-sharp, G-flat, A, and B major chords). Be sure to acknowledge the specified sharps and flats per each chord. Also, when playing the C-sharp–major chord, notice the white key E-sharp. Please refer to **FIGURE 17-2**.

FIGURE 17-2:
Root position
major chords

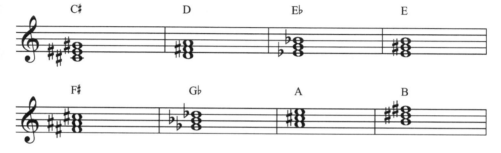

Minor Chords

The intervallic structure of all minor chords is comprised of two intervals: a minor third followed by a major third. For example, the D-minor chord has a minor third from the root, D, up to the third, F. This minor third interval is comprised of a whole step from D to E and a half-step from E to F. The D-minor chord has a major third from the third of the chord, F, up to the fifth, A. This major third interval is comprised of two whole steps, from F to G and G to A.

Here's a table showing the construction of minor triads (chords) starting with various roots.

TABLE 17-2

Root	Third	Fifth
C	E-flat	G
C-sharp	E	G-sharp
D	F	A
E-flat	G-flat	B-flat
E	G	B
F	A-flat	C
F-sharp	A	C-sharp
G	B-flat	D
A	C	E
B-flat	D-flat	F

Please note that all of the above minor chords have the same intervallic structure: a minor third followed by a major third.

The right-hand fingering of these minor chords is the same as the fingering used when playing major chords: thumb on the root, second finger on the third, and fifth finger on the fifth. With that in mind, please play the chords as shown in **FIGURE 17-3**.

FIGURE 17-3:
Root position major chords

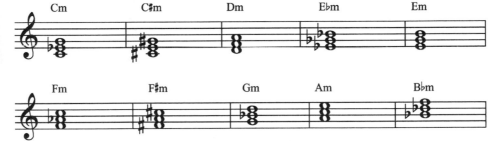

Chords in a Major Key

When you played the C-major scale, you played the scale degrees from the root C up one or two octaves. A piece of music written in the key of

C major can use all or some of the chords within the key. Chords in the key of C major are built on each scale degree.

Here's a table of the chords in the key of C major and their intervallic structures and chord qualities.

TABLE 17-3

Scale Degree	Chord Number	Root	Third	Fifth	Quality
1st	I	C	E	G	major
2nd	ii	D	F	A	minor
3rd	iii	E	G	B	minor
4th	IV	F	A	C	major
5th	V	G	B	D	major
6th	vi	A	C	E	minor
7th	vii	B	D	F	diminished

Notice that each chord has a number and that all of the chords have their own root, third, and fifth. The major chords in the key of C are the I, IV, and V chords. They are major because they are comprised of two intervals: a major third and a minor third. For instance, the IV chord F has a major third from the root F to A and a minor third from A to C. To refresh your memory, the interval of a major third is comprised of two whole steps, and the interval of a minor third is comprised of one whole step and a half-step.

The minor chords in the key of C are the ii, iii, and vi chords. To make it easier to differentiate between the major and minor chords in a given key, the major chord numbers are in uppercase roman numerals, and the minor chords are in lowercase roman numerals. The D-, E-, and A-minor chords are minor because they are comprised of a minor third and a major third. Using the ii chord D minor for example, it's a whole step from D to E and a half-step from E to F (which makes up the interval of a minor third) and from F to G and G to A are two whole steps (which makes up the interval of a major third).

Diminished Chords

Chords built on the seventh scale degree are called diminished chords, which are a half-step smaller than minor chords. The intervallic structure of all diminished chords is comprised of two minor intervals. For instance, the B-diminished chord has a minor second from B to D (a half-step from B to C and a whole step from C to D) and another minor second from D to F-natural (a whole step from D to E and a half-step from E to F).

The chords in the key of C major are:

C major
D minor
E minor
F major
G major
A minor
B diminished

EXERCISE 17-1 utilizes some of the chords in the key of C played by the right hand.

There are twelve chords in this exercise. The rhythmic pattern is the same throughout—two quarter note chords followed by a half note chord per measure. As you can see, the chords are comprised of three-note triads, and the notes are stacked up together, making the chord. The sequence of chords is called a chord progression.

Please look at **TABLE 17-4** carefully before playing **EXERCISE 17-1**.

Augmented Chords

Augmented notes are raised a half-step above the standard position in chords or scales. An augmented chord contains a root, a major third, and an augmented fifth. It's almost an ordinary major chord, but the fifth is one half-step higher.

Try playing a C-major chord: C, E, and G. Now raise the G a half step to G-sharp. C, E, and G-sharp is an augmented chord.

TABLE 17-4

Chord	Notes in the Chord	Chord Quality	Fingering
1st	C–E–G	I (major)	thumb-C, 2nd-E, 5th-G
2nd	B–D–G*	V (major)	thumb-B, 2nd-D, 5th-G
3rd	A–C–E	vi (minor)	thumb-A, 2nd-C, 5th-E
4th	A–C–E	vi (minor)	thumb-A, 2nd-C, 5th-E
5th	B–D–F	vii (diminished)	thumb-B, 2nd-D, 5th-F
6th	C–E–G	I (major)	thumb-C, 2nd-E, 5th-G
7th	C–F–A**	IV (major)	thumb-C, 2nd-F, 5th-A
8th	D–G–B**	V (major)	thumb-D, 2nd-G, 5th-B
9th	E–A–C**	vi (minor)	thumb-E, 2nd-A, 5th-C
10th	E–A–C**	vi (minor)	thumb-E, 2nd-A, 5th-C
11th	D–G–B**	V (major)	thumb-D, 2nd-G, 5th-B
12th	E–G–C*	I (major)	thumb-E, 2nd-G, 5th-C

* first inversion

** second inversion

As the fingering indicates above, the right hand uses the same finger configuration for all of the chords in this exercise (thumb, second finger, and fifth finger).

EXERCISE 17-1

Let's add a left-hand bass line to the same chord progression for **EXERCISE 17-2**.

EXERCISE 17-2

Adagio ♩ = 69

Root Position and First- and Second-Inversion Chords

The first, third, fourth, fifth, and sixth chords in **EXERCISE 17-2** are in root position, meaning that the first note in each chord is the root of the chord, followed by the third and fifth. However, the second chord and the chords in measures 3 and 4 are not in root position. The second chord in the first measure is in a first-inversion position, meaning that the first note in the chord is not the root, but the third, followed by the fifth and the root. Indicated with one asterisk in Table 17-4, the first note in the G-major chord is B, the third, followed by the fifth, D, and the root, G.

Chords seven through eleven are in a position called second inversion, meaning that the first note of the chord is the fifth, followed by the root and the third. Looking at Table 17-4, the second-inversion chords have two asterisks by their letter names. For example, in measure 3, the first note in the F-major chord is C, which is the fifth of the chord. Similar to the second chord in the first measure, the last chord in the exercise is also in a first-inversion position (the first note of the chord is the third, followed by the fifth and the root).

Chords in a Minor Key

When you played minor scales in Chapters 15 and 16, you played natural minor scales—notes that observe the key signature. For example, when you played the E-minor scale, you acknowledged the F-sharp key signature and played the series of notes E, F-sharp, G, A, B, C, D, and the octave E. That's the E-natural–minor scale.

When building chords on the scale degrees of E-natural minor we get the following chords:

TABLE 17-5

Scale Degree	Chord Number	Root	Third	Fifth	Quality
1st	i	E	G	B	minor
2nd	ii	F-sharp	A	C	diminished
3rd	III	G	B	D	major
4th	iv	A	C	E	minor
5th	v	B	D	F-sharp	minor
6th	VI	C	E	G	major
7th	VII	D	F-sharp	A	major

As you can see by doing a comparison with the chords built on major scale degrees, the quality of chords are different in a natural minor key.

Chords built on major scale degrees have the following qualities:

- Major chords: I, IV, V
- Minor chords: ii, iii, vi
- Diminished chords: vii

Chords built on natural minor scale degrees have the following qualities:

- Major chords: III, VI, VII
- Minor chords: i, iv, v
- Diminished chords: ii

Harmonic minor scales are different from natural harmonic scales because of one scale degree: the seventh scale degree is sharp in a harmonic minor scale. As you already know, the seventh scale degree in a natural minor scale is not sharp, it's natural. Using E minor as an example, the seventh scale degree is D-natural in E-natural minor, and D-sharp in E-harmonic minor. When applying the sharp seventh scale degree to chords in E-harmonic minor, the III chord (G) becomes augmented, the V chord (B) becomes major, and the vii chord (D) becomes diminished because of the D-sharp.

When building chords on the scale degrees of E-harmonic minor, we get the following chords:

TABLE 17-6

Scale Degree	Chord Number	Root	Third	Fifth	Quality
1st	i	E	G	B	minor
2nd	ii	F-sharp	A	C	diminished
3rd	III	G	B	D-sharp	augmented
4th	iv	A	C	E	minor
5th	V	B	D-sharp	F-sharp	major
6th	VI	C	E	G	major
7th	vii	D-sharp	F-sharp	A	diminished

Here's a comparison of chord qualities between natural minor scale degrees and harmonic minor scale degrees:

	Natural Minor	Harmonic Minor
Major chords:	III, VI, VII	V, VI
Minor chords:	i, iv, v	i, iv
Diminished chords:	ii	ii, vii
Augmented chords:		III

The most striking difference between these two different minor scales is the quality of the fifth scale degree. As you may recall from Chapter 15, the fifth scale degree is called the dominant. The dominant/tonic relationship is harmonically very strong because the dominant chord, built on the fifth scale degree, wants to resolve to the tonic, the root. This is referred to as tension/resolution in harmonic terms. Using E-harmonic minor as an example, the tension is caused by the D-sharp, which is the third in the V chord B major (please see Table 17-6). Harmonically, the D-sharp wants to resolve to the tonic E. In the E-natural–minor scale, the fifth scale degree is B minor, with D-natural as the third in the B minor chord. The harmonic tension is less between B minor and E minor because of the D-natural.

The next two exercises illustrate these harmonic differences.

In **EXERCISE 17-3**, you will be playing chords in E-natural minor, acknowledging the D-natural in the root position VII chord (first half note chord in the second measure) and the root position v chord (first half note chord in the fourth measure). Likewise, the left hand plays a D-natural (second quarter note in the fourth measure).

Before playing the exercise take a close look at the following table.

TABLE 17-7

Chord	Notes in the Chord	Chord Quality/ Position	Fingering
1st	E–G–B	i-minor/root	thumb-E, 2nd-G, 5th-B
2nd	E–A–C**	iv-minor/2nd	thumb-E, 2nd-A, 5th-C
3rd	D–F#–A	VII-major/root	thumb-D, 2nd-F#, 5th-A
4th	E–G–B	i-minor/root	thumb-E, 2nd-G, 5th-B
5th	B–E–G**	i-minor/2nd	thumb-B, 2nd-E, 5th-G
6th	A–C–E	iv-minor/root	thumb-A, 2nd-C, 5th-E
7th	B–D–F#	v-minor/root	thumb-B, 2nd-D, 4th-F#
8th	B–E–G**	i-minor/2nd	thumb-B, 2nd-E, 5th-G

** second-inversion chords

As you can see, **EXERCISE 17-3** has a repeat sign. As also indicated, play this exercise the first time with only the right hand. If you need to, keep repeating only the right-hand part. Once you have the right-hand part worked out, play only the left-hand part. Then play the piece as written: once with the right hand only, the second time with both hands. Please use the numbered fingering for the left hand.

EXERCISE 17-3

EXERCISE 17-4 utilizes chords built on the E-harmonic–minor scale degrees, acknowledging the D-sharp. As you can see, the sharp sign is written on the staff just before the D, telling you to play the D up a half-step. Unlike the F-sharp, the sharp sign is written before each D note because D-sharp is not in the key signature of E minor. Be prepared to play the D-sharp in the first-inversion V chord (first half note chord in measure 2) and the second-inversion V chord (first half note chord in measure 4). Likewise, be sure to play the D-sharps in the left hand (second quarter note in the second and fourth measures).

Before playing **EXERCISE 17-4**, take a close look at the following table.

TABLE 17-8

Chord	Notes in the Chord	Chord Quality/ Position	Fingering
1st	E–G–B	i-minor/root	thumb-E, 2nd-G, 5th-B
2nd	E–A–C**	iv-minor/2nd	thumb-E, 2nd-A, 5th-C
3rd	D#–F#–B*	V-major/1st	thumb-D# 2nd-F#, 5th-B
4th	E–G–B	i-minor/root	thumb-E, 2nd-G, 5th-B
5th	D–G–B**	III-major/2nd	thumb-D, 2nd-G, 5th-B
6th	E–A–C**	iv-minor/2nd	thumb-E, 2nd-A, 5th-C
7th	F#–B–D#**	V-major/2nd	thumb-F#, 2nd-B, 4th-D#
8th	G–B–E*	i-minor/1st	thumb-G, 2nd-B, 5th-E

* first-inversion chords

** second-inversion chords

As you can see, this exercise also has a repeat sign. As indicated, play this exercise the first time with only the right hand. If you need to, keep repeating only the right-hand part. Once you have it worked out, then play only the left-hand part. When you have both parts worked out independently, then play the piece as written: once with the right hand only, the second time with both hands. Please use the numbered fingering for the left hand.

EXERCISE 17-4

EXERCISE 17-4 utilizes both first- and second-inversion chords. Inverted chords serve two purposes: They make the fingering easier in the chord progression, and the voices of one chord flow stepwise to the next chord. For instance, in the second measure, the first half note chord (the V chord B major) in second-inversion position has the notes D-sharp, F-sharp, and B. To get to the next chord (the root position E minor), the thumb and second finger simply move up a half-step from D-sharp to E and F-sharp to G. What's even easier is the B played by the fifth finger—it plays the top note B in the B-major chord and plays the top note B in the E-minor chord (B being the common tone in both chords).

Another example is the first-inversion B-major chord in the fourth measure with the notes F-sharp, B, and D-sharp. To get to the first-inversion E-minor chord, you simply move your thumb a half-step from F-sharp to G, and your fourth finger a half-step from D-sharp to E. The second finger stays put and plays the B in the B-major chord and then plays the same B in the E-minor chord. Here again, B is the common tone in both chords.

Playing chords only in root position is difficult and requires a lot of moving up and down the keyboard. Unlike inverted chords, when playing only root position chords in a chord progression, the changing notes from chord to chord don't flow smoothly.

A Harmonic Relationship

Let's take a look at **EXERCISE 17-3** and see what the harmonic relationship is between the chords in the right hand and the bass line in the left hand. In the first measure, the bass plays the quarter note E, located an octave below the root-position chord E minor in the right hand. It then jumps down an octave to play the second quarter note E. Both of these notes are playing the root of the chord (E) in two different octaves. It then goes back up and plays the half note E, while the right hand plays the second-inversion A-minor chord. This half note E sounds good because E is a note in the A-minor chord. Instead of playing the root (A), it's playing the fifth (E) in the A-minor chord.

In the second measure, the left hand plays exactly the same as it did in the first measure. However, the chords in the right hand are different. The right hand plays a half note D-major chord over the two quarter notes E in the left hand. This creates harmonic tension because there are no common tones between the D-major chord and the bass note E. But the tension is quickly resolved in the third beat of the same measure when the right hand plays the root-position E-minor chord, and the left hand plays E. The D-major chord over the E in the bass is sometimes referred to as a pedal tone; the pitch remains the same in the left hand while the right hand plays different chords.

In measure 3, the bass again plays an E, supporting the E-minor chord in the right hand, and then plays a passing quarter note G before playing the half note A. The passing note G works well harmonically for two reasons: G is the third in the E-minor chord, and scale-wise, leads directly to the A.

In measure 4, the left hand plays the quarter notes B and D, which are the root and third in the B-minor chord played by the right hand, and lands on the root E with the E-minor chord played by the right hand.

In summary, in **EXERCISE 17-3**, the left hand plays the root of the chords, with the exception of the first two beats in the second measure. And it plays two passing notes, both of which are notes in the chords played by the right hand.

In **EXERCISE 17-4**, the left hand plays the root of the chords and passing notes, which are also notes in the chords played by the right hand. As you can see, the left-hand bass line plays roots, fifths, and thirds of the chords played by the right hand, while the right hand plays chords in all three positions (root, first inversion, or second inversion).

The Use of Chords in the Right Hand

So far, the exercises in this chapter have dealt with playing chords with the right hand, while the left hand plays bass lines. Playing chords in the right hand is used primarily for accompaniment purposes—when accompanying a singer or solo instrumentalist. This is because the melody is being sung by the singer or played by the instrumentalist. In this scenario, the piano provides the chordal, harmonic, and rhythmic support for the melody.

Now let's put the chords in the left hand and melody in the right hand.

The Use of Chords in the Left Hand

A pianist can play melody, harmony, and bass on the piano. The right hand can play the melody and/or chords, and the left hand can play the bass line or chords, and can also play melody.

When the piano is not in the accompaniment role, but rather in the solo role, the left hand usually plays a combination of bass lines and chords, while the right hand usually plays the melody and chords. This is the case with piano sonatas, piano concertos, and instrumental piano pieces.

In the next two exercises you will play chords in the left hand and melody in the right.

In **EXERCISE 17-5**, the left hand plays chords supporting the melody in the right hand. Take a close look at the following table before playing **EXERCISE 17-5**.

TABLE 17-9

Chord	Notes in the Chord	Chord Quality/ Position	Fingering
1st	D–F#–A	I-major/root	5th-D, 2nd-F#, thumb-A
2nd	D–G–B**	IV-major/2nd	5th-D, 2nd-G, thumb-B
3rd	D–F#–A	I-major/root	5th-D, 2nd-F#, thumb-A
4th	C#–E–A*	V-major/1st	4th-C#, 3rd-E, thumb-A
5th	D–F#–B*	vi-minor/1st	5th-D, 2nd-F#, thumb-B
6th	D–G–B**	IV-major/2nd	5th-D, 2nd-G, thumb-B
7th	D–G–B**	IV-major/2nd	5th-D, 2nd-G, thumb-B
8th	C#–E–A*	V-major/1st	4th-C#, 3rd-E, thumb-A
9th	D–F#–A	I-major/root	5th-D, 2nd-F#, thumb-A

* first-inversion chords

** second-inversion chords

Please notice that **EXERCISE 17-5** is in 3/4 time, the tempo is andante (slowly), and as the two-sharp key signature indicates, it's in the key of D major (F-sharp and C-sharp). Be sure to play all Fs and Cs sharp in both the right- and left-hand parts. As Table 17-9 indicates, most of the chords are inverted, making the harmony smooth and the fingering easy. As always, play the right- and left-hand parts separately before playing them together.

If it helps, write the left-hand chord fingering in the left-hand part.

EXERCISE 17-6 is written in D-harmonic minor. That's why there's a sharp sign before the C in the first-inversion V chord in the second measure. A natural sign appears before the C in the second-inversion IV chord in the third measure, canceling out the previous C-sharp. However, the C-sharp returns again in the fourth measure. Please look closely at Table 17-10 before playing the exercise.

QUIET SUNDAY

TABLE 17-10

Chord	Notes in the Chord	Chord Quality/ Position	Fingering		
1st	D–F–A	i-minor/root	5th-D,	2nd-F,	thumb-A
2nd	D–G–B♭**	iv-minor/2nd	5th-D,	2nd-G,	thumb-B♭
3rd	D–F–A	i-minor/root	5th-D,	2nd-F,	thumb-A
4th	C#–E–A*	V-major/1st	4th-C#,	3rd-E,	thumb-A
5th	D–F–B♭*	VI-major/1st	4th-D,	2nd-F#,	thumb-B♭
6th	C–F–A**	III-major/2nd	5th-C,	2nd-F,	thumb-A
7th	C#–E–A*	V-major/1st	4th-C#,	2nd-E,	thumb-A
8th	D–F–A	i-minor/root	5th-D,	2nd-F,	thumb-A

* first-inversion chords
** second-inversion chords

EXERCISE 17-6 is in 4/4 time, and the tempo is andante (metronome marking: quarter note equals 80). This makes the tempo in this exercise slower than the tempo in **EXERCISE 17-5**. Similar to **EXERCISE 17-5**, most of the chords in **EXERCISE 17-6** are inverted.

In the third measure, there's a crescendo sign from *mp* to *f* followed by a decrescendo sign in the fourth measure, bringing the volume back down to *mp*. Please observe the repeat sign. This time start with only playing the left hand. Add the right hand once you have your left-hand chords in place.

CHANGING C's

You have covered a lot of new material in this chapter. And now for the questions . . .

1. Why am I answering these questions?

2. What is harmony?

3. What's another word for a three-note chord?

4. How many intervals are there in a major chord?

5. What type of intervals are they?

6. What note is a fifth above A-flat?

7. What note is a major third above C-sharp?

8. What is the relationship between an F-sharp–major chord and a G-flat–major chord?

9. What is E-sharp's enharmonic equivalent?

10. What types of intervals comprise minor chords?

11. What note is a minor third above F?

12. What note is a fifth above F-sharp?

13. What is the third chord in the key of C major?

14. What is the seventh chord in the key of C major?

15. What is a root-position chord?

16. What is a first-inversion chord?

17. What is a second-inversion chord?

18. What is the sequence of letter note names of a first-inversion A-major chord?

19. What is the sequence of letter note names of a second-inversion E-minor chord?

20. What is the fifth chord in the key of E-natural minor?

21. What is the seventh chord in the key of E-natural minor?

22. What chord is diminished in the key of E-natural minor?

23. What chords are diminished in the key of E-harmonic natural minor?

24. Why is the fifth chord in E-harmonic minor a major chord?

25. Why are chords inverted?

(Answers can be found in Appendix A.)

CHAPTER 18

Listening and Basic Music Theory

B y now, you're familiar with reading piano music. But you may not realize that your eyes are taking in information both vertically and horizontally—the vertical reading of singular notes and chords, and the horizontal reading of melodies and the flow of notes (voices) within chord progressions. This chapter will show you how it all works together.

Listen to the Music

There's a big difference between hearing and listening. You hear a lot of sounds all day long. People might ask you, "Did you hear that?" Your response could be, "I'm not sure." But when someone has something important to say to you, they might preface it by saying, "Listen very carefully."

Listening is an acquired skill. It requires full attention, being focused, and not being distracted. Listening to music is very important. Not just hearing music as background music, but focused listening. And with repeated listening to the same piece of music, you will hear things you didn't hear the first or second time.

Listening is so important that some music schools have a required class for music major students called ear training. It's designed to develop one's listening skills. Through the process of taking ear training classes, the student can more easily recognize and identify intervallic relationships, chord qualities and chord progressions, and the harmonic relationship between melody and harmony.

When you're playing a piece of music on your keyboard, give it your full listening attention. Listen to the melody; listen to the harmony and bass line. Listen to the parts individually, and listen to them collectively. Good musicians are very good listeners.

Analyze the Piece of Music

Before playing any piece of music, it's always best to analyze all of the parts: the key signature, tempo/metronome marking, time signature, the right-hand part, the melody, the left-hand part, the harmony, the fingering, the rhythm, and dynamic markings. The vast majority of piano pieces don't have the right- and left-hand fingering written in the part. So, you have to go through the piece and determine which fingers to use for each hand.

This preparation helps with your ability to play a piece of music as written and anticipate what's coming. It's always good practice for your eyes to be slightly ahead of your fingers. For instance, when you're playing the first measure, your eyes should be looking at measures 2 and 3.

Piano pieces can be written in a specific style or left open for your own stylistic adaptation. Musical styles cover a wide range, including baroque, classical, romantic, impressionistic, ragtime, stride, abstract, jazz, bebop, boogie-woogie, rhythm and blues, country, gospel, rock and roll, show tunes (Broadway musicals), pop, soul, disco, funk, reggae, and New Age. If specified, try to play the piece in the style it's written in.

While reading and playing music, you're mentally registering what you're seeing. At the same time, you're also hearing what you're reading (seeing) and playing. These multi-sensory events are taking place all at once. Playing music is a multi-sensory experience utilizing the visual, audio, physical, and mental facilities. It's interesting to note that some pianists have very strong reading skills, can read any style and multiple parts simultaneously, but have difficulty playing without the written music in front of them. On the other hand, some pianists possess strong listening skills; they can hear a piece of music and replicate it without the written music. But when they try to read the same piece of music, they find it difficult, and the attempt to read impairs their playing ability. Some pianists "play by ear" while others play by reading. Then there are those very fortunate pianists who are gifted with having both very sharp eye and ear skills.

Repetition is a very effective methodology that helps when learning a piece of music. When playing the same piece of music repeatedly, it becomes more committed to one's memory. As a result of repeated practicing, some pianists can memorize lengthy pieces of music.

Four-Note Chords

Both the right hand and left hand can play four-note chords. They are based on the span of an octave, usually from the root of the chord up eight notes to its octave, along with the third and fifth of the chord in between. Four-note chords also include the first and second inversions of the root-position chords.

Using some of the three-note chords (triads) from Chapter 17, let's make them four-note chords. Following Table 18-1 below, you can see the octave has been added for each of the chords.

TABLE 18-1

Chord	Root	Third	Fifth	Octave
C major	C	E	G	C
D major	D	F-sharp	A	D
E-flat major	E-flat	G	B-flat	E-flat
F major	F	A	C	F
G major	G	B	D	G
A major	A	C-sharp	E	A
B major	B	D-sharp	F-sharp	B

The following table shows the same chords in the first-inversion position.

TABLE 18-2

Chord	Third	Fifth	Root	Third
C major	E	G	C	E
D major	F-sharp	A	D	F-sharp
E-flat major	G	B-flat	E-flat	G
F major	A	C	F	A
G major	B	D	G	B
A major	C-sharp	E	A	C-sharp
B major	D-sharp	F-sharp	B	D-sharp

Notice that with four-note first-inversion chords, the octave occurs from the low third to the high third, eight notes above.

Here are the same chords in the second-inversion position.

TABLE 18-3

Chord	Fifth	Root	Third	Fifth
C major	G	C	E	G
D major	A	D	F-sharp	A
E-flat major	B-flat	E-flat	G	B-flat
F major	C	F	A	C
G major	D	G	B	D
A major	E	A	C-sharp	E
B major	F-sharp	B	D-sharp	F-sharp

Notice that with four-note second-inversion chords, the octave occurs from the low fifth to the high fifth, eight notes above.

Right Hand

When playing four-note chords with the right hand, the fingering of the notes that make up the chord is consistently the same for each chord:

Root: Thumb
Third: Second finger
Fifth: Third finger
Octave: Fifth finger

The same fingering applies to first- and second-inversion chords played by the right hand. While the fingering is the same, the sequence of the notes in the chord change as follows:

First-Inversion Chords—Right Hand
    Third: Thumb
    Fifth: Second finger
    Root: Third finger
    Third: Fifth finger

Second-Inversion Chords—Right Hand
    Fifth: Thumb
    Root: Second finger
    Third: Third finger
    Fifth: Fifth finger

As you can see, when playing four-note first-inversion chords with the right hand, there's an octave from the third played by the thumb to the third played by the fifth finger, eight notes above. When playing four-note second-inversion chords, an octave occurs from the fifth of the chord to the fifth, eight notes above.

Left Hand

When playing four-note chords with the left hand, the fingering of the notes that make up the chord is also consistently the same for each chord:

Root: Fifth finger
Third: Third finger
Fifth: Second finger
Octave: Thumb

The same fingering applies to first- and second-inversion chords played by the left hand. While the fingering is the same, the sequence of the notes in the chord changes as follows:

First-Inversion Chords—Left Hand
    Third: Fifth finger
    Fifth: Third finger
    Root: Second finger
    Third: Thumb

Second-Inversion Chords—Left Hand
    Fifth: Fifth finger
    Fifth: Fifth finger
    Third: Second finger
    Fifth: Thumb

Here again, when playing four-note first-inversion chords with the left hand, there's an octave from the third played by the fifth finger to the third played by the thumb, eight notes above. When playing four-note second-inversion chords, an octave occurs from the fifth of the chord to the fifth, eight notes above.

Four-Note Chord Exercises

In **EXERCISE 18-1**, you will play four-note chords with your right hand. Please use the same fingering for each chord: root–thumb; third–second finger; fifth–third finger; octave–fifth finger.

In **EXERCISE 18-1**, all of the chords are major chords: C major, D major, and E-flat major. As a group, these chords don't belong to one specific key signature. Therefore, no key signature is written on the staff. Generally speaking, when there isn't a sharp or flat key signature that means the music is in the key of C major or A minor. However, this is not the case here because we are using major chords from more than one key signature, and we're even mixing sharp (the D-major chord) and flat (the E-flat–major chord) major chords together. Be sure to acknowledge the F-sharp in the D-major chord, and the E- and B-flats in the E-flat–major chord.

In **EXERCISE 18-2**, a rhythmic bass line is added to the same chord progression. This bass line, played by the left-hand thumb, stays on the C note, an octave below middle C. As you can see, there is a curved line called a tie, which ties together the first quarter note with the first eighth note in the second beat of measures 1, 2, 3, and 4. The tie means the first eighth note is heard but not played because it is tied to the quarter note. But you do play the second eighth note, which is the subdivision of the second beat in the measure.

To get a feel for the tied rhythm played by the left hand, count out loud the following:

ONE	two	**AND**	**THREE**	four
(Quarter	eighth	**eighth**	**half**	**)**

The above numbers in bold and the corresponding note values represent the beats and notes to play with the left hand in **EXERCISE 18-2**. When counting out loud, put an emphasis on *one*, *and*, and *three*. As you recall, two eighth notes equal one quarter note. A subdivision is simply dividing a single quarter beat into two eighth beats.

Harmonically, the moving right-hand chords over the repeated C in the bass creates tension in measures 2, 3, and 4, and then resolves in the fifth measure with the left hand playing the root of the C-major chord, doubled down an octave. The harmonic tension in measures 2, 3, and 4 is created because the bass note C is not a note within the triadic structure of the D and E-flat chords. As a reminder, the triadic structure of a chord is comprised of the root, third, and fifth.

As indicated, the right-hand chords have their letter names written above each chord.

EXERCISE 18-2

Another name for a tied rhythm is a dotted rhythm. The value of a dotted note is equal to the note's value plus half its value. For example, a dotted quarter note equals one quarter beat plus a half beat, or in other words, a beat and a half. As you can see in **EXERCISE 18-2**, the quarter note tied to the eighth note equals a beat and a half. So another way of writing the exact same rhythm is to use a dotted quarter note followed by a single eighth note, instead of a quarter note tied to an eighth note. Please refer to **EXERCISE 18-3**.

EXERCISE 18-3

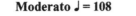

The rhythm of the bass line in **EXERCISE 18-3** is exactly the same as the rhythm of the bass line in **EXERCISE 18-2**. However, as you can see, there is a difference between these two exercises: In **EXERCISE 18-3**, the pitches are different in the second, third, and fourth measures.

Now let's move on to playing four-note chords with the left hand.

In **EXERCISE 18-4**, the left hand plays the following four-note chords: C major, D major, and E major (not E-flat major). Please be sure to acknowledge the sharps in the D- and E- major chords. The left-hand fingering of all of the chords in this exercise is: root–fifth finger; third–third finger; fifth–second finger; octave–thumb. Also notice that the last chord (E major) played in measure 7 is tied to the same chord in measure 8. Play the E-major chord in measure 7, keep it held down, and let it sustain through the end of measure 8.

EXERCISE 18-4

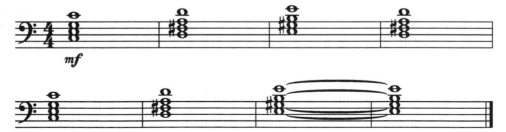

As you can see in the next exercise, a dotted, or tied, rhythm is played by the right hand. The rhythm is written in two different ways: a quarter note tied to an eighth note (measures 1 and 4) and a dotted quarter note (measures 2, 3, 5, and 6). The rhythm in measures 1 through 6 is exactly the same, and sounds the same, even though the rhythm is written in two different ways.

This dotted rhythm is the same rhythm that the left hand played in Exercises 18-2 and 18-3, with one exception: The rhythm is different in the seventh measure. The rhythm of the third and fourth beats in the seventh measure is also a tied (dotted) rhythm (the fourth beat is tied to the preceding quarter note; the *and* of the fourth beat, the second eighth note, is played).

It's exactly the same rhythm as the first two beats in the measure.

Let's look at the harmonic relationship between the right-hand melody and left-hand chords in **EXERCISE 18-5**. The repeated E note played by the right hand is harmonically consonant (resolved) with the chords played by the left hand in measures 1, 3, 5, 7, and 8. This is because the note E is also the third in the C-major chord and the root and octave in the E-major chord. Because both the C- and E-major chords have the note E in their triadic structure, E is referred to as the common tone between the two chords. In measures 2, 4, and 6, the E note in the right hand creates some tension against the D chord because the E note is not a pitch that makes up the D-major triad.

EXERCISE 18-5

Breaking It Down

EXERCISE 18-6 is comprised of a simple melody in the right hand and moving four-note chords in the left hand. It's the moving harmony of the chords juxtaposed to the simple melody that makes this exercise interesting.

The following table identifies the quality, position, and fingering of the chords used in **EXERCISE 18-6**.

TABLE 18-4

Measure	Notes in the Chord	Quality/Position	Fingering
1	E♭–G–B♭–E♭	I-major/root	5th-E♭, 3rd-G, 2nd-B♭, thumb-E♭
2	E♭–G–B♭–D	I-major 7th/root	5th-E♭, 3rd-G, 2nd-B♭, thumb-D
3	C–E♭–G–C	vi-minor/root	5th-C, 3rd-E♭, 2nd-G, thumb-C
4	C–E♭–A♭–C*	IV-major/1st	5th-C, 3rd-E♭, 2nd-A♭, thumb-C
5	C–F–A♭–C**	ii minor/2nd	5th C, 3rd F, 2nd-A♭, thumb-C
6	D♭–F–A♭–D♭^	VII-major/root	5th-D♭, 3rd-F, 2nd-A♭, thumb-D♭
7	D–F–B♭–D*	V-major/1st	5th-D, 3rd-F, 2nd-B♭, thumb-D
8	E♭–G–B♭–E♭	I-major/root	5th-E♭, 3rd-G, 2nd-B♭, thumb-E♭

* first-inversion chords

** second-inversion chords

^ lowered seventh chord

There are two new chords introduced in **EXERCISE 18-6**. In the second measure, the chord is E-flat–major seventh. It's called a major seventh chord because the distance between the root E-flat and D is an interval of a major seventh. This interval is added on to the E-flat major triad. In the sixth measure, the chord is D-flat major. This is an altered chord because in the key of E-flat major, the seventh scale degree is D-natural, not D-flat. Even though D-flat is not in the key of E-flat major, this chord works well because the D-flat is a stepwise, passing tone from C to D. Additionally, F minor and D-flat major have two common tones: F and A-flat. We will discuss altered chords more extensively in Chapter 19.

While all the notes of the chords provide harmony for the melody, take a look at the top note in each chord. The top notes of the chords measure by measure are: E-flat, D, C, C, C, D-flat, D-natural, and E-flat. This top harmonic voice moves smoothly in a stepwise motion while the other notes (voices) in the chord move beneath it. This top note is also strong harmonically because it is doubled an octave lower throughout the chord progression with the exception of the second measure. When notes are doubled and played in octaves, their sounds dominate the other notes in the chord.

Play only the left-hand chords several times before adding the right-hand melody. In doing so, you will discover common tones among the chords and smooth harmonic changes by playing inversions. As indicated, **EXERCISE 18-6** is in the key of E-flat major. Be sure to play all the flats as indicated in the key signature.

SAFE and SOUND?

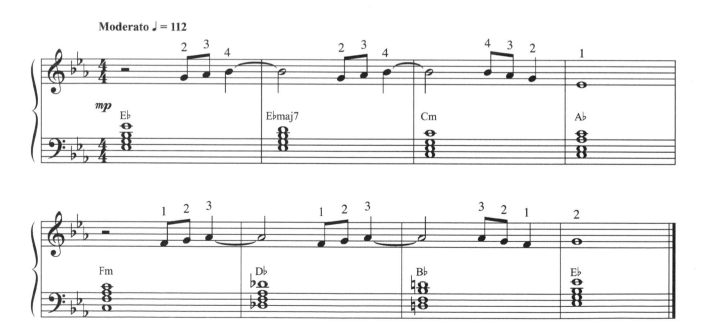

Pulling It All Together

EXERCISE 18-7 is in 6/8 time. That means that there are six eighth notes, or the equivalent thereof, per measure. When counting the eighth notes, count 1-2-3, 2-2-3 for each measure, with an accent on the first eighth note in each group of three. This gives the 6/8 time signature a two-beat feel with three eighth-note subdivisions per beat. When playing this piece with a two-beat feel, the tempo is largo, which is slow. Keep in mind that there are two sets of three even eighth notes per beat.

Because **EXERCISE 18-7** is in the key of D-harmonic minor, the seventh scale degree is C-sharp. As indicated in measures 4 and 8, the C-sharp makes the V chord A major. The dotted quarter note chords equal three eighth notes (two eighth notes in a quarter plus the dot equals half the value of a quarter note, which is an eighth). The dotted half note chords equal two dotted quarter notes or six eighth notes. The left hand plays four-note chords throughout the piece except for the very last D-minor chord, which is a three-note chord. This occurs because the right hand plays the top note D. The fingering of the chords in the left hand is the same throughout: fifth finger, third finger, second finger, and thumb, except for the last chord, played with the fifth finger, third finger, and second finger. The G-minor chord in measures 2, 3, 6, and 7 are second inversions, starting with the fifth of the chord D, followed by G, B-flat, and D. The A chord in measures 4 and 8 are first inversions, starting with the third of the chord C-sharp, followed by E, A, and C-sharp.

Play only the left-hand chords several times. Take time, practice the chords, listen to the four voices that make up the chord and how the voices change from chord to chord. You'll hear the common tone (D) between D minor and G minor, and how the first-inversion A chord makes a smooth harmonic progression to D minor.

Once you have the chords worked out comfortably with your left hand, play only the melody with your right hand. Notice how measures 5, 6, and 7 are exactly the same as measures 1, 2, and 3.

And please observe the D-minor key signature and play all Bs flat.

UNDERGROUND

To help you absorb the material covered in this chapter, please answer the following questions.

1. What should you do before playing any piece of music?

2. When reading music, where should your eyes be?

3. What is listening?

4. What are four-note chords based on?

5. What is the sequence of notes in a four-note, first-inversion, E-flat–major chord?

6. What is the sequence of notes in a four-note, first-inversion, E-minor chord?

7. What is the sequence of notes in a four-note, second-inversion, B-major chord?

8. What is the sequence of notes in a four-note, second-inversion, D-minor chord?

9. Compared to four-note root-position chords, how does the fingering change when playing their first inversion with the right hand?

10. Where does the octave occur when playing four-note second-inversion chords?

11. Why is there no key signature in Exercise 18-1?

12. What happens when notes are tied together?

13. In Exercise 18-2, do you play the eighth notes that are tied to the quarter note?

14. Why is there harmonic tension between the D- and E-flat–major chords and the C in the bass in Exercise 18-2?

15. What's another way of writing a tied rhythm?

16. How many eighth notes are there in a dotted quarter note?

17. In Exercise 18-5, is the rhythm the same in measures 1 and 2?

18. What is a common tone?

19. C-major and E-major chords have a common tone. What is it?

20. What are the common tones between C-minor and A-flat–major chords?

21. What are the common tones between F-minor and D-flat–major chords?

22. What are the common tones between D-flat–major and B-flat–major chords?

23. How many eighth notes are there in a dotted half note?

24. Why does a 6/8 time signature feel like two beats per measure?

25. Why does the left hand only play a three-note chord at the end of Exercise 18-7?

(Answers can be found in Appendix A.)

CHAPTER 19

Advanced Chord Structures

At this point, you are familiar with most major and minor chords in root position and first and second inversions. In this chapter, we will be adding notes to the basic chord structure, which will allow you more freedom to express yourself through music.

Major Sevenths

Major seventh chords are consonant. They are built on major key scale degrees. In major key scales, the seventh scale degree is a half-step below the octave.

As you know, chords are comprised of thirds: a major third and a minor third equal a major triad; a minor third and a major third equal a minor triad. Going up another third from the fifth of a chord gives us the seventh. For example, the notes in a C-major chord are C (root), E (third), and G (fifth). A major third above G is B. When you stack up the thirds in a C-major seventh chord you have: C, E, G, B (C to E is a major third, E to G is a minor third, and G to B is a major third). So the formula for all major seventh chords is a sequence of a major third, minor third, and major third.

The following table shows you the notes and consecutive thirds in major seventh chords.

TABLE 19-1

Chord	Root	Third	Fifth	Seventh
D-major 7th	D	F-sharp	A	C-sharp
F-major 7th	F	A	C	E
G-major 7th	G	B	D	F-sharp
A-major 7th	A	C-sharp	E	G-sharp
B-major 7th	B	D-sharp	F-sharp	A-sharp

In keeping with the major seventh formula, notice that the interval from the root to the third with all of the chords is a major third, from the third to the fifth is a minor third, and from the fifth to the seventh is a major third.

When playing the D-, G-, A-, and B-major seventh chords in Table 19-1 with the right hand, the fingering is:

Root: Thumb
Third: Second finger
Fifth: Third finger
Seventh: Fourth finger

The fingering is slightly different for the F-major seventh chord:

Root: Thumb
Third: Second finger
Fifth: Third finger
Seventh: Fifth finger

The difference in the fingering is because of the following: When the seventh in a major seventh chord is located on a black key, the fourth finger plays the seventh because it is longer than the fifth finger and can easily reach the black key. However, when the seventh in a major seventh chord is located on a white key, the fifth finger is a better choice. (For those of you who have small hands, you might not be able to reach the seventh on a black key with your fourth finger. In that case, try using your fifth finger.)

In **EXERCISE 19-1**, play the major seventh chords in Table 19-1 with your right hand.

EXERCISE 19-1
Major seventh chords

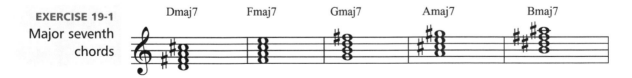

When playing the chords with your left hand, the fingering is:

Root: Fifth finger
Third: Third finger
Fifth: Second finger
Seventh: Thumb

This left-hand fingering applies to all major seventh chords, black and white keys alike. When playing sevenths that are on black keys, you're going to have to play deeper into the keys, moving your hand toward the fallboard. In doing so, it will be easier for your relatively short thumb to reach the black keys.

In **EXERCISE 19-2**, play the major seventh chords in Table 19-1 with your left hand.

EXERCISE 19-2:
Major seventh
chords

In **EXERCISE 19-3** you're going to build major seventh chords following the major third, minor third, major third formula. Build up from the roots starting with middle C. (Reminder: The major seventh is a half-step below the octave.)

EXERCISE 19-3

Constructing Major Seventh Chords

	Root	Third	Fifth	Seventh
C				
E-flat				
F-sharp				
A				
B-flat				

Now that you have constructed the chords, play them with your right hand in **EXERCISE 19-4**.

EXERCISE 19-4:
Major seventh chords

Minor Seventh Chords

The following minor seventh chords are built on natural minor scale degrees. The seventh scale degree in natural minor scales is a whole step below the octave.

The stacking up of thirds for natural minor seventh chords follows this formula: minor third, major third, and minor third.

The following table shows you the notes and consecutive thirds in natural minor seventh chords.

TABLE 19-2

Chord	Root	Third	Fifth	Seventh
C-minor 7th	C	E-flat	G	B-flat*
D-minor 7th	D	F	A	C
E-minor 7th	E	G	B	D
F-minor 7th	F	A-flat	C	E-flat*
G-minor 7th	G	B-flat	D	F
A-minor 7th	A	C	E	G
B-minor 7th	B	D	F-sharp	A

Please note that all of the chords in Table 19-2 follow the natural minor seventh formula—from the root to the third is a minor third, from the third to the fifth is a major third, and from the fifth to the seventh is a minor third.

When playing minor seventh chords with the right hand, the fingering is the same as playing major seventh chords. As indicated with one asterisk in Table 19-2, the sevenths that are on black keys are played using the fourth finger. All of the other sevenths, which are on white keys, are played using the fifth finger.

In **EXERCISE 19-5**, play the chords in Table 19-2 with your right hand.

EXERCISE 19-5:
Minor seventh chords

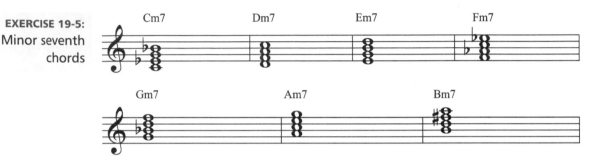

When playing minor seventh chords with the left hand, the fingering is the same as playing major seventh chords.

In **EXERCISE 19-6**, play the minor seventh chords in Table 19-2 with your left hand.

EXERCISE 19-6:
Minor seventh chords

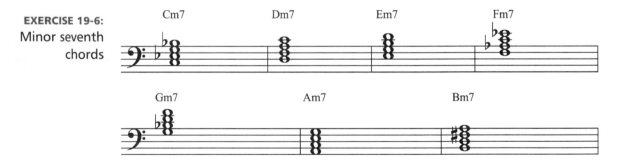

In **EXERCISE 19-7**, build natural minor seventh chords following the minor third, major third, minor third formula. Start with the root, E-flat. (Reminder: The minor seventh is a whole step below the octave.)

EXERCISE 19-7

Constructing Minor Seventh Chords

	Root	Third	Fifth	Seventh
E-flat				
F-sharp				
A				
B-flat				

Now that you have constructed the chords, play them with your right hand in **EXERCISE 19-8**.

EXERCISE 19-8:
Minor seventh
chords

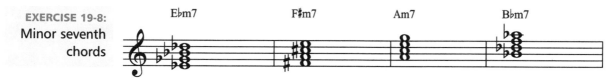

Harmonic Minor Sevenths

Minor seventh chords with an interval of a major seventh from the root to the seventh are built on harmonic minor scale degrees. The seventh scale degree in harmonic minor scales is a half-step below the octave.

The stacking up of thirds for harmonic minor seventh chords follows this formula: minor third, major third, and major third. Rather than calling them harmonic minor seventh chords, they are commonly referred to as minor chords with a raised seventh—raised because the seventh is a half-step higher than the natural minor seventh. For example, the notes in a G-minor seventh chord are G, B-flat, D, and F. In a G minor with a raised seventh, the notes are: G, B-flat, D, and F-sharp. The shorthand version chord symbol for harmonic minor chords is Gm+7. The "+" is shorthand for raised.

The difference between major seventh chords and minor chords with a raised seventh is only one pitch: the third of the chord. For example, the notes in a C-major seventh chord are C, E, G, and B. The notes in a C minor with a raised seventh are C, E-flat, G, and B. The simple change of a lowered half-step with the third of the chord makes a big difference in the way these two chords sound.

To illustrate this difference, alternate playing between C-major seventh and C minor with a raised seventh. Use middle C as the root of both chords.

Dominant Seventh Chords

The seventh chords we have covered so far are all built on the first scale degree—the root. Dominant seventh chords are built on the fifth scale degree—the dominant.

In the key of C major, the dominant seventh is G7. This chord is comprised of the G-major triad plus a minor seventh interval from the root G up to F. The notes in the G7 chord are G, B, D, and F. Dominant seventh chords want to resolve to the root. When playing in a major key, C major for instance, the G7 also has a sense of resolution by going to the vi chord, A minor. The formula for all dominant seventh chords is a sequence of a major third, minor third, and minor third.

Dominant seventh chords are also used in harmonic minor keys. For example, in the key of E-harmonic minor, the V chord is B major. B major becomes B7 by adding the note A. The notes in the B7 chord are B, D-sharp, F-sharp, and A.

In the next exercise, build dominant seventh chords following the major third, minor third, minor third formula. Start with the root E, two whole steps above middle C. (Reminder: The minor seventh is a whole step below the octave.)

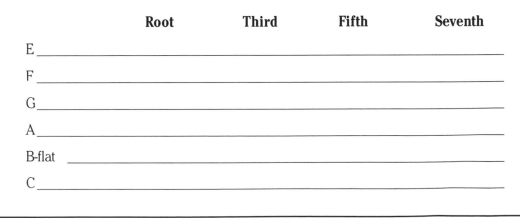

EXERCISE 19-9
Constructing Dominant Seventh Chords

	Root	Third	Fifth	Seventh
E				
F				
G				
A				
B-flat				
C				

When you have constructed the dominant seventh chords in **EXERCISE 19-9**, play them with your right hand in **EXERCISE 19-10**.

EXERCISE 19-10:
Dominant seventh chords

Seventh-Chord Inversions

Seventh chords can be inverted to first, second, or third positions. With a first-inversion, E-dominant seventh chord, the notes are G-sharp, B, D, and E. In a second-inversion, C-major seventh, the notes are G, B, C, and E. The first note in a third-inversion chord is the seventh. For example, the notes in an F-major seventh third-inversion chord are E, F, A, and C.

The following table shows seventh chords in third-inversion positions.

TABLE 19-3

Chord	Seventh	Root	Third	Fifth
C-minor 7th	B-flat	C	E-flat	G
D-major 7th	C-sharp	D	F-sharp	A
E-dominant 7th	D	E	G-sharp	B
F-minor 7th	E-flat	F	A-flat	C
G-major 7th	F-sharp	G	B	D
A-minor +7th	G-sharp	A	C	E
B-major 7th	A-sharp	B	D-sharp	F-sharp

Play the chords in Table 19-3 with your right hand in **EXERCISE 19-11**. The fingering is the same for all of the chords:

Seventh: Thumb
Root: Second finger
Third: Third finger
Fifth: Fifth finger

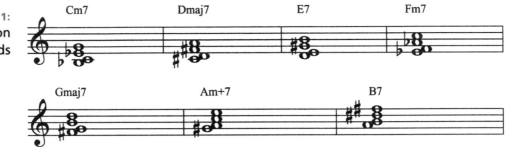

EXERCISE 19-12 uses a variety of seventh chords in the right hand over a rhythmic bass line. Table 19-4 identifies the chord qualities and their positions.

TABLE 19-4

Measure	Chord	Notes	Quality	Position
1	C-major 7th*	E–G–B	I-major 7th	1st inversion
2	F-major 7th	E–F–A–C	IV-major 7th	3rd inversion
3	E major**	E–G#–B	V-dominant	root position
4	A minor	E–A–C	iv-minor	2nd inversion
5	F-major 7th*	E–A–C	IV-major	3rd inversion
6	E-dominant 7th**	E–G#–B–D	V-dominant 7th	root position
7	A minor	E–A–C	iv-minor	2nd inversion
8	A minor	E–A–C–E	iv-minor	2nd inversion

* root in bass

** borrowed dominant

The table for **EXERCISE 19-12** reveals new harmonic information. Up until now, you have been playing closed-position chords. In the next exercise you will be playing two open-position chords.

Looking at the very first chord (C-major seventh), it looks like the right hand is playing an E-minor chord. But when you add the root of the chord, C, played by the bass, the E-minor chord becomes a C-major seventh chord. Likewise, in measure 5, the root of the F-major seventh chord is played by the bass. The voicings of the C-major seventh and F-major seventh chords are good examples of open-position chords, where the notes that make up the chord are played in different octaves. All other chords in **EXERCISE 19-12** are closed-position chords.

As indicated with two asterisks, the E-major and E-dominant seventh chords are borrowed dominants from the key of A minor. In the key of C major, the iii chord is minor. By making it major, it becomes the V chord in the key of A minor. In doing so, we move from the key of C major to A minor. **EXERCISE 19-12** starts in the key of C major, but after two measures, transposes to the key of A minor and stays in that key for the remainder of the piece.

In the left-hand part, notice the dotted rhythm on the first two beats of every measure except for the last measure. The rhythm of the bass part in measure 1 is repeated in measures 3, 4, 6, and 7. A variation of this rhythm takes place on the fourth beat in measures 2 and 5.

There is a common tone among all of the chords in this exercise. One note is played in the same position throughout the chord progression. It's the note E, which is the first note in every chord played by the thumb in the right hand.

Play only the right-hand chords several times. Then play only the left-hand bass part several times. When you're ready, play with both hands together. You'll notice when you add the bass part to the chords in measures 1, 2, and 5 how significantly the sound of the harmony changes.

MOVING ON

Andante ♩ = 96

Ninth Chords

An octave is eight notes above any given pitch. A whole step above an octave is a ninth. For example, starting with the root G, eight notes above is the octave G, a whole step above the octave G is A, which is the ninth.

Ninths can be added to all types of major chords and all minor chords. With that in mind, add the ninth to the following chords. (Reminder: The ninth is a whole step above the octave.)

EXERCISE 19-13

Constructing Ninth Chords

Root/Chord	Third	Fifth	Ninth
C major	E	G	_____
D minor	F	A	_____
E-flat major	G	B-flat	_____
F minor	A-flat	C	_____
F-sharp major	A-sharp	C-sharp	_____
G minor	B-flat	D	_____
A major	C-sharp	E	_____
B-flat minor	D-flat	F	_____

Ninths can also be added to all types of seventh chords. Add the ninth to the following seventh chords:

EXERCISE 19-14

Adding Ninths to Seventh Chords

Root/Chord	Third	Fifth	Seventh	Ninth
C-sharp minor 7th	E	G-sharp	B	_____
D-major 7th	F-sharp	A	C-sharp	_____
E-minor 7th	G	B	D-sharp	_____
F-dominant 7th	A	C	E-flat	_____
G-minor 7th	B-flat	D	F	_____
A-major 7th	C-sharp	E	G-sharp	_____
B-dominant 7th	D-sharp	F-sharp	A	_____

There are also flat ninth chords. The flat ninth chord is built on a dominant seventh chord.

It's flat because the ninth is lowered a half-step. Using an F-dominant seventh chord as an example, by adding a G-flat, it becomes a flat ninth chord. The notes in the chord are F, A, C, E-flat, and G-flat. The abbreviated chord symbol for flat ninth chords is F7♭9. Flat ninth chords are very dissonant.

EXERCISE 19-15 has a variety of seventh and ninth chords in various positions with a bass line that leaps octaves every now and then.

Table 19-5 identifies the chord qualities, notes in the chord, and their positions.

TABLE 19-5

Measure	Chords	Notes	Position
1	A-major 7, 9*	C#–E–G#–B	1st inversion
	A major	C#–E–A	1st inversion
	A-major 7th*	C#–E–G#	1st inversion
	A major	C#–E–A	1st inversion
2	B-minor 7th*	D–F#–A	1st inversion
	E-dominant 7th	D–E–G	3rd inversion
3	A-major 7, 9*	C#–E–G#–B	1st inversion
	A major	C#–E–A	1st inversion
	A-major 7th*	C#–E–G#	1st inversion
	A major	C#–E–A	1st inversion
4	B-minor 7th*	D–F#–A	1st inversion
	E-dominant 7th	D–E–G	3rd inversion
5	F-sharp minor	F#–A–C#	root
6	D-major 7th*	F#–A–C#	1st inversion
7	B minor	D–F#–B	1st inversion
	B-minor 7th*	D–F#–A	1st inversion
8	E-dominant 7th	D–E–G#	3rd inversion
	E major	E–G#–B	root
9	A-major 7, 9*	C#–E–G#–B	1st inversion
	A major	C#–E–A	1st inversion
	A-major 7th*	C#–E–G#	1st inversion
	A major	C#–E–A	1st inversion
10	B-minor 7th*	D–F#–A	1st inversion
	E-dominant 7th	D–E–G	3rd inversion
11	A-major 7, 9*	C#–E–G#–B	1st inversion
	A major	C#–E–A	1st inversion
	A-major 7th*	C#–E–G#	1st inversion
	A major	C#–E–A	1st inversion
12	B-minor 7th*	D–F#–A	1st inversion
	E-dominant 7th	D–E–G	3rd inversion
13	A-major 7th	E–G#–A–C#	2nd inversion

* root in bass

As you can see by looking at the key signature, **EXERCISE 19-15** is in the key of A major; be sure to play all Fs, Cs, and Gs sharp. The tempo of this piece is adagio (quarter note equals 72).

In this piece, the right hand plays both chords and melody. The top note in the chords, along with the passing eighth notes, make up the melody. Isolating the melody, the notes in the first two measures are: (measure 1) B, A, G-sharp, and A, and (measure 2) A, G-sharp, F-sharp, G-sharp, A, and B. This two-bar phrase melody, along with the chord progression and bass line, is repeated in measures 3 and 4, 9 and 10, and 11 and 12.

EXERCISE 19-15 has two parts. The first part is the two-bar phrase, repeated in measures 3 and 4. The second part is measures 5 through 8. This second part starts on A major's relative minor, F-sharp minor, and works its way back to the first part, which is repeated in measures 9 through 12. In terms of form, this exercise follows an abbreviated A-B-A form—A: part one; B: part two; A: part one repeated.

When playing the A-major ninth chords in measures 1, 3, 9, and 11, the root of the chord is in the bass. Likewise, in the B-minor seventh chords in measures 2, 4, 10, and 12, the root is in the bass.

For the purpose of illustration, the rhythm of the bass part in measure 5 is the same as the rhythm in measure 6. The dotted half note in measure 5 equals three beats; the half note tied to the quarter note in measure 6 also equals three beats.

The thumb and the second finger of the right hand play the bottom two notes of the chords, while the third, fourth, and fifth fingers play the chords' third and fourth notes. Additionally, as indicated in the right-hand part, the second, third, fourth, and fifth fingers also play the melody's passing eighth notes.

Play only the right-hand chords several times before adding the left-hand part.

EXERCISE 19-15

KEEP ON TRYING

Suspended Chords

Suspended chords include the second and fourth scale degrees in major and minor chords. The written shorthand for suspended chords is sus. They are called suspended chords because the suspended pitch (note) wants to resolve to either the root, third, or fifth of the chord. For example, a C sus2 chord contains the second scale degree D. The D can resolve to either C (the root) or E (the third). A C sus4 chord contains the fourth scale degree F. The F can resolve to E (the third) or G (the fifth). The second (D) resolves by either going up a whole step to E or down a whole step to the root; the fourth (F) resolves by moving down a half-step to E or up a whole step to G.

The following table includes a variety of suspended chords.

TABLE 19-6

Root/Chord	Sus2	Third	Sus4	Fifth
C-minor sus2	D			G
D-major sus4			G	A
E-minor sus4			A	B
F-major sus2	G			C
G-major sus4			C	D
A-minor sus4			D	E
B-major sus2	C#			F#

As you can see in the table above, when playing sus2 or sus4 chords, the third of the chord is not included. Chord progressions that contain suspended chords generally move from a suspended chord to a resolved chord that includes the third.

Diminished Chords

If you recall from Chapter 17, chords built on the seventh scale degree in major keys are diminished chords. Diminish means to make smaller.

Diminished chords are a half-step smaller than minor chords. For example, the two third intervals that make up a G-minor chord are a minor third (from G to B-flat) and a major third (from B-flat to D). By lowering the major third a half-step and making it a minor third, we have two minor thirds that equal a diminished chord. The notes in a G-diminished chord are G, B-flat, and D-flat.

Adding to the two minor third triads that make up a diminished chord (by adding another minor third on top of the fifth), we get a diminished seventh chord. Using the G-diminished triad, a minor third above the fifth is F-flat.

Diminished chords are dissonant and want to resolve. For example, a G-diminished seventh chord can resolve to A-flat major or its relative minor, F minor. Note by note, this is how the G-diminished chord resolves to A-flat:

G moves to A-flat
B-flat moves to A-flat
D-flat moves to C
F-flat moves to E-flat

Diminished chords are similar to dominant (V) seventh chords. For example, the dominant seventh chord in the key of A-flat major is E-flat (E-flat, G, B-flat, D-flat). The first three notes in a G-diminished chord are the same as the last three notes in the E-flat dominant seventh chord: G, B-flat, D-flat. To further illustrate this similarity, play a G-diminished chord with the right hand (G, B-flat, D-flat) and add an E-flat with your left hand. By adding the E-flat, the G-diminished chord becomes an E-flat dominant seventh (E-flat, G, B-flat, D-flat). The shorthand for writing diminished chords is dim. (G dim.7).

Augmented Chords

You may recall that the III chord built on a harmonic minor scale is an augmented chord. Augment means to make larger. Augmented chords are a half-step larger than a major triad. For example, the two third intervals that make up a D-major chord are a major third (from D to F-sharp) and a minor third (from F-sharp to A). By raising the minor third a half-step and making it a major third, we have two major thirds that equal an augmented chord. The notes in a D-augmented chord are D, F-sharp, and A-sharp.

Augmented chords are also dissonant chords that want to resolve. For example, the D-augmented chord wants to resolve to G major. Note by note, this is how a D-augmented chord resolves to G major:

D stays on D (common tone with both chords)
F-sharp moves to G
A-sharp moves to B

The shorthand for writing augmented chords is aug. (A aug).

Arpeggio Chords (Broken Chords)

In contrast to the way you have been playing chords thus far, another way of playing chords is to arpeggiate, or break up, the notes that make up the chord and play each note individually. The Italian word *arpeggio* means "harp-like." Arpeggio chords can be played by either the right hand or the left hand.

The next exercise uses broken chords in the left hand with a simple melody in the right hand. The following table identifies the chords and their qualities in **EXERCISE 19-16**.

TABLE 19-7

Measure	Chords	Notes	Position
1	C major	C–E–G–C	root
	C-major 7	C–E–G–B	root
2	F major	F–A–C–F	root
	F minor	C–F–A–C	2nd inversion
3	B-dim. 7	A♭–B–A♭–C	2nd inversion
	G-dominant 7	D–F–G–B	2nd inversion
4	C major	C–E–G–C	root

TABLE 19-7 (*continued*)

5	A minor	C–E–A–C	1st inversion
	A minor	C–E–A–C	1st inversion
6	D major	D–F#–A–D	root
	D 7	D–F#–A–C	root
7	D-minor 7	D–F–A–C	root
	D-minor 7	D–F–A–C	root
8	G 7 sus4	D–F–G–C	2nd inversion
	G 7	D–F–G–B	2nd inversion
9	F major	C–F–A–C	2nd inversion
10	F minor	C–F–A♭–C	2nd inversion
11	D-minor 7	D–F–A–C	root
	G-dominant 7	D–F–G–B	2nd inversion
12	C major	C–E–G–C	root
13	C major	C–E–G–C	root
	C-major 7	C–E–G–B	root
14	F major	C–F–A–C	2nd inversion
	F minor	C–F–A♭–C	2nd inversion
15	B-dim. 7	D–F–A♭–B	1st inversion
	G-dominant 7	D–F–G–B	2nd inversion
16	C major	C–E–G–C	root

The broken chord pattern in **EXERCISE 19-16** is comprised of a series of eighth notes, with the exception of half notes representing the third and fourth beats in measures 4, 8, 12, and 16. The eighth notes should be played evenly, giving them all the same equal value. Each set of four eighth notes represents one chord. For example, the first set of four eighth notes in measure 1 (C, E, G, C) represents the C-major chord. Likewise, the first set of eighth notes in measure 5 (C, E, A, C) represents the A-minor chord in first-inversion position.

EXERCISE 19-16

BACK ON TRACK

Notice that the right-hand melody part in measures 9 through 12 is exactly the same as the right-hand notes in measures 1 through 4. What's different is the harmony—the chords in the left-hand in measures 9 through 12 play chords that are different than those played in measures 1 through 4. In measures 13 through 16, the melody is repeated once again.

Also notice the fourth eighth notes in measures 9 and 10 are tied to half notes. Simply play the fourth eighth note and hold it down, giving it the full combined value equal to five eighth notes (the half note C equals four eighth notes plus the tied eighth note C).

In measures 3 and 15, you can see how the first-inversion, B-diminished seventh chord resolves to the G-dominant seventh chord. Also note how the second-inversion, G 7 sus4 chord in measure 8 resolves to the second-inversion, G-dominant seventh chord.

The left-hand fingering of the set of four ascending eighth notes is the same throughout the piece: 5, 3, 2, 1.

Play only the left-hand part several times; try to play the eighth notes evenly. When you have the fingering and timing worked out, add the right-hand melody part.

And now for the questions . . .

1. What is the formula for building major seventh chords?

2. How far is a major seventh from the octave?

3. What note is a major seventh above E-flat?

4. What are the notes in a root-position, A-flat–major seventh chord?

5. How far is a minor seventh from the octave?

6. What note is a minor seventh above F-sharp?

7. What are the notes in a root-position, F-sharp–minor seventh chord?

8. What are the notes in a root-position, A-harmonic–minor seventh chord?

9. What are the notes in a root-position, B-flat–minor seventh chord?

10. What are the notes in a root-position, E-dominant seventh chord?

11. What are the notes in a second-inversion, C-major seventh chord?

12. What are the notes in a first-inversion, B-natural–minor seventh chord?

13. What are the notes in a second-inversion, F-sharp–dominant seventh chord?

14. What are the notes in a third-inversion, C-natural–minor seventh chord?

15. What are the notes in a third-inversion, A-major seventh chord?

16. What is an open-position chord?

17. What is a borrowed dominant chord?

18. What interval is a whole step above an octave?

19. What are the notes in a root-position, E-natural–minor 7, 9 chord?

20. What are the names of the two suspended chords?

21. A suspended fourth resolves to what note in a triad?

22. A suspended second resolves to what note in a triad?

23. What's the difference between a minor chord and a diminished chord?

24. What are the notes in a B-diminished seventh chord?

25. What's the difference between a major chord and an augmented chord?

26. What's another word for broken chords?

(Answers can be found in Appendix A.)

CHAPTER 20

Applying Music Theory to Playing the Piano

As you know, there's practice and there's theory. In practical terms, theory by itself doesn't accomplish much. It is the application of the theory to the keyboard that makes the theory come to life, and makes the practice of playing the piano easier to grasp.

Abbreviated Chord Symbols

Every chord has a symbol representing its quality. The following list is an example of chords, their quality, and their corresponding symbol.

Chord/Quality	Symbol
C major	C*
D-major seventh	Dmaj.7
E-dominant seventh	E7**
F minor	Fm
G-minor seventh	Gm7
A-flat–major ninth	A♭9
A-minor ninth	Am9
B-suspended second	Bsus2
C-suspended fourth	Csus4
D diminished	Ddim.
E-flat–diminished seventh	E♭dim.7
F augmented	Faug.
B-flat minor, raised seventh	B♭min+7
C-dominant seventh, flat nine	C7♭9

*: A letter name without any abbreviations or numbers represents a major chord.
**: A letter name followed by a seven represents a dominant seventh chord.

Some piano music has the melody, harmony (chords), and bass line written out in fine detail. This is the case with classical pieces. With jazz, pop, and rock piano music, sometimes the specific harmony is not written. Instead, chord symbols are written above the melody. The sequence of chords is called a chord progression.

Playing a chord chart requires a lot of keyboard experience and the ability to construct chords based on chord symbols. The pianist has to know all of the notes that belong in the chord and which position to play the chord: root, first inversion, second inversion, or third inversion.

The first step in this process is to go through the entire chord progression and figure out the fingering and positions of the chords with the left hand. Once that is accomplished, then add the melody with the right hand.

Take a look at **EXERCISE 20-1**, which has only a melody with chord symbols above it. The following table identifies the chord qualities and the notes for each chord in this exercise.

TABLE 20-1

Measure	Chords	Notes
1	D-major 7th	D–F#–A–C#
2	A-major 7th	A–C#–E–G#
3	B-minor 7th	B–D–F#–A
4	A-major 7th	A–C#–E–G#
5	B-minor 7th	B–D–F#–A
6	F-sharp minor	F#–A–C#
7	D major	D–F#–A
8	A major	A–C#–E

With your left hand, try to figure out the fingering and position of the chords. As you know, first and second inversions make it easier to go from one chord to another, minimizing the repositioning of the hand and fingers. When playing a chord chart, the rhythm of the chords also has to be determined. With **EXERCISE 20-1**, simply play one dotted half note chord per measure. Start with the D-major seventh in root position, building up from D, one whole step above middle C.

As indicated in the key signature, **EXERCISE 20-1** is in the key of A major and is in 3/4 time.

NIKKI

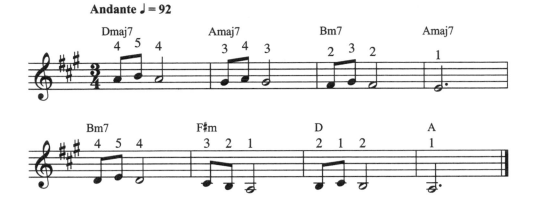

If you had difficulty constructing the chords in **EXERCISE 20-1**, the following table shows the positions of the chords in the progression.

TABLE 20-2

Measure	Chords	Notes	Position
1	D-major 7th	D–F#–A–C#	root
2	A-major 7th	C#–E–G#–A	1st inversion
3	B-minor 7th	B–D–F#–A	root
4	A-major 7th	A–C#–E–G#	root
5	B-minor 7th	B–D–F#–A	root
6	F-sharp minor	A–C#–F#	1st inversion
7	D major	A–D–F#	2nd inversion
8	A major	A–C#–E	root

Improvisation

Some chord charts have no written melody or harmony at all. The rhythm is indicated by slanted slash marks. This type of chord chart is used primarily by pianists who accompany singers or solo instrumentalists. The singer or instrumentalist sings or plays the melody while the pianist provides the chordal (harmonic) rhythmic accompaniment. In order to do this successfully, it usually requires years of keyboard experience and working with other musicians—soloists and singers alike. It also requires the ability to improvise or fill in. A keyboard player in a band typically plays solos. When playing from a chord chart that has no written notes to play, the pianist has to improvise; in other words, the pianist has to make up solos on the spot.

Improvisation is a very special skill. Some pianists can acquire and develop this skill.

Other pianists have difficulty improvising and prefer to play from much more detailed written music. Playing from chord charts is certainly for the advanced keyboard player who knows how to improvise.

The next exercise is an example of a chord chart with no written melody or harmony. Each slanted slash mark represents a quarter beat. It's a fast moving, bouncy, bright little piece. Go right ahead and play with it; start slowly and figure out the fingering and chords and gradually work your way up to tempo (allegro). Play the chords with your right hand, and play the root of the chords with your left hand. There's an introduction in the first four measures, with changing chords every two beats. Repeat it as often as you like.

EXERCISE 20-2

BOUNCING BACK

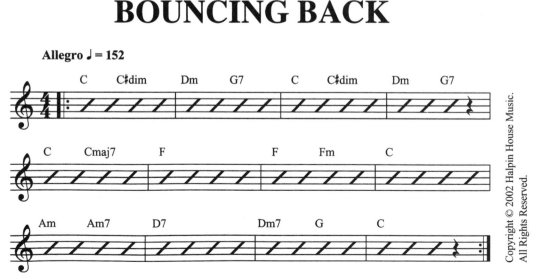

Chord Formulas

The following table identifies the formulas for constructing the chords we have covered in this book. The sequence of thirds starts from the root of the chord and builds up accordingly.

TABLE 20-3

Major Chord	dominant 7	dominant 7, 9	major 7	major 7, 9
		major third		minor third
	minor third	minor third	major third	major third
minor third	minor third	minor third	minor third	minor third
major third	major third	major third	major third	major third

Minor chord	minor 7	minor 7, 9	minor +7	minor +7, 9
		major third		minor third
	minor third	minor third	major third	major third
major third	major third	major third	major third	major third
minor third	minor third	minor third	minor third	minor third

diminished	dim. 7	augmented	aug. 7	aug. 7, 9
				minor third
	minor third		minor third	minor third
minor third	minor third	major third	major third	major third
minor third	minor third	major third	major third	major third

One of the most dissonant chords in the table above is the augmented 7, 9 chord. The tension is caused by the raised (augmented) fifth in the chord. The notes in a C aug. 7, 9 are C, E, G-sharp, B, and D.

Tied Rhythm

The next exercise has a tied rhythm in the melody over chords played with the left hand. As you already know, another way of writing this tied rhythm is a dotted rhythm—a dotted quarter note followed by an eighth note. With a dotted rhythm, you don't see the second beat; whereas with the tied rhythm, you can see the second beat, even though you don't play it.

EXERCISE 20-3 begins with a two-bar introduction, which sets up the key of B-flat major, the 4/4 time signature, and the melody. As you can see in the second measure, the melody begins with the two quarter pick-up notes C and D. In the fourth measure, there are accent marks above and below the chords and melody. Acknowledge the accent marks by playing these notes and chords forcefully.

The following table contains the notes in the chords, quality, position of the chords, and left-hand fingering for **EXERCISE 20-3**.

TABLE **20-4**

Measure	Chords	Notes/Fingering	Position
1	B♭ major	B♭–D–F–B♭ 5 3 2 1	root
	E♭ major	B♭–E♭–G–B♭ 5 3 2 1	2nd inversion
2	B♭ major	B♭–D–F–B♭ 5 3 2 1	root
3	C-minor 7th C-minor 7th	C–E♭–G–B♭ C–E♭–G–B♭ 5 3 2 1	root root
4	F major F major	C–F–A C–F–A 5 2 1	2nd inversion 2nd inversion
5	B♭ major B♭ major	B♭–D–F B♭–D–F 3 2 1	root root
6	B diminished	B-natural–D–F 3 2 1	root

TABLE 20-4 *(continued)*

7	C-minor 7th	C–E♭–G–B♭	root
	C-minor 7th	C–E♭–G–B♭	root
		5 3 2 1	
8	F major	C–F–A	2nd inversion
	F major	C–F–A	2nd inversion
		5 2 1	
9	B♭ major	B♭–D–F–B♭	root
		5 3 2 1	
	F major	C–F–A	2nd inversion
		5 2 1	
10	E♭ major	E♭–G–B♭	root
		3 2 1	
11	C-minor 7th	C–E♭–G–B♭	root
	C-minor 7th	C–E♭–G–B♭	root
		5 3 2 1	
12	F major	C–F–A	2nd inversion
	F major	C–F–A	2nd inversion
		5 2 1	
13	B♭ major	B♭–D–F–B♭	root
		5 3 2 1	
	E♭ major	B♭–E♭–G–B♭	2nd inversion
		5 3 2 1	
14	B♭ major	B♭–D–F–B♭	root
		5 3 2 1	

In terms of compositional form, there two patterns in **EXERCISE 20-3**. The first pattern takes place in the first two measures: the tied rhythm in the melody followed by a half note over the I (B-flat), IV (E-flat), and I (B-flat) chords. This is repeated with some variation in measures 9 and 10: the same rhythm with different pitches in the melody over the I (B-flat), V (F), and IV (E-flat) chords. The same pattern is repeated again in

POSITIVE

Moderato ♩ = 112

measures 13 and 14: the same rhythm with different pitches in the melody over the I (B-flat), IV (E-flat), and I (B-flat) chords.

The second pattern begins with the two pick-up quarter notes C and D in the second measure followed by the tied rhythm in the melody in measure 3, and concludes with the two accented quarter notes F in measure 4. In this pattern, the left hand plays Cm7 and F chords. This pattern is repeated in measures 6, 7, and 8. It is repeated once again, with different pitches in the melody, in measures 10, 11, and 12.

The third beat in the right-hand part in measures 4, 8, and 12 is a quarter rest. This rest lets the melody take a breath and sets up the pick-up notes in the fourth beat.

With that in mind, play **EXERCISE 20-3**. Be sure to raise the B-flat to B-natural in the left-hand B-diminished chord in measure 6. As always, play only the left hand several times. Then play only the right hand several times. The fingering for the right hand is written above the melody. Please refer to Table 20-4 for the left-hand fingering. When you have both parts worked out individually, play the exercise with both hands.

Suspensions and Resolutions

EXERCISE 20-4 has a busy right-hand part, playing chords, broken chords with suspensions, and the melody. The left-hand part simply plays steady quarter notes and a few whole notes. This piece uses a harmonic structure of suspensions and resolutions throughout the piece.

In **EXERCISE 20-4** there are two suspensions in the melody. The top note in the first chord in measures 1, 2, 5, 6, 9, 10, 17, 18, 21, and 22 is a suspended fourth, and the second eighth note in the third beat is a passing suspended second, which resolves to the root in the fourth beat. The melodic pattern emphasizes the eighth notes that play the fourth, third, second, and root. For example, in the first measure, the eighth notes C, B, A, and quarter note G make up the melody. The other eighth notes, D and G, are notes in the G-major broken chord. This melodic pattern is repeated with different chords throughout the piece.

The following table identifies the right-hand chords played on the first beat in each measure of **EXERCISE 20-4**.

TABLE 20-5

Measure	Chord/Quality	Notes	Position
1	G sus4	D–G–C	2nd inversion
2	G sus4	D–G–C	2nd inversion
3	C maj.7*	E–G–B	1st inversion
4	C maj.7*	E–G–B	1st inversion
5	Am sus4	E–A–D	2nd inversion
6	Am sus4	E–A–D	2nd inversion
7	G	D–G–B	2nd inversion
8	D	D–F–A	root
9	Em sus4	B–E–A	2nd inversion
10	Em sus4	B–E–A	2nd inversion
11	Bm	B–D–F#	root
12	Bm	B–D–F#	root
13	Am 7, 9*	C–E–G–B	1st inversion
14	Am 7, 9*	C–E–G–B	1st inversion
15	D7sus	C–D–G	3rd inversion
16	D7	C–D–F#	3rd inversion
17	G sus4	D–G–C	2nd inversion
18	G sus4	D–G–C	2nd inversion
19	C maj.7*	E–G–B	1st inversion
20	C maj.7*	E–G–B	1st inversion
21	Am sus4	E–A–D	2nd inversion
22	Am sus4	E–A–D	2nd inversion
23	D sus	D–G–A	root
24	G	D–G–B	2nd inversion

* root in bass

The left hand plays the root of the chord in every measure except measure 7, where it plays the fifth (D) of the G-major chord. As you can see in measures 1, 2, 3, 4, 5, 6, 9, 10, 17, 18, 19, 20, 21, and 22, the left hand plays the lower octave on the fourth quarter note beat.

The second measure is exactly the same as the first, the fourth measure is exactly the same as the third, and the sixth measure is exactly the same as the fifth. Measures 17 through 22 are an exact repetition of measures 1 through 6.

EXERCISE 20-4 has two different sections: section A (measures 1 through 8) and section B (measures 9 through 16). Section A is repeated in measures 17 through 24. This exercise follows an A-B-A form.

You'll discover that the fingering pattern in the right hand feels very natural and makes it easy to play the part. **EXERCISE 20-4** is a light piano piece, thus the *mp* dynamic marking.

Staccato

EXERCISE 20-5 is in the key of C-sharp minor. The tempo is a quick-paced moderato (quarter note equals 120) in 4/4 time. As you can see, the left-hand part has small dots written above and below the introductory quarter notes in measures 1 and 2, all of the following chords (with the exception of measure 18), and the very last note in measure 26. When any note or chord is articulated with dots, it means to play the value of the note shorter. In other words, the dots above and below the quarter notes and chords in the left-hand part do not get their full quarter note values. Instead, the value is closer to that which equals an eighth note. Staccato is the musical term that describes playing notes and chords shorter than their written values.

EXERCISE 20-5 is written in A-B-A form. After a two-bar introduction played by the left hand, the A section is stated in measures 3 through 10. As indicated by repeat signs, measures 3 through 10 are repeated. After playing the repeat, we move on to the B section, which is stated in measures 11 through 18. The A section returns in measures 18 through 26 (which is a repetition of measures 3 through 10), with the addition of the final quarter note played by the left hand in measure 26.

TIME

Chord symbols are written above the left-hand chords. By now, you should be able to figure out the fingering for the left-hand chords. Start by using the following fingers from the bottom note of the chord and going up: fifth, third, second, and thumb. Notice that the F-minor chord in measures 4, 6, 7, 13, 17, 20, 22, and 23 are second inversions, and in measure 9, the B chord is in second-inversion position. Be sure to play the A-sharp in the second-inversion F-sharp–major chord in measures 12 and 16 and to acknowledge the natural sign before the A note in the second-inversion F-sharp–minor chords in measures 13 and 17, canceling out the preceding A-sharp in measures 12 and 16. Also notice the raised B-sharp in the second-inversion G-sharp 7 chord in the third and fourth beats in measure 14. In measure 18, the A-major chord is in first-inversion position, followed by the first-inversion B chord. And in measure 25, notice that the B chord is in second-inversion position.

The right-hand fingering is written in the part. Be sure to use the second-finger-over-the-thumb technique for the first and last eighth notes in measure 9. In contrast to the rhythm played by the right hand in section A, the rhythm of the right-hand part is a dotted rhythm in the B section: dotted quarter note followed by an eighth note. As you know, the dotted quarter note equals the first beat and half of the second beat. To emphasize the ending of the musical phrase and resolution on the E-major chord (C-sharp minor's relative major), as indicated by accent marks in measures 10 and 26, play the staccato E chords and left-hand E notes with force.

Now that we have analyzed **EXERCISE 20-5**, start with working out the left-hand chords. Be sure to acknowledge the staccato marks and to play them short. The right-hand melody should fall into place without any difficulty.

As indicated by the dynamic marking *f*, play this piece loudly.

FREEDOM MARCH

Syncopated Rhythm

EXERCISE 20-6 is in the key of D major and B minor and is in 4/4 time. The tempo is andante, with a metronome marking of a quarter note equaling 104. The exercise starts off with a four-bar chord introduction, followed by the A section in measures 5 through 8. The B section takes place in measures 9 through 16, followed by a repeat of the four-bar introduction. As indicated by the repeat signs, after playing the chords in measures 17 through 20, go back to measure 5 and play to the end (measure 20).

The right hand plays a syncopated rhythm and plays both chords and melody while the left hand plays even quarter and half notes. What makes the right-hand part syncopated is the tied notes. For example, in measures 5 through 16, the second eighth note in the second beat is tied to the third beat. Additionally, in measures 9, 10, 11, 13, 14, and 15, the second eighth note in the third beat is tied to the fourth beat. The syncopation occurs with the bass part playing the third and fourth beats and the right hand playing only the second eighth, the second part of the third and fourth beats.

The following table identifies the qualities and positions of the chords in **EXERCISE 20-6**.

TABLE 20-6

Measure	Chords	Notes	Position
1	G major	D–G–B	2nd inversion
	A major	E–A–C#	2nd inversion
2	B minor	F#–B–D	2nd inversion
3	G major	D–G–B	2nd inversion
	A major	E–A–C#	2nd inversion
4	D major	F#–A–D	1st inversion
5	D major	A–D–F#	2nd inversion
	A major	E–C#–A	arpeggio
6	G major	B–D–G	1st inversion
	D major	A–D–F#	2nd inversion
7	E minor	B–E–G	1st inversion
	B minor	F#–D–B	arpeggio

TABLE 20-6 *(continued)*

8	G major	B–D–G	1st inversion
	F# major	C#–F#–A#	2nd inversion
9	B minor	D–F#–B	1st inversion
	B minor sus 2*	C#–D (no 5th)	open
10	G maj. 7*	D–F#–B	2nd inversion
	G maj. 7, sus 4*	C#–D (no 3rd)	open
11	E minor 7	E–G–D	root
12	F# major sus 4	C#–F#–B	2nd inversion
	F# major*	A# (no 5th)	open
13	B minor	D–F#–B	1st inversion
	B minor sus 2*	C#–D (no 5th)	open
14	G maj. 7*	D–F#–B	2nd inversion
	G maj. 7, sus 4*	C#–D (no 3rd)	open
15	E minor 7	E–G–D	root
16	F# major sus 4	C#–F#–B	2nd inversion
	F# major*	A# (no 5th)	open
17	G major	D–G–B	2nd inversion
	A major	E–A–C#	2nd inversion
18	B minor	F#–B–D	2nd inversion
19	G major	D–G–B	2nd inversion
	A major	E–A–C#	2nd inversion
20	D major	F#–A–D	1st inversion

* root in bass

Before you play **EXERCISE 20-6**, take a close look at the melody and bass line. The top note of the right-hand chords is the melody. In measures 5 and 7, the right hand plays arpeggio chords in the third and fourth beats; in measures 6 and 8, there's a quick suspended second in the second eighth note in the first beat. We modulate to B minor on the first beat in measure 9, using the borrowed dominant F-sharp from B minor in the previous measure. Therefore, the A is raised a half-step to A-sharp on the fourth beat in measure 8.

HOPEFUL

Andante ♩ = 104

In measure 9, once the B-minor chord is established in the first beat, the fifth of the chord (F-sharp) is no longer played. This creates an open sound with the bass playing the root in the lower octave. Another open sound with no third takes place in measure 10 and with no fifth in measure 12. Also in measure 9, the right hand plays a suspended second in the melody, which resolves up to D. This occurs while the bass, on the fourth beat, goes to the passing note A on its way down to G in measure 10.

The second G-major seventh chord in measure 10 is also in the open position with the root in the bass. In that same measure, notice that the suspended fourth in the melody is C-sharp. This is caused by the C-sharp in the D-major key signature. Notice that the bass on the fourth beat goes to the passing note F-sharp on its way down to E in measure 11. As you can see, the right hand is playing a repeated pattern in measure 10, with a pitch variation (the passing note C-sharp in the melody) in measure 11, and a harmonic resolution and rhythm change in measure 12.

In measure 11, notice that the bass note on the fourth beat is E-sharp, which is a passing note to the F-sharp in measure 12. Measures 13 through 16 are exactly the same as measures 9 through 12.

By now, you should be able to figure out the fingering for the left hand. The fingering for the top note melody in the right hand is as indicated in the part.

Use your newfound knowledge to answer the following questions.

1. What is the abbreviated chord symbol for a D-dominant seventh chord?

    ....

2. What is the abbreviated chord symbol for an E-minor seventh chord?

    ....

3. What is the abbreviated chord symbol for a C-dominated seventh, flat 9 chord?

    ....

4. What are the notes in a first-inversion, A-major seventh chord?

    ....

5. When reading a chord chart that has no written melody or chords, what does the pianist have to do?

    ....

6. What is the sequence of triads that make a dominant seventh chord?

7. What is the sequence of triads that make a major seventh, ninth chord?

    ....

8. What is the sequence of triads that make a minor raised seventh chord?

9. What is the sequence of triads that make a diminished seventh chord?

10. What is the sequence of triads that make an augmented seventh chord?

11. What is the sequence of triads that make an augmented seventh, ninth chord?

12. What are the notes in a C-augmented 7, 9 chord?

13. What does the word *staccato* mean?

14. How does Exercise 20-6 begin?

15. What type of rhythm does the right hand play in Exercise 20-6?

16. What makes it syncopated?

17. What note is suspended in a B-minor suspended second chord?

18. What note is suspended in an F-sharp–major suspended fourth chord?

19. The borrowed dominant F-sharp–major chord belongs to what key?

20. What causes the C-sharp in the G-major seventh, suspended fourth chord in measure 10?

(Answers can be found in Appendix A.)

APPENDIX A
Quiz Answers

Chapter 13

1. Four.
2. Four.
3. One.
4. Quarter notes.
5. Four.
6. Bar lines.
7. Treble clef; also called a G clef.
8. The first three fingers of the right hand.
9. A quarter rest; one beat.
10. A half rest; two beats.
11. A double bar line; the end of the exercise or piece of music.
12. A time signature.
13. It means that there are four beats per measure, and the quarter note gets the beat (and the quarter rest gets the silent beat).
14. Tempo; the rate of speed at which the exercise is to be played.
15. Moderately (not too fast; not too slow).
16. Mezzo forte; medium loud.
17. Because the notes are on the B line of the staff and higher.
18. A repeat sign.
19. It means to repeat playing the music between the repeat signs.
20. Twice; however, in this exercise, because the written text says repeat three times, it is played three times.
21. Exercise 13-8 is an octave higher than Exercise 13-1.
22. A two-bar pattern.
23. The fingering.
24. Ten.
25. Ten.
26. Four.
27. Three.

Chapter 14

1. A, F, D, B, G.
2. G, E, C, A.
3. One ledger line above the staff.
4. Fast.
5. Loud.
6. Slow.
7. An octave is the distance of eight notes between two pitches.
8. The fifth finger and the thumb.
9. Two.
10. 2, 4, 7, and 9.
11. The third and fourth beats.
12. Review "Practicing Techniques When Playing with Both Hands."
13. It ties the treble and bass staffs together.
14. They read music vertically and horizontally at the same time.
15. When playing descending bass notes.
16. So you don't run out of fingers; so you can play all of the descending bass notes.
17. When playing ascending bass lines
18. In the first bar, two eighth notes followed by two quarter notes, two more eighth notes, and a whole note in the second bar.

Chapter 15

1. None.
2. A minor.
3. The sixth.
4. Natural.
5. The root.
6. G major and E minor.
7. A half-step.
8. A whole step.
9. A half-step.
10. A downbeat.
11. Three quarter beats.
12. They equal their combined value.
13. Moderately slow.
14. A metronome marking.

15. It tells you the rate of speed of the quarter note.
16. Yes.
17. Review "Practicing Techniques When Playing with Both Hands" (Chapter 14).
18. D major and B minor.
19. The fourth finger.

Chapter 16

1. A circle of fourths.
2. They lower a pitch down a half-step.
3. The fourth scale degree.
4. The sixth scale degree.
5. F major, D minor.
6. It's the black key between the white keys A and B.
7. Because of the octaves played by the left hand.
8. Gradually play louder.
9. Gradually play softer.
10. Pick-up notes.
11. A two-bar sequence.
12. Three.
13. D-flat.
14. Four.
15. Fast.
16. From the E-flat down to the A-flat.
17. While resting, it is waiting and prepared to play the notes in measure 9.
18. Play only the right-hand part several times.
19. Five.
20. They are enharmonic equivalents.
21. Yes.
22. A-sharp minor.

23. G-flat major.
24. E-flat minor.
25. G-sharp.
26. C-flat.

Chapter 17

1. To get a better understanding of how melody, harmony, and bass lines work together to make piano music.
2. A combination of sounds considered pleasing to the ear.
3. A triad.
4. Two.
5. A major third followed by a minor third.
6. E-flat.
7. E-sharp.
8. They are enharmonic equivalents.
9. F.
10. A minor third followed by a major third.
11. A-flat.
12. C-sharp.
13. E minor.
14. B diminished.
15. A chord that starts with the root followed by the third and fifth.
16. A chord that starts with the third followed by the fifth and root.
17. A chord that starts with the fifth followed by the root and third.
18. C-sharp, E, A.
19. B, E, G.
20. B minor.
21. D major.

22. The ii chord: F-sharp diminished.
23. The ii and vii chords.
24. Because of the D-sharp.
25. To make the fingering easier; to make the notes from one chord to another flow smoothly by moving a half- or whole step.

Chapter 18

1. Analyze all of its parts.
2. Two or three measures ahead of your fingers.
3. An acquired skill.
4. The span of an octave.
5. G, B-flat, E-flat, G.
6. G, B, E, G.
7. F-sharp, B, D-sharp, F-sharp.
8. A, D, F, A.
9. The fingering doesn't change; it's exactly the same as playing four-note root-position chords.
10. From the fifth to the fifth.
11. Because the chords don't belong to one specific key signature.
12. You play their combined value.
13. No.
14. Because C is not a note in the triadic structure of D-major and E-flat–major chords.
15. Writing a dotted rhythm.
16. Three.
17. Yes.
18. When two or more chords have the same note in their triadic structure.
19. E.
20. C and E-flat.

21. F and A-flat.
22. There's only one: F.
23. Six.
24. Because the two beats include three eighth notes per beat.
25. Because the fourth note, D, is played by the right hand.

Chapter 19

EXERCISE 19-3

Root/Chord	Ninth
C major	D
D minor	E
E-flat minor	F
F minor	G
F-sharp minor	G-sharp
G minor	A
A minor	B
B-flat minor	C

EXERCISE 19-4

Root/Chord	Ninth
C-sharp minor 7th	D-sharp
D-major 7th	E
E-minor 7th	F
F-dominant 7th	G
G-minor 7th	A
A-major 7th	B
B-dominant 7th	C-sharp

1. From the root of a chord, build a major third (root to third), minor third (third to fifth), and a major third (fifth to seventh).
2. A half-step.
3. D.

4. A-flat, C, E-flat, G.
5. A whole step.
6. E.
7. F-sharp, A, C-sharp, E.
8. A, C, E, G-sharp.
9. B-flat, D-flat, F, A-flat.
10. E, G-sharp, B, D.
11. G, B, C, E.
12. D, F-sharp, A, B.
13. C-sharp, E, F-sharp, A-sharp.
14. B-flat, C, E-flat, G.
15. G-sharp, A, C-sharp, E.
16. When the notes of a chord are spread out in more than one octave.
17. It's a V chord that belongs to the new key; it's a pivotal chord that moves from one key to another.
18. A ninth.
19. E, G, B, D, F-sharp.
20. Suspended fourth and suspended second.
21. The third.
22. The root or the third.
23. The fifth in a diminished chord is lowered by a half-step.
24. B, D, F, A-flat.
25. The fifth in an augmented chord is raised a half-step.
26. Arpeggio chords.

Chapter 20

1. D7.
2. Em7.
3. C7♭9.

4. C-sharp, E, G-sharp, A.
5. Construct the chords, determine their position, and improvise.
6. Major third, minor third, minor third.
7. Major third, minor third, major third, minor third.
8. Minor third, major third, major third.
9. Minor third, minor third, minor third.
10. Major third, major third, minor third.
11. Major third, major third, minor third, minor third.
12. C, E, G-sharp, B, D.
13. To play the dotted notes shorter than their written values.
14. With a four-bar introduction.
15. A syncopated rhythm.
16. The tied notes over even quarter notes in the bass.
17. C-sharp.
18. B.
19. B minor.
20. The D-major key signature.

APPENDIX B

Resources

Music Schools

For those of you interested in pursuing a formal music education, here is a list of some music institutions that offer diplomas and degrees in music.

Berklee College of Music
1140 Boylston Street
Boston, MA 02215-3693
(617) 266-1400

Boston Conservatory
8 The Fenway
Boston, MA 02215
(617) 536-6340

Cal State Northridge Department of
Music
18111 Nordhoff Street
Northridge, CA 91330
(818) 885-3181

California Institute of the Arts
School of Music
24700 McBean Parkway
Valencia, CA 91355
(805) 253-7818

Columbia University
Department of Music
703 Dodge Hall
New York, NY 10027
(212) 854-3825

Curtis Institute of Music
1726 Locust Street
Philadelphia, PA 19103
(215) 893-5252

Eastman School of Music
26 Gibbs Street
Rochester, NY 14604
(716) 274-1000

The Hartford Conservatory
of Music
834 Asylum Avenue
Hartford, CT 06105
(860) 246-2588

The Hartt School of Music
The University of Hartford
200 Bloomfield Avenue
West Hartford, CT 06117
(860) 768-4454

Julliard School of Music
60 Lincoln Center Plaza
New York, NY 10023
(212) 799-5000

The Manhattan School of Music
120 Claremont Avenue
New York, NY 10027
(212) 749-2802

Mannes College of Music
150 West 85th Street
New York, NY 10024
(212) 580-0210

New England Conservatory of
Music
290 Huntington Avenue
Boston, MA 02115
(617) 262-1120

Oberlin Conservatory of Music
Conservatory of Music
Oberlin, OH 44074
(216) 775-8200

UCLA Department of Music
Los Angeles, CA 90024
(213) 825-4761

UCSB Department of Music
Santa Barbara, CA 93106
(805) 893-3261

University of Cincinnati
Conservatory of Music
Cincinnati, OH 45221
(513) 556-3737

For a less formal education, contact music store listings in your local yellow pages.

Pianos Online

The following list of Web sites sell new and used pianos. The digital list includes retail outlets that also sell synthesizers.

New Pianos

www.artisticpianos.com
www.baldwinatlanta.com
www.baldwinpiano.com
www.beethovenpianos.com
www.creighton-tweedie.com
www.critchetts.com
www.dibros-piano.com
www.ellispiano.com
www.fieldspianos.com
www.hansmusic.com
www.horinespianosplus.com
www.jordankitts.com
www.kawaius.com
www.kreftingpianos.com
www.mathismusic.com
www.milliganmusic.com
www.musicproducts.com
www.nhpianos.com
www.pianoliquidator.com
www.pianooutpost.com
www.pianosinc.net
www.pianosource.com
www.pianosthatplay.com
www.premierpiano.com
www.shermanclay.com
www.steinway.com
www.steinwaythebayarea.com
www.templeofmusic.com
www.thepianoexchange.com
www.vintagepianos.com
www.wilmingtonpiano.com
www.yamaha.com

New and Used Pianos

www.abcpiano.com
www.atlantagrandpianos.com
www.bnpiano.com
www.cooperpiano.com
www.cranespiano.com
www.daytonpiano.com
www.farleyspianos.com
www.gravespianos.com
www.jmlmusic.com
www.kurtzmusic.com
www.leswhitemusic.com
www.mipiano.com
www.musicloversshoppe.com
www.musicmallinc.com
www.newenglandpiano.com
www.newusedpianosofnynjct.com
www.pianoco.com
www.pianomart.com
www.pianopiano.com
www.pianowholesalers.com
www.pianoworld.com
www.rawlingsmusic.com
www.reederpianos.com
www.rickjonespianos.com
www.rjpianos.com
www.scottwray.com
www.spordonepiano.com
www.toonshopmusic.com
www.wrightsounds.com

Digital Pianos

www.academicenterprises.com
www.allaboutpianos.com
www.casio.com
www.generalmusic.com
www.gentrymusic.com
www.gottsmusic.com
www.hendersonmusic.com
www.instruments-to-go.com
www.kepplermusic.com
www.korg.com
www.kurzweilmusicsystems.com
www.lancastermusic.com
www.pianobid.com
www.pianodepot.com
www.scottwray.com
www.viscountus.com
www.wojnar.com
www.yamaha.com

Index

A

A-flat major key, 188–190
A-major key, 170–171
A-minor key, 156–159, 185
accordion, 6, 8
acoustic piano. *See* piano
action
   in piano, 69–70
   in pianoforte, 3
adagio, 145
adults
   teachers for, 104–105
   when to start lessons, 103
allegro, 144
altered chord, 227
amplifiers, 115
analog synthesizers, 81–82
andante, 164
arpeggio chords, 252–255
Ashby, Irving, 57
audiocassette decks, 112–113
augmented chords, 201–203,
   251–252

B

B-flat major key, 180–183, 185
B-flat minor key, 191–192
B-major key, 172–173

B-minor key, 166–169
Babcock, Alpheus, 5
Bach, Johann Sebastian, 3, 17
backposts, 73
Baldwin pianos, 90–91
bar, defined, 127
bar lines
   use of, 131–132
   defined, 126
Bartok, Bela, 18
bass line
   defined, 126
   learning to play, 142–147
beat, defined, 126
Beatles, 20–23, 24
bebop, 52
Bechstein pianos, 91
Beethoven, Ludwig van
   concertos of, 18
   sonatas of, 10, 14–15, 32
benches, piano, 107
big band music, 52
Blutner pianos, 91, 92
Borge, Victor, 30–31
Boston pianos, 90, 91
Brahms, Johannes
   concertos of, 17, 18
   Liszt and, 42
Brendel, Alfred, 30–31
bridge, of piano, 70–71

broken chords, 252–255
Brown, Ray, 57
Brubeck, Dave, 20
Brunner-Schwer, Hans Gerg, 57
Buchbinder, Rudolph, 28
Busch, Adolf, 49

C

C-major key, 156–159, 185
   chords in, 199–203
C-minor key, 183–187
C-sharp minor key, 171–172
cabinet/casing, of piano, 66
celesta, 6
Charles, Ray, 53–54
Charles Walter pianos, 91, 92
children
   encouragement of, 105–106
   teachers for, 103
   when to start lessons,
      102–103, 104
Chopin, Fryderyk François
compositions of, 16, 17
   concertos of, 18
   life of, 36–37
chords, advanced, 233–256
   abbreviated symbols for,
      258–260
   arpeggio, 252–255

C, 183–187
C sharp, 171–172
D, 178–179
D sharp, 174–175
E harmonic, 162–165,
  206–208
F, 188–190
F sharp, 170–171
G, 180–183
natural versus harmonic,
  204–208
minor sevenths chords,
  237–239
minor thirds, 196
mix-down deck, 118
mixing, 122–123
moderato, 134
Moody Blues, 24
Moog, Robert, 82
Mozart, Wolfgang Amadeus
  concertos of, 17, 18
  sonatas of, 12, 28
multitracking, 121–122
music desk, 66

N

natural minor keys. *See* minor
  keys
natural notes, 156
ninth chords, 245–249
notes
  defined, 127
  names of, 128–129

notes, value of, 127, 138
  eighth, 146–147, 229
  half, 138
  quarter, 131, 138
  six-eighth, 229
  three-quarter, 163–164
  whole, 138

O

octaves, 136, 146
open-position chords, 243
operas
  of Elton John, 62
  of Scott Joplin, 55
organs, 6, 7–8
Oscar Peterson Trio, 57
overdubbing, 121–122

P

Paderewski, Ignancy Jan,
  43–47
  political life of, 46
Paganini, Nicolò, 41
Pass, Joe, 58
pedals
  practice, 69
  soft (damper), 3, 68, 148
  sostenuto, 68, 73, 148
  sustain, 4, 68, 72–73, 148
Pederson, Niels, 58
Perahia, Murray, 28
Perlman, Itzhak, 30–31

Peterson, Oscar, 55–58
pianists
  classical, 27–34
  jazz/pop, 51–62
  romantic, 35–49
  see also repertoires
piano
  care of, 95–99
  choosing of, 87–94
  history of, 1–5
  manufacturers of, 5–6,
    90–93
  parts of, 66–73
  types of, 63–65, 74
  see also electronic
    keyboards
pianoforte, 2
pin block, 73
pitch, defined, 127
playing by ear, 219
polyphony, 80
pop compositions. *See*
  jazz/pop compositions
posture, at piano, 107
practice, 101
  concentration and, 106–107
  habits and, 108
  listening and, 218–219
  pedal for, 69
  posture for, 107
  time needed for, 105–106
Presley, Elvis, 21
Prokofiev, Sergei, 17, 18
prop sticks, for piano lid, 67

suspended chords, 250
suspensions, 266, 268, 269
sustain pedal, 4, 68, 72–73, 148
syncopated rhythm, 272–275
synthesizers, 6, 81
   analog, 81–82
   contrasted to acoustic
      piano, 84–85
   digital, 83–84
   MIDI, 84
   recording of, 120–122
Szokolay, Balazs, 29

T

Tatum, Art, 58–59
   Peterson and, 56
Taupin, Bernie, 61–62
Tchaikovsky, Peter, 18
teacher
   for adults, 104–105
   for children, 103
tempo, 134
   defined, 127
Thigpen, Ed, 57
three-quarter time notes,
   163–164
thumb, moving around
   fingers, 150–151
tied rhythm, 223–227, 263–266,
   267
time signature, 134
   defined, 127
tone poem, 17

Toscanini, Arturo, 39–40
Treemonisha (Joplin), 55
triads. *See* chords, three-note
tuning, of piano
   after move, 90, 98
   importance of professional,
      98
   universal, 118
tuning pins, 73
two-hand fingering techniques,
   148–153

U

upright pianos, 65, 89
used pianos
   buying, 93–94
   selling, 99–100

V

virginal, 6, 7
Vivaldi, Antonio, 17
voicing, of hammers, 72, 98

W

Waller, Fats, 52
Webb, Jimmy, 23
whole note, 138
whole rest, 138
Wonder, Stevie, 25
Wornum, Robert, 5

Y

Yamaha pianos, 91, 92
Young & Chang pianos, 91, 92

Z

Zumpe, Johannes, 4

THE EVERYTHING GUITAR BOOK

By Peter Rubie and Jack Wilkins

Play Like a Pro in No Time

THE EVERYTHING GUITAR BOOK

From buying the right guitar to mastering your favorite songs

Jack Wilkins and Peter Rubie

Trade paperback,
$14.95 ($22.95 CAN)
1-58062-555-X, 304 pages

The Everything® Guitar Book is filled with clear, step-by-step instructions, finger position diagrams, and tons of professional tips. Guitar legend Jack Wilkins and former guitar instructor Peter Rubie walk you through the basics—from buying the right guitar to playing your favorite songs. This easy-to-follow book teaches you how to tune and strum your guitar, read music, and develop an ear for the right chords. *The Everything® Guitar Book* also explains what gear to buy and how to use it, including cases, picks, capos, amplifiers, effects pedals, straps, and strings.

OTHER *EVERYTHING*® BOOKS BY ADAMS MEDIA CORPORATION

BUSINESS

Everything® **Business Planning Book**
Everything® **Coaching & Mentoring Book**
Everything® **Home-Based Business Book**
Everything® **Leadership Book**
Everything® **Managing People Book**
Everything® **Network Marketing Book**
Everything® **Online Business Book**
Everything® **Project Management Book**
Everything® **Selling Book**
Everything® **Start Your Own Business Book**
Everything® **Time Management Book**

COMPUTERS

Everything® **Build Your Own Home Page Book**
Everything® **Computer Book**

Everything® **Internet Book**
Everything® **Microsoft® Word 2000 Book**

COOKING

Everything® **Bartender's Book, $9.95**
Everything® **Barbecue Cookbook**
Everything® **Chocolate Cookbook**
Everything® **Cookbook**
Everything® **Dessert Cookbook**
Everything® **Diabetes Cookbook**
Everything® **Low-Carb Cookbook**
Everything® **Low-Fat High-Flavor Cookbook**
Everything® **Mediterranean Cookbook**
Everything® **One-Pot Cookbook**
Everything® **Pasta Book**
Everything® **Quick Meals Cookbook**
Everything® **Slow Cooker Cookbook**

Everything® **Soup Cookbook**
Everything® **Thai Cookbook**
Everything® **Vegetarian Cookbook**
Everything® **Wine Book**

HEALTH

Everything® **Anti-Aging Book**
Everything® **Dieting Book**
Everything® **Herbal Remedies Book**
Everything® **Hypnosis Book**
Everything® **Menopause Book**
Everything® **Stress Management Book**
Everything®**Vitamins, Minerals, and Nutritional Supplements Book**
Everything® **Nutrition Book**

HISTORY

Everything® **American History Book**

All Everything® books are priced at $12.95 or $14.95, unless otherwise stated. Prices subject to change without notice.
Canadian prices range from $11.95–$22.95 and are subject to change without notice.

Everything® **Civil War Book**
Everything® **World War II Book**

HOBBIES

Everything® **Bridge Book**
Everything® **Candlemaking Book**
Everything® **Casino Gambling Book**
Everything® **Chess Basics Book**
Everything® **Collectibles Book**
Everything® **Crossword and Puzzle Book**
Everything® **Digital Photography Book**
Everything® **Drums Book (with CD),**
 $19.95, ($31.95 CAN)
Everything® **Family Tree Book**
Everything® **Games Book**
Everything® **Guitar Book**
Everything® **Knitting Book**
Everything® **Magic Book**
Everything® **Motorcycle Book**
Everything® **Online Genealogy Book**
Everything® **Playing Piano and**
 Keyboards Book
Everything® **Rock & Blues Guitar**
 Book (with CD), $19.95,
 ($31.95 CAN)
Everything® **Scrapbooking Book**

HOME IMPROVEMENT

Everything® **Feng Shui Book**
Everything® **Gardening Book**
Everything® **Home Decorating Book**
Everything® **Landscaping Book**
Everything® **Lawn Care Book**
Everything® **Organize Your Home Book**

KIDS' STORY BOOKS

Everything® **Bedtime Story Book**
Everything® **Bible Stories Book**
Everything® **Fairy Tales Book**
Everything® **Mother Goose Book**

NEW AGE

Everything® **Astrology Book**

Everything® **Divining the Future Book**
Everything® **Dreams Book**
Everything® **Ghost Book**
Everything® **Meditation Book**
Everything® **Numerology Book**
Everything® **Palmistry Book**
Everything® **Spells and Charms Book**
Everything® **Tarot Book**
Everything® **Wicca and Witchcraft Book**

PARENTING

Everything® **Baby Names Book**
Everything® **Baby Shower Book**
Everything® **Baby's First Food Book**
Everything® **Baby's First Year Book**
Everything® **Breastfeeding Book**
Everything® **Get Ready for Baby Book**
Everything® **Homeschooling Book**
Everything® **Potty Training Book,**
 $9.95, ($15.95 CAN)
Everything® **Pregnancy Book**
Everything® **Pregnancy Organizer,**
 $15.00, ($22.95 CAN)
Everything® **Toddler Book**
Everything® **Tween Book**

PERSONAL FINANCE

Everything® **Budgeting Book**
Everything® **Get Out of Debt Book**
Everything® **Get Rich Book**
Everything® **Investing Book**
Everything® **Homebuying Book, 2nd Ed.**
Everything® **Homeselling Book**
Everything® **Money Book**
Everything® **Mutual Funds Book**
Everything® **Online Investing Book**
Everything® **Personal Finance Book**

PETS

Everything® **Cat Book**
Everything® **Dog Book**
Everything® **Dog Training and Tricks**
Everything® **Horse Book**
Everything® **Puppy Book**
Everything® **Tropical Fish Book**

REFERENCE

Everything® **Astronomy Book**
Everything® **Car Care Book**
Everything® **Christmas Book, $15.00,**
 ($21.95 CAN)
Everything® **Classical Mythology Book**
Everything® **Divorce Book**
Everything® **Etiquette Book**
Everything® **Great Thinkers Book**
Everything® **Learning French Book**
Everything® **Learning German Book**
Everything® **Learning Italian Book**
Everything® **Learning Latin Book**
Everything® **Learning Spanish Book**
Everything® **Mafia Book**
Everything® **Philosophy Book**
Everything® **Shakespeare Book**
Everything® **Tall Tales, Legends, &**
 Other Outrageous Lies Book
Everything® **Toasts Book**
Everything® **Trivia Book**
Everything® **Weather Book**
Everything® **Wills & Estate Planning**
 Book

RELIGION

Everything® **Angels Book**
Everything® **Buddhism Book**
Everything® **Catholicism Book**
Everything® **Judaism Book**
Everything® **Saints Book**
Everything® **World's Religions Book**
Everything® **Understanding Islam Book**

SCHOOL & CAREERS

Everything® **After College Book**
Everything® **College Survival Book**
Everything® **Cover Letter Book**
Everything® **Get-a-Job Book**
Everything® **Hot Careers Book**
Everything® **Job Interview Book**
Everything® **Online Job Search Book**
Everything® **Resume Book, 2nd Ed.**
Everything® **Study Book**

All Everything® books are priced at $12.95 or $14.95, unless otherwise stated. Prices subject to change without notice.
Canadian prices range from $11.95–$22.95 and are subject to change without notice.

WE HAVE EVERYTHING . . . .

SPORTS/FITNESS

Everything® **Bicycle Book**
Everything® **Fishing Book**
Everything® **Fly-Fishing Book**
Everything® **Golf Book**
Everything® **Golf Instruction Book**
Everything® **Pilates Book**
Everything® **Running Book**
Everything® **Sailing Book, 2nd Ed.**
Everything® **T'ai Chi and QiGong Book**
Everything® **Total Fitness Book**
Everything® **Weight Training Book**
Everything® **Yoga Book**

TRAVEL

Everything® **Guide to Las Vegas**
Everything® **Guide to New England**
Everything® **Guide to New York City**
Everything® **Guide to Washington D.C.**

Everything® **Travel Guide to The Disneyland Resort®, California Adventure®, Universal Studios®, and the Anaheim Area**
Everything® **Travel Guide to the Walt Disney World® Resort, Universal Studios®, and Greater Orlando, 3rd Ed.**

WEDDINGS & ROMANCE

Everything® **Creative Wedding Ideas Book**
Everything® **Dating Book**
Everything® **Jewish Wedding Book**
Everything® **Romance Book**
Everything® **Wedding Book, 2nd Ed.**
Everything® **Wedding Organizer, $15.00** ($22.95 CAN)

Everything® **Wedding Checklist,** $7.95 ($11.95 CAN)
Everything® **Wedding Etiquette Book,** $7.95 ($11.95 CAN)
Everything® **Wedding Shower Book,** $7.95 ($12.95 CAN)
Everything® **Wedding Vows Book,** $7.95 ($11.95 CAN)
Everything® **Weddings on a Budget Book, $9.95** ($15.95 CAN)

WRITING

Everything® **Creative Writing Book**
Everything® **Get Published Book**
Everything® **Grammar and Style Book**
Everything® **Grant Writing Book**
Everything® **Guide to Writing Children's Books**
Everything® **Writing Well Book**

ALSO AVAILABLE:
THE EVERYTHING® KIDS' SERIES!

Each book is 8" x 9¼", 144 pages, and two-color throughout.

Everything® **Kids' Baseball Book, 2nd Edition, $6.95** ($10.95 CAN)
Everything® **Kids' Bugs Book, $6.95** ($10.95 CAN)
Everything® **Kids' Cookbook, $6.95** ($10.95 CAN)
Everything® **Kids' Joke Book, $6.95** ($10.95 CAN)
Everything® **Kids' Math Puzzles Book, $6.95** ($10.95 CAN)
Everything® **Kids' Mazes Book, $6.95** ($10.95 CAN)
Everything® **Kids' Money Book, $6.95** ($11.95 CAN)

Everything® **Kids' Monsters Book, $6.95** ($10.95 CAN)
Everything® **Kids' Nature Book, $6.95** ($11.95 CAN)
Everything® **Kids' Puzzle Book $6.95,** ($10.95 CAN)
Everything® **Kids' Science Experiments Book, $6.95** ($10.95 CAN)
Everything® **Kids' Soccer Book, $6.95** ($10.95 CAN)
Everything® **Kids' Travel Activity Book, $6.95** ($10.95 CAN)

Available wherever books are sold!
To order, call 800-872-5627, or visit us at everything.com

Everything® is a registered trademark of Adams Media Corporation.